Children's Language

Children's Language

Consensus and Controversy

Ray Cattell

CASSELL

London and New York

#4/674433

Cassell
Wellington House, 125 Strand, London WC2R OBB
370 Lexington Avenue, New York, NY 10017–6550

http://www.cassell.co.uk

First published 2000

British Library Cataloguing-in-Publication Data
A catalogue record for this book is available from the British Library.

ISBN 0-304-70128-9 (hardback)
      0-304-70681-7 (paperback)

Library of Congress Cataloging-in-Publication Data
Cattell, N.R.
        Children's language: consensus and controversy / Ray Cattell.
            p.   cm.
        Includes bibliographical references and indexes.
        ISBN 0–304–70128–9 (hb). — ISBN 0–304–70681–7 (pb)
        1. Language acquisition. I. Title.

        P118.C384   2000
        401'.93—dc21   99–38234
                                                                          CIP

Typeset by York House Typographic Ltd, London
Printed and bound in Great Britain by Biddles Ltd, Guildford and King's
Lynn

Contents

Figures   vii

Acknowledgements   viii

1. Getting to rub two words together   1
   (Getting started with language)

2. Catching fire   12
   (Starting to make fast progress)

3. Do we *teach* children to speak?   30
   (B. F. Skinner and behaviourism)

4. Learning through touching and feeling   44
   (Jean Piaget: learning is based on handling objects)

5. What goes on in the mind?   62
   (Mentalism as a school of thought. Noam Chomsky)

6. A close look at Chomsky's theories   83
   (Some of Chomsky's work on language acquisition)

7. Do we *help* children to speak?   104
   ('Motherese' or child-directed speech)

8. Learning how to mean   129
   (Michael Halliday's views on how language develops)

9. The two hemispheres of the brain – A   151
   (Their functions in relation to language)

10. The two hemispheres of the brain – B   169
    (Modern discoveries about them)

11. The bounds of language acquisition   183
    (What is and what isn't natural language acquisition?)

12. Was Dr. Dolittle lying?   201
   (Animals and language)

13. 'Bootstrapping' – A   216
   (New knowledge about infant knowledge)

14. 'Bootstrapping' – B   227
   (Bootstrapping in vocabulary)

15. The best of both worlds?   240
   (The work of Annette Karmiloff-Smith)

16. Conclusion   255
   (Drawing the threads together)

   References   261

   Index   273

Figures

4.1   Piaget: simple reversibility test   53

4.2   Piaget: test for conservation of discontinuous quantity: 54
lines of same length

4.3   Piaget: test for conservation of discontinuous quantity: 54
lines of different length

4.4   Piaget: test for conservation of continuous quantity   55

4.5   Piaget: test of seriation   57

8.1   Halliday: Nigel at 12 months   140

9.1   The two hemispheres of the human brain, viewed from   152
above

9.2   The left side of the human brain, showng Broca's and   155
Wernicke's areas

11.1   American Sign Language: minimal contrasts involving   187
hand configuration, place of articulation, and movement

12.1   Communication among bees: the orientation of the   203
dance under different conditions

13.1   Infant perception test: schematic depictions of the   218
habituation display, and the test displays of a partly
occluded object

14.1   The 'basic' level in hierarchy   234

Acknowledgements

This book would have been impossible without the help of the people named below. I greatly value the help they willingly gave me when I asked for it.

I owe deep and strong gratitude to Neil Smith of University College London, whose advice has been invaluable. He not only read each chapter in two different drafts and offered superb criticisms and suggestions on each one, but carried out each such task with great rapidity and good humour, and often with sharp wit. He also suggested the title that I finally chose for the book. And when, occasionally, I wouldn't change things that he thought ought to be changed, it didn't seem to dent our long-standing friendship. It's the sort of help that money can't buy.

Two of my former colleagues in the Department of Linguistics at the University of Newcastle, New South Wales, helped considerably at a stage when help was really needed. Peter Peterson, Head of the Department, read an early draft and made detailed and penetrating comments which affected some of the lines the book took. I greatly valued his perceptive remarks. Alison Ferguson read the same draft and also made some very helpful and encouraging comments. Because she's in charge of the speech pathology section of the department, her comments were of particular interest and value to me.

I am especially grateful to Michael Halliday, whose contribution to child language studies is described in Chapter 8. At my request, he vetted that chapter when it was in draft form and gave very generously of his time and his ability, making detailed and careful comments on what I had written. Without that, I'm sure the chapter wouldn't have been as accurate an account of his ideas as I believe it now is. But if any mistakes have crept in, I am, of course, entirely responsible.

I'd like to express my thanks as well to contributors to the Systemic-Functional e-mail lists, Sys-func and Sysfling, while I was 'listening' during and before the writing of Chapter 8.

Carolyn Newton, Margaret Shanley, and James and Russell Shanley contributed in crucial ways to the knowledge on which Chapter 11 draws. I can't thank them enough.

Catherine Snow kindly pointed me in the right direction for some of the references I've used in the chapter on motherese. I greatly appreciate her help.

Likewise, I owe grateful thanks to Annette Karmiloff-Smith for giving me the references to some important discussions of her work, which were very useful in the preparation of Chapter 15.

Various members of the Piagetian e-mail list provided me with very useful discussion, both on-line and off-line, but I especially want to thank Leslie Smith, Trevor Bond, Michael Commons, George Forman and Herman Epstein, all of whom helped me to become more knowledgeable about things Piagetian. But I also learnt a lot from everybody else who contributed to the list while I was tuned in.

I gained enormous help from the bulletin board and other services of Childes, the most important on-line focus of child language studies, which runs under the superb guidance of Brian MacWhinney. The Childes bibliography is outstandingly useful, thanks to Roy Higginson, who does the updates.

The staff of Better Hearing Australia at Waratah, Newcastle, New South Wales, gave me welcome help in providing information relevant to Chapter 11.

Janet Joyce, director of Cassell Academic, who acted as my editor, did everything to help me write the best book I could, accepting my numerous changes to the title, contents and shape of the book with admirable equanimity. Working with her was an enjoyable experience. I am also grateful to Marion Blake and Peter Harrison at Cassell for their very efficient editorial help.

Bob Wilson, of Astam Books, helped me to find a publisher and provided me with continuing information about forthcoming books. My thanks to him for this very useful service.

I'm also grateful to Laura Maaske, the medical illustrator who did the diagrams of the brain, both for her excellent work and for her interest in the project beyond the strict call of duty.

John Giles was able to elucidate the mathematical concept of a morphism for me, for the chapter on Piaget, when my own books contained no useful account of it. Thanks, John.

I suppose it must be family modesty that makes me put my wife, Jan Angel, last. It can't be for any other reason. She has been a tower of strength. I drew on her deep knowledge of and experience in clinical procedures in the treatment of aphasia for Chapters 9 and 10. She also read the manuscript several times and provided me with extremely helpful comments. At the crucial closing stage of my completion of the manuscript, she insisted on keeping me out of the kitchen and the garden while she worked twice as hard as usual. And throughout the whole project she provided constant loving support and encouragement. My debt to her is immeasurable.

All the people named above had a great many other things to do in their busy lives besides helping me, but they managed to do it anyway. I'll be forever grateful.

Oh, and another thing. They're not responsible for any mistakes that might be in the book. I am.

Ray Cattell
May 1999

For my sons, Simon, Gavin and Rohan, who, when they were children, filled me with wonderment and delight as they came to have language.

1. Getting to rub two words together

1.1 Introduction

A baby of my acquaintance has been visiting us periodically since he was born, some 21 months ago. As he lives in a different city from us, several months often go by before he decides to drop in again. And that means we see marked changes in his development and behaviour each time he comes.

Although we've both had the experience of seeing babies develop before, my wife and I are still as impressed as anyone else at the miraculous changes – just as if the baby were doing something original. Well, it's not original, but it's still mind-boggling.

In the beginning he was a withered little prune of a fellow, and yet the attention of everybody focused on him all the time he was here. And this in spite of the fact that his social comportment could often only be described as regrettable. But the next time he came, he smiled a lot and you didn't mind what else he did.

One of the things that's happened since we first met him is that he's started the process of acquiring language. Now *that's* miraculous; yet at the same time it's the most ordinary thing in the human world. Unless there's something seriously wrong, we expect all babies, sooner or later, to start talking. And we're rarely disappointed.

The talk usually starts (on average) somewhere about 1 year of age. Yes, it's true that a few babies get started as young as 6 months and some hang back till as late as 2 years or more, but it averages out at about a year, and in fact most babies keep to about that schedule. Anxious parents and relatives are often sure the baby's about to burst into fluent speech months before (s)he really starts (and even then it's not very fluent for quite a while). So the time from birth to the first word can be a long, frustrating time for parents who are eager for that landmark.

And, of course, if the baby isn't talking by about the age of 1 year, the parents can become *very* anxious, especially if a neighbour says that her child said its first word at 6 or 8 months. But they can relax. More or less. Although a child who speaks early isn't likely to be dull, if your child doesn't speak till late, it doesn't mean that (s)he's *definitely* dull. (You've still got a fighting chance.) In fact, some famous people who afterwards became quite eloquent in their adult life started to talk late. Maybe your child is shrewd enough to be just listening and learning about what sort of family it's got itself into before it commits itself to any public utterances.

1.2 Crying

Although the first word mightn't come before about a year, that doesn't mean there isn't any development in that time.

'In the beginning was the word,' it says in the Gospel according to St John; but as far as babies are concerned, in the beginning is the cry. A baby cries as soon as it's born, and for quite a while that's its main vocal accomplishment.

But consider what an important thing for babies the ability to cry is. When they're born, they aren't capable of making many movements; in particular, they can't change the position they're lying in: they have to stay wherever they're put, and in whatever orientation they're put. So if they're uncomfortable for some reason, they can't do anything about it, directly. But they cry, to complain about their discomfort. And with any luck (which they usually have), an adult will come along and pick them up, check if there's any obvious reason why they're uncomfortable, and if there is, fix it. Then they may be laid in a new position. Thus, from the very beginning, babies exert some influence, and often control, over their universe. Vocal communication has begun.

The discomfort may not just be from an unsatisfactory lying position. It could be from an unfortunately placed safety-pin (used less and less now), or from internal discomfort from digestive problems. And it's always a possibility that there's some serious organic problem.

Apart from discomfort and pain, there's another main reason why babies cry: hunger. If there doesn't seem to be any other reason why the baby should be in discomfort, feeding it will often bring relief to the family's ears. Like the telephone, babies' cries are very difficult to ignore – and that, of course, has great value in their battle to survive. They're literally playing a game of life and death, so crying is no trivial matter. There's some evidence that mothers can identify their own baby in hospital when her/his cries are heard from another room.

The normal cry comes in brief bursts of about a second, with pauses in between. Each burst of sound falls in pitch as it goes on. It's been said that the quality of sound is like that of the vowel [a], and it often is (though not always). The sound changes according to how worked up the baby is. If the cries are ignored, (s)he can get *very* worked up indeed.

A reasonable question might be whether the quality of sound in the cry differs according to which language is spoken around the child, but the answer appears to be no.

Certain properties of the cries, however, will continue to be important when the baby develops speech; for instance, the rhythm of the recurring bursts of sound and the different pitches produced by the vibrations of the vocal cords. (The greater the frequency of the vibration, the higher the pitch.)

Some people have observed that the typical rising-then-falling pitch pattern of an infant's cry is similar to the intonation pattern (pattern of pitch changes) of a typical declarative statement in adult speech, and that another pattern, which rises in pitch at the end, resembles the intonation pattern of adult questions in some varieties of English. It's difficult to know how to assess this, but it's true that intonation (change of pitch) is a crucial part of adult speech in all languages, and that virtually all babies show the ability to use it. A baby has to have something pathologically wrong not to have intonational change.

1.3 Cooing

At about 2 months, most babies start to make 'cooing' or, if you like, 'gooing' sounds[1] as well as crying sounds. They start with a variable consonant-like sound, made towards the back of the mouth cavity, followed by a variable vowel-like sound. At somewhere around 3 months of age (give or take a little), the baby usually begins to emit sequences of cooing sounds. The sequences can be of differing lengths, and sometimes there may be a dozen or more. Cooing doesn't have the same distressed quality as cries often have, and in fact it seems like a pleasurable activity. Eventually (perhaps around 4 months) the baby will give little chuckles and laughs.

In producing cooing sounds, the lips and tongue and other speech organs move in ways that are comparable with the movements they'll later make in actual speech. The sounds are more speech-like, too, but they aren't yet sounds belonging to the specific language that members of the baby's family speak.

At somewhere between 5 and 8 months of age, the baby begins to explore the sounds it can make; and again this activity seems to be enjoyable. It explores different consonants and vowels and different *kinds* of consonants and vowels – for example, nasalized ones, fricative ones, etc., arranging them in CV (consonant + vowel) syllables.

An interesting question is whether the consonants and vowels develop in any particular order, but the evidence for that isn't strong. As Lise Menn and Carol Stoel-Gammon (1995: 347) point out, the age at which children master particular sounds (and classes of sounds) varies from one child to another, and the order in which they acquire them does, too.

There seems to be a lot of individuality in the paths by which babies work towards the sounds that they'll use in speech.

1.4 Babbling

As the sounds begin to emerge (from about 8 months or a little later), cooing turns gradually into babbling, which involves patterns of sounds. It especially tends to involve reduplication, e.g. babababa, gagagaga. The patterns become more complex and more varied as time goes on. Babbling continues to about 1 year or more (even up to 18 months), and it doesn't stop when speech begins.

1.5 The first words

Eventually, the magic moment arrives when the baby says her/his first word. But it isn't always clear-cut. Often you can't really be sure whether it was a word or just a short babble. It mightn't sound much like any adult word. But if you find that the baby makes the same sound sequence under the same conditions repeatedly, it's safe to assume that an attempt is being made to produce a word. Many babies do say what sounds like 'Mum-mum' as their first word. They're assisted in this by the fact that they're used to making sucking movements with the lips. If they press the lips together firmly and then open them, it can very easily sound like 'Mum-mum' if they leave the voice motor running. A delighted mother then usually smiles and responds so pleasantly that the baby soon manages to do it again.

Some may find it surprising, though, that the first word doesn't *have* to be 'Mum-mum'. The first word one of my own children used was 'light', pronounced /laː/ (to rhyme with 'Pa'). I used to carry him around in my arms, especially if he'd been upset. In order to distract him, I'd draw his attention to various objects, including, on one occasion, the light switch. Either that time or the next, he reached out towards it. The next few times, when we passed the light switch and I said 'light', he reached out even more eagerly, and then eventually said /laː/, even imitating my rising intonation.

Now, of course, no adult would say /laː/ for 'light', but the circumstantial evidence was fairly strong that this was what the child was trying to say, especially as he continued to use this sequence every time we passed the light and I said the word. Crestfallen mother.

The first few words may be learnt in that fashion, repeating them after an adult – perhaps even the first few dozen; but I will maintain, in a later chapter (Chapter 3), that that isn't the way children learn most of the words they acquire, and it isn't the way they gain the ability to put words together into grammatical structures.

Up to about 18 months, new words are added only slowly. This is probably because the child is learning by imitating the adults and older children in the immediate environment, and hasn't yet moved into the main word-acquisition phase which I will describe in Chapter 2.

During this initial period of comparatively slow word acquisition, the repertoire of words that the child seems to know varies from time to time. Not only are new words added, but some words seem to drop out, only to reappear again a good deal later. At this stage, the child may build up a vocabulary of up to about 50 words (sometimes more, sometimes fewer). But remember, the phonetic form of those words won't necessarily be the same as adults produce.

Then a fairly dramatic change occurs. Up to this point, a linguist or a parent could easily keep a list of vocabulary items that have been heard, but within a short space of time so many new words are being added that it's difficult to keep up with recording them. This is often referred to as a 'vocabulary explosion'. In fact, it is more than that, since other aspects of language also 'explode' at about this time.

Following close upon the heels of the 'explosion' of words, two-word utterances begin – utterances such as *shoe off, light off, cup hot, more juice, Daddy go* . . . We'll turn to those shortly.

Sometimes the child might seem to have entered the stage of two-word utterances before (s)he really has. *All gone*, for example, might seem like a two-word utterance to an adult, who is conscious of the spelling, but to the child it's probably a single lexical item: *allgone*. Only if the child sometimes replaces one part of the sequence with other items will we assume that *allgone* is two words. For instance, if the child says not only *all gone*, but also *car gone, Daddy gone*, etc., then we may assume that *all gone* is being analysed by the child as two words – especially if *all* is heard in other contexts too. *Byebye* is also a single lexical item with internal reduplication, rather than two words.

It isn't until real two-word utterances begin that we can say that syntactic (grammatical) constructions have started to form. I'd better explain why I just put 'grammatical' in brackets after 'syntactic'. The word 'grammar' and its related word 'grammatical' are used differently by different linguists. One school uses them for all aspects of the description of language, so that they include phonology (roughly, the study of sounds), semantics (the study of meanings) and syntax (the study of the relationships to each other of words in a sentence). Other linguists, including traditional ones, use the word 'grammar' only for what I've just described as syntax. In this book I'll follow the first school, and use 'grammar' to include phonology, semantics and syntax; but I'll remind you from time to time that that's what I'm doing.

Until you have two words to rub together, then, there isn't any syntax, because syntax is about the relationships *between* words in a sentence.

Some linguists have challenged this notion by claiming that single-word utterances are really 'holophrastic sentences'; in other words, the single word stands for a sentence. One strong version of this claim is that children have a mental representation of a fuller sentence structure, but can say only one word at first. They will fill in the gaps in the structure as they develop.

Those who think that single-word utterances are actually holo-phrastic sentences cite pieces of supporting evidence.

In the first place, the same word can be uttered in different contexts with different stress and intonation, which makes it seem possible that the meanings are different on the different occasions. It's been shown that adults listening to babies' one-word utterances have a high level of agreement as to whether they'd classify particular examples as declarative, interrogative or emphatic utterances, based on what they themselves would mean if they used the particular intonation contour. For example, 'car' said with a rising intonation contour might well mean 'Is this a car?', and with a falling contour might mean 'This is a car'. That might suggest that the different utterances of this single word are being used for fuller meanings. But even if that is so, it doesn't have to imply that they represent specific, different syntactic forms, as suggested by the citation of 'Is this a car?' and 'This is a car'.

Another piece of evidence that children might use single words as holophrastic utterances is that they often use gestures to augment the single word; for example, arms raised while saying 'Up' apparently means 'Will you lift me up?'

McNeill (1970: 24) cites some work carried out by Patricia Greenfield, who kept a diary of her daughter's early speech. At 12 months 20 days, the child, Lauren, said 'Ha!' when something hot was put in front of her. A month later, she said 'Ha!' about an empty coffee-cup and a stove that was turned off. The implication is that she used 'Ha!' not only to label hot objects, but also to label objects that could be hot. That means she was labelling a property.[2]

At 14 months 28 days, Lauren pointed to the top of her grandparents' refrigerator and said 'Nana!'. There were no bananas on the refrigerator at the time, but at home her mother kept bananas on the top of the fridge. McNeill (p. 24) claimed that 'Nana!' was being used not merely as a label, but as an indicator of location. However, Greenfield herself disagreed with McNeill's analysis of this utterance, saying (Greenfield and Smith, 1976: 214):

> Even though we agree that the child is relating the banana to its habitual location, the word *nana* represents not the location but the object. Thus, we would classify this utterance as an Object Associated with Another Object or Location.

Bloom (1973: 94) raised the question of whether Lauren could be using the word *nana* to refer to the refrigerator by association, because she didn't know the word *refrigerator*. But on other occasions she used it to refer to bananas that were not on the refrigerator. Besides, as Greenfield and Smith point out (1976: 214), Lauren on this occasion was not

7

looking in the direction of the refrigerator, but specifically at its top. It would seem, then, that she was now using words to indicate the normal location of objects.

Bloom (1973: 61) disputes the idea that one-word utterances are holophrastic sentences:

> single-word utterances are not sentences. Children in the first half of the second year do not use phrases and sentences – they say only one word at a time. When single-word utterances are successive, within the bounds of a single speech event, there is some evidence to indicate that the child is aware of relational aspects of experience. But children do not use syntax [at this stage].

You should be beginning to see how very difficult it is to analyse a child's one-word utterances. Far from being simple to analyse, they're complex, because the linguist has to use imagination to work out what the child's doing.

It would be reasonable to think that children's language should be easier to analyse than adult language, since it appears to be simpler. In fact, it might seem that studying the 'simple' language of little children should give us a flying start towards being able to analyse the complexities of adult language. But that isn't the case. Noam Chomsky, a very famous linguist, once said (1964a: 35), 'It seems that the attempt to write a grammar for a child raises all of the unsolved problems of constructing a grammar for adult speech, multiplied by some rather large factor.'

1.6 Two-word utterances

Somewhere around 18 months (give or take a bit, because there are marked individual differences), children start to make two-word utterances.

At first, they often seem to make two separate but adjacent one-word utterances. As Lois Bloom (1973: 41) says,

> The prosodic pattern that distinguished such words as these said in succession, as single-word utterances, was unmistakable. Each word occurred with terminal falling pitch contour, and relatively equal stress, and there was a variable but distinct pause between them, so that utterance boundaries were clearly marked.

It's worth noting, though, that not all examples of this phenomenon involve 'terminal falling pitch contour' (a fall in pitch at the end of the utterance). Sometimes the pitch contours can rise, as if with question intonation: *light↗ off↗*.

But whatever the exact details, the two words uttered as separate but adjacent utterances soon come together, and are accommodated within the same sentence contour. Typical examples are *Mummy shoe*, *allgone milk*, *Daddy go*, etc. As these examples indicate, very few inflections (grammatical endings) are used – that is, there are usually no plural, genitive or tense endings. There is also a dearth of so-called function-words: the 'bits of grammatical cement' such as prepositions, conjunctions, determiners, etc.[3]

Yet surely you would think that when a child's at the two-word stage, and there's so little structure to analyse, it would be simple. But again, this isn't the case. The fact that there's so little structure to analyse is one of the problems. The apparent simplicity seems to conceal unseen complexities. In any case, no one has been able to come up with a very satisfying account of two-word utterances.

An early attempt to provide a system of analysis for them was that of Martin Braine (1963b), who gives an account of a study done with three children. (Also see Braine, 1963a.) Braine claimed that a comparatively small number of words tended to recur in the same position in two-word utterances; for example, utterances like *see sock*, *see boy*, *see light* show that the same word can occupy the first position in a number of two-word utterances – and the list can be greatly extended. Another example of the same sort is provided by utterances like *allgone man*, *allgone train*, *allgone flower*, etc. Braine used the term 'pivot class' to label the words, such as *see* and *allgone*, which seemed to have a fixed position.

But there were also words that tended to recur in the second position of two-word utterances; for example, *off*, in *sock off*, *shoe off*, *pants off . . .*, and *come*, in *Daddy come*, *boy come*, *Mummy come*. So *off*, *come*, etc. were second-position pivot words. To distinguish between the two pivot classes, he called the ones like *see* and *allgone* Class P1 and those like *off* and *come* Class P2.

But what about the other words in two-word utterances – the ones that could occur sometimes in first position and sometimes in second position? An example is *sock*, which occurs in *see sock*, *sock off*, etc. Braine said that these belong to a special 'open' class, which he labelled 'Class X', whereas the pivot classes P1 and P2 are 'closed' classes.

9

Linguists use the term 'open class' to refer to any grammatical category which is always 'open' to new members. In adult English, nouns, verbs and adjectives are open classes, since new ones are constantly added to the language and old ones sometimes die out. Think of the new nouns, verbs and adjectives which are constantly spawned in teenage slang, and which usually disappear after they've had a vogue, and are replaced by new ones.

Closed classes, by contrast, are ones which hardly ever accept new members. These are grammatical categories like prepositions, conjunctions and determiners. It's been a long time since English acquired a new preposition, and even teenage slang usually doesn't introduce new ones.

So Braine claimed that the 'X' class was open to new members, but that the pivot classes P1 and P2 were a more or less fixed set, though a particular child would sometimes add one to his/her usage. The open class was a large one, containing nearly all the words the children used. Any one of those words occurs less frequently than any of the pivot words.

According to Braine, there are certain combinations of these classes that occur in two-word utterances, and certain ones that don't. The ones that do occur are P1 + X; X + P2; X; X + X. The ones that don't occur are *X + P1; *P2 + X; *P; *P1 + P2; *P2 + P1. (In linguistics, an * indicates that what follows is ungrammatical.)

It would have been nice, in a way, if pivot grammars had turned out to be valid, because then we would have had a neat system for describing what grammar operates at the two-word stage. And that would perhaps have provided a springboard into subsequent development. But wishful thinking is usually destined to fail in research, and pivot grammars were too good to be true.

Pretty soon, evidence began to come in that tended to refute pivot grammars. Lois Bloom (1970) documented the fact that the two-word utterances used by three children she studied did not consistently conform to the patterns predicted by pivot grammar. Further evidence in that direction was given by Brown (1970, 1973), Bowerman (1973) and Slobin (1971).

There does seem to be *some* tendency for two-word utterances to conform to the requirements of pivot grammar, but there are too many exceptions for us to feel any confidence that it is the right grammar. It isn't true that pivots occur in rigidly fixed positions, or that they never occur in combination with other pivots, or that they never occur as single-word utterances.

Again, we must be struck by how difficult it is to get off the ground in analysing children's early utterances. You may have started reading this book with the idea that they would be simple to analyse; but if so, hopefully you're beginning to see that there's much more involved than you thought.

Notes

1. Notice that the initial consonants in 'coo' and 'goo' are both velar sounds, made by contact between the back of the tongue and the velum, or soft palate. They differ in that /g/ is a voiced sound and /k/ isn't.
2. But see Greenfield and Smith (1976: 130), where Greenfield disagrees with McNeill's analysis of these facts.
3. The name 'telegram style' has often been used for this way of speaking, but now that telegrams are extinct, a new name is needed. Neither 'fax style' nor 'e-mail style' will serve, however. Perhaps the nearest thing is 'headline style', but it's not very near.

2. Catching fire

2.1 Making faster progress

The so-called 'vocabulary explosion', which occurs, on an average, at about 18 months,[1] and the two-word utterances that follow it, aren't the only indications that the process of acquiring language accelerates towards the end of the child's second year or the first half of the third year. In this chapter we'll look at some of the areas in which the children 'catch fire' during this period.

2.2 Multiple-word utterances

Most children go through a two-word stage, but after that it's hardly worth distinguishing a three-word stage, a four-word stage, and so on. We'll just assume that the next stage is a 'multiple-word' one.

We saw that, even with two-word utterances, the problem of analysing what's going on is by no means simple. With multiple-word utterances, it becomes tremendously complex; not just four or five times more complex, but, at an estimate, hundreds of times more so. Just a few decades ago, attempts even by good linguists to analyse the grammar of children's multiple-word sentences were not very successful. And although a great deal of progress has been made in those few decades, there are still plenty of problems.

So the grammar of a small child's sentences seems to be a tough nut to crack. But what is surprising is that the child progresses and keeps producing sentences which become more and more complex in their grammar, without seeming to have a great deal of difficulty. It is claimed that by the age of 4, most children acquiring English have mastered the central structures of English syntax. They haven't finished acquiring English, of course, and more complex structures take them longer to acquire (maybe up to about 10; see Carol Chomsky, 1969). But by the age of 4, or soon after, many children can handle passive constructions like 'Daddy was stopped by a policeman', as well as quite complex questions like 'Who was Daddy with?', 'What are you doing that for?' and 'What did you tell me to do?' The question is, how they come to be able to do this at such a young age. Truly, they seem to have 'caught fire'.

Many linguists have tried to make sense of what children do in their progression from simple two-word sentences to fully formed and quite lengthy ones. The most discussed question has been how they come to handle the verb system, because it involves a number of interlocking puzzles.

One of them concerns the system of tenses. Like many other languages, English makes a distinction between 'present' tense and 'past' tense. To get started, it will do if you think of these as referring to different 'times', though we'll soon move on from that. So we have the contrast between (1a) and (1b):

1a   Bob owns a Ferrari.
1b   Bob owned a Suzuki.

The sentence in (1a) tells us something about the present; the one in (1b) tells us something about a time in the past. If you are a fluent speaker of English, you know that in (1a) it's the -*s* on the end of *own* that signals that we're talking about 'now', and in (1b) it's the -*ed* on the end of the same verb that signals that we're talking about the past.

But it isn't as simple as it seems, as the sentences in (2) show:

2a   My trip starts on Sunday.
2b   So he asks me, 'What do you think you're doing?'

In (2a), the time referred to is the future, although it is the 'present-tense' ending (-*s*) that appears on *start*. And in (2b) the time referred to is the past, even though it is, once again, the 'present-tense' ending (-*s*) that appears on *ask*. This is an example of the so-called 'historic' or 'narrative' present, which is very common in anecdote-telling in popular speech. The fact that some people object to it is a social fact about them, rather than a fact about language. This use of the present tense is, in fact, a device for bringing immediacy to the story, and thus making it more vivid.

13

Now, if the so-called 'present tense' can be used to refer to past, present or future time, tense can't be the same thing as time. Strictly speaking, *starts* and *started* are different forms of the same verb, which can be interpreted in different ways with respect to time, depending on the circumstances. Similar remarks apply to *asks* and *asked*. Tense, then, is a matter of the form of the verb, not of the meaning. Of course, it's still true that there's a strong tendency for 'present' tense to correlate with a 'present' time-reference.

'Past' tense, as you know, is frequently signalled by the ending -*ed*. But in certain circumstances, even that can refer to future time:

3   If you called in tomorrow afternoon, I could give it to you then.

If we regard *called* as being a so-called 'past tense' form of the verb, the ending -*ed* signals a particular form of the verb, but does not indicate past time. It would be less confusing, in fact, if we called this the 'preterit' tense, which is an alternative name for it.

This is part of what children have to master, then, when they're acquiring English as a first language. But wait, there's more. Not all verbs show their tense-forms in the same way. As you already know, there are verbs like *go*, *get*, *come* and *cut*, which don't form the preterit tense by simply adding -*ed* on. The correct forms are *went*, *got*, *came* and *cut*. Such verbs are called 'irregular' ones, while the -*ed* ones are called 'regular' verbs. The preterit form of the irregular ones is not predictable from the present-tense form, and has to be learnt separately for each one. That is also part of what children have to learn before they will have mastered English. And they do it before the age of about 4, without real help. Even if parents do try to help, children often turn a deaf ear to what they're saying, until they have arrived at their own pace.

Sometimes small children put the regular endings on the stems of irregular verbs: *Daddy goed/comed*, etc. This shows that they're aware of the regular endings and know how to form regular past tenses. Sooner or later they correct to *went*, *came*, etc., showing that they've now realized that there are special forms for these verbs.

Don't go away yet. What I've been discussing so far are simple verbs, but there are also complex ones which involve the auxiliaries *be*, *have* and *do*:

4a   Scott <u>is going</u> to bed.
4b   The baby <u>has finished</u> her food.
4c   Mummy <u>has been combing</u> her hair.

14

You can't just put any auxiliary anywhere. The sequences shown in (5) are deviant:

5   *Scott has going to bed.
      *The baby has finishing her food.
      *Mummy is been combing her hair.

(An asterisk indicates a sentence that is not well formed.) The child has to master the quite intricate ways in which combinations can be constructed so as to produce acceptable sentences.

There's a lot more that children have to master at this period of their lives (say, their third and fourth years). One of the hurdles for them is to learn how to make negative utterances:

6a   Scott isn't going to bed.
6b   The baby hasn't finished her food.
6c   Mummy hasn't been combing her hair.

This mightn't seem too difficult. Once the child understands that there are auxiliaries (*is*, *has*, etc.), it's just a matter of attaching -*n't* (or *not*) to the end of the first one. But at first they haven't acquired auxiliaries. And even when they have, there's a problem. How do you turn the following sentence into its negative form?

7   The cat scratched the baby.

If you're a native speaker, or even a fluent speaker, of English, you know what the answer is:

8   The cat didn't scratch the baby.

But put yourself in the place of a baby. How does (s)he work out what's happening here? It's actually quite difficult. A form of the auxiliary *do* has been inserted from nowhere. The past-tense ending that occurred on the end of scratch in (7) has been removed, and it is the (irregular) past tense form of *do* that's used instead. Finally, the negative element -*n't* has been attached to that auxiliary. You can see that there's quite a lot for the small child to learn. And no one tells him/her that that's how you do it. The parents probably don't consciously know how they do it.

There have been various attempts to trace the steps by which children learn this process. Klima and Bellugi-Klima (1966) and Bellugi (1967) reported some research in which three children seemed to go through three stages in learning negation. The youngest was 18 months when the study began and 26 months when it finished. The other two were 26 and 27 months respectively when it began and were both 4.0 years when it finished. These were the three stages:

1. The negative was placed outside the main part of the utterance: *No the sun shining; no fall!* At this stage, no auxiliaries had been acquired, so none were used.
2. In the second stage, sentences like those in the first stage continued to occur, but ones like the following also occurred: *I can't catch you; I don't like him; He not little, he big; He no bite you.* In other words, only two auxiliaries were used in the negative form: *can't* and *don't; not* also occurred within the sentence, and occasionally *no*.
3. In the third stage, all the auxiliaries had been acquired, and were put inside the main part of the sentence. The negative element *not* or *-n't* is put straight after the auxiliary, as in adult speech.

The direction of development therefore seemed to be from having the negative element external to the main part of the sentence to having it internal to the main part, attached to auxiliaries.

However, Lois Bloom (1991: 144–5) gives a rather different interpretation to the facts described by Bellugi (1967), and reported above. She said that, like most acquisition researchers at that time, Bellugi ignored meaning,[2] and consequently didn't look at the context to see what the negative sentences meant; she only took note of the form of words used. According to Bloom, then, Bellugi 'had not done the critical analysis'. But Peter and Jill de Villiers (1979) did do it subsequently, and found that very few of the sentences had subjects in them – that is, they lacked the crucial markers for deciding whether the negative element was internal or external to the main part of the sentence. The de Villiers also recorded utterances by their own son when he was between 23 and 29 months old. He WAS putting subjects in his sentences. An example was *no Mommy do it*, and an analysis of the circumstances in which it was said showed that the meaning was '[I] no [want] Mommy do it'. This meant that the 'no' was targeting not *Mommy do it* but the unexpressed verb (or meaning) *want*. Furthermore, they found that all except one of the sentences where the negative might seem to be outside the main part of the sentence were of this kind. It's further evidence that the task of investigating children's language is never easy.

Another crucial grammatical device which develops at about the same time in children's acquisition of the language is the form of questions. I won't go into that development in great detail here, but it's worth mentioning that there are two main types of questions in English: 'yes–no' questions and 'Wh' questions. Yes–no questions are ones like the following, to which the answer can be (among other things) 'Yes' or 'No':

9a Have you asked her yet?
9b Is John going to the party?
9c Did you finish that game?

Like negation, they involve auxiliaries, and the dummy auxiliary *do*, but additionally involve reversing the order of the subject and the first auxiliary (*have you* as compared with the statement form *you have*).

These are simpler than Wh questions, which are ones starting with a so-called 'Wh' word: *when, where, why*, etc. And even though it doesn't start with 'wh', *how* is also regarded as belonging to the Wh words, because it functions similarly:

10a Where has Daddy gone?
10b When will Daddy come?
10c How do you make those?

I said that yes–no questions were simpler than Wh questions. Nevertheless, they're more complex than simple negation, such as I discussed above.

There are a good many other syntactic (grammatical) constructions that a child acquires by the age of 4, but I hope I've said enough to give you an idea of the way syntax 'catches fire' between about 2 and 4.

2.3 Acquiring words

It isn't only in sentence structure that the children 'catch fire'. They also do it, spectacularly, in the way they learn new words.

One of the problems that babies face is that there are no 'spaces' between the words in normal connected speech – no gaps in the sound to mark where one word ends and the next one begins. This will possibly come as a surprise to some readers, because we're so conscious of how words look when they're printed that we tend to imagine that there are gaps. But if you listen to speech around you, you'll soon convince yourself that words in connected speech aren't regularly separated by gaps. There are, of course, some silences as the speaker pauses; but these are not predictable, and certainly don't occur between every pair of words in the running stream. So the baby first has to discover what the boundaries are to each word.

Mothers and others try to help with this problem by sometimes speaking words in isolation, bringing out the separateness of words from each other. It's plausible that this helps, though even that isn't certain. (See Chapter 7 on 'motherese'.)

But even when the baby realizes that there are words, there's still the question of their meanings – both their individual meanings and their combined meanings when they occur in sequence.

After a slow start until about the age of 18 months to 2 years, children absorb new words with astonishing speed. Susan Carey, in a memorable paper (1978: 264) makes this challenging statement:[3]

> By age six the average child has learned over 14,000 words. On the assumption that vocabulary growth does not begin in earnest until the age of eighteen months or so, this works out to an average of about nine new words a day, or almost one per waking hour.

In a footnote, Carey explains that 'The estimate of 14,000 words includes inflected and derived words and is based on comprehension vocabulary. For root words[4] only, the estimate falls to around 8,000, or roughly five new root words a day.' But even so, this is a staggering estimate, and it has been widely referred to ever since. Most researchers find it credible.

As Carey says, it represents a puzzle, because a great deal of information must be stored in order to learn even a single word. Here are some of the kinds of information:

- that it *is* a word. Even as adults, we usually become aware that there *is* a particular word that some people use, before we come to learn other information about it;
- the syntactic word class to which it belongs (noun, verb, etc.);
- the subclass to which it belongs (count noun, intransitive verb, etc.);

- its semantic properties (properties of meaning). For instance, the verb *drink* has the semantic property that it implies an actor (a person or animal to do the drinking). Another of its semantic properties is that it implies that the object of that action will be a liquid;
- its place in the child's system of concepts. For instance, the child may have the concept 'physical object', which will apply to a word like *stone*;
- its relationship to other words in the child's vocabulary. For example, *bigger* is lexically related to *big*; *am* is lexically related to *be*; *give* is semantically related to *have*; and so on.

This list is by no means exhaustive. Of course, children don't learn all this information at once; it probably takes years before such complete information is absorbed. Nevertheless, they seem to latch on to words quickly – enough, apparently, to get the general drift of their meaning.

Although linguists and psychologists[5] have put many years of research effort into the question of how babies crack the verbal code, there's still a great deal that isn't known about it. If you've ever listened to a broadcast in a language you don't understand, you'll have some idea of the enormity of the task that infants face before they know any words. Somebody looking from the outside at what's happening would probably assume that the first hurdle would be for them to realize that the sounds they hear from the mouths of adults and others around them aren't simply noise but mean something. Note that this isn't a problem that faces *us* when we listen to a foreign language we don't understand. We assume it means something; we just don't understand the code.

People look at babies while they're talking to them, smile and make other gestures of endearment, and play verbal games which involve the repetition of something simple and attention-getting like 'Boo!'. At the same time, there's some action which the baby can't ignore: perhaps the adult suddenly parts her hands to reveal her face, or (in other verbal games) buries her head in the baby's stomach, or tickles the baby under the arms. One way and another, there are indications that the adult is *addressing* the baby – trying to say something *to* it. So it isn't surprising that babies come to realize that the noises coming from the adult's mouth *mean something*.

But the task of working out WHAT they mean is much more difficult, and is achieved only over time. In Chapter 14, 'Bootstrapping', we'll again take up the question of the acquisition of vocabulary.

2.4 The sounds of the language

At the same time as the child is acquiring words, (s)he's acquiring the sounds of the language – a task that takes quite a long time to fully master. My aim here is to make you aware of what the child has to absorb about sounds and about the organization that lies behind them. It will be necessary for you to try to free yourself from the grip of spelling when you're thinking about words in this section, and listen to the sounds.

Let's consider the consonants first, and some of the complexities about them which babies have to learn to cope with, if they're ever going to understand and use the language. Consonants are sounds which involve an obstruction or constriction to the stream of air coming from the lungs. Different kinds of obstruction or constriction produce different sounds; thus in the first sound in *tea*, the obstruction is caused by placing the tip of the tongue in contact with the back of the gum ridge, just above the top teeth. To produce the first sound in *pet*, on the other hand, we form a temporary obstruction by pressing the two lips together, and in the first sound in *call*, the obstruction is caused by contact between the back of the tongue and the soft palate. So these closures are in three different places in the mouth cavity.

In each case we let the air build up briefly behind the obstruction, and then release it. These three sounds ('t', 'p' and 'k') are often called 'stops', because the flow of air is stopped completely, if only briefly. They're also sometimes called 'plosives', because of the little explosion of air that they involve. The initial consonant in both cases is said to be aspirated (accompanied by a little puff of air).

In order to describe speech sounds as accurately as possible, linguists use one or other of several phonetic alphabets. The best known is the International Phonetic Alphabet, or IPA for short. In the United States, other alphabets are used more often. I'm not going to attempt to give you a course in phonetics in this chapter, or to instruct you in any extensive way in how to represent sounds by phonetic symbols. If you're reading this book as part of a course in linguistics, it's highly likely that there'll be a section of the course devoted to phonetics. But I'll mention a few significant things about phonetic representation whenever it seems relevant to do so for present purposes.

The sound at the beginning of *call* is represented in the phonetic alphabet by [k], not [c]. The letter 'c' has two different pronunciations in English: the sound at the beginning of *call* and the one in the middle of *receive*. Since they're different sounds, they must be represented by different symbols: the former is represented by **[k]** and the latter by **[s]** (in all the alphabets).

Notice that the **[t]** on the end of *pet* is pronounced differently from the one at the beginning of *tea*. In *pet*, there's no little puff of air and usually no release. In fact, if you wish, you can say the **[t]** at the end of *pet* by making a closure with your tongue on the teeth ridge and never taking your tongue away again, or never opening your mouth again. (True, these would be eccentric and unlikely eventualities.) My point is that the final 't' on *pet* is in principle not exploded. The same isn't true of the one at the beginning of *tea*.

A similar contrast occurs between the **[p]** at the beginning of 'pet' and the one at the end of *stop*, in that the latter needn't be, and usually isn't, exploded. The same sort of contrast also occurs between the sound **[k]** at the beginning of *call* and the one at the end of *back*. Notice that although I've referred to the 'sound' **[t]**, the 'sound' **[p]** and the 'sound' **[k]** in these two positions, and have so far used the same symbols to represent them in both positions, it's implicit in what I've been saying that the members of each pair are not *exactly* the same sounds at all. They aren't formed in exactly the same way, and they don't sound exactly the same, either. How can the members of each pair be 'the same sound' and at the same time 'not the same sound'? This is an important paradox, one to which we'll return soon.

Let's pause to notice that already, with these few simple facts, we've described some important things that little children must absorb by the time they learn to talk reasonably well. If they are to learn to understand and use words, they must come to hear the different acoustic effects of the different types of closures in consonants. It isn't an optional extra. The children must get to be able to tell the sounds apart and to use them, if they're to know the difference between *tap* and *cap*, *cap* and *cat*, or *pick* and *kick*.[6]

Some consonants have a less complete blocking of the airstream than the stops do. For a start, there are the so-called fricatives, in which there's a partial constriction, so that the air's allowed to escape through it with an audible friction (hence the name 'fricative'). They include sounds like the consonant at the beginning of *fat*, **[f]**, formed by making a light contact between the upper teeth and the lower lip, and the sound at the beginning of *thin*, **[θ]**, usually formed by a light contact between the tongue and either the upper teeth or both sets of teeth.

Then there are the nasal sounds: **[m]**, in which the two lips are pressed together while air's allowed to escape through the nose; **[n]**, in which the tip of the tongue comes into contact with the back of the teeth ridge and air is released through the nose; and **[ŋ]**, which is the last sound in *sing*. In spelling, it's represented by two letters, but in fact it's only one sound. So if you said 'doin' and 'havin' when you were a child and your parents told you you were dropping your 'g's, they were giving only a spelling description of what you were doing. The phonetic description would be that you were substituting one sound for another: you were using the sound **[n]** instead of the sound **[ŋ]**.

If you think of other consonant sounds, like **[l]**, **[w]**, **[s]**, **[r]**, and numerous others, you'll realize that there are other ways of forming constrictions and of releasing air. We're not going to pursue all of those, because it's already clear that what the baby has to learn about consonant sounds is intricate.

Obstruction of the airstream isn't the only factor involved in the production of consonants; for instance, some pairs of consonants are distinguished from each other by the fact that voice is used in the production of one, but not the other.[7] So the difference in pronunciation between *tip* and *dip* is just that the 't' in *tip* is not accompanied by voice, whereas the 'd' in *dip* is.

If you say these sounds in isolation, you may feel that they're both voiced, because you can hear voice on both occasions. But the explanation is as follows: if you say what's supposed to be the sound of 't' in isolation (as you possibly did when you were learning to read in first grade), you actually say what is phonetically represented as **[tə]**. In other words, you say a sequence of two sounds, the consonant and a vowel (the 'neutral' vowel which we shall discuss shortly). The reason this is (rather misleadingly) used as the 'sound' of 't' in elementary reading classes is that the sound **[t]** by itself wouldn't be heard very clearly in the classroom, since it consists of just the sound of air escaping from the closure between the tongue and the teeth ridge.

But since the second sound in each case is a vowel (a sound made without obstruction to the airstream), and since voice is used in the production of all vowels, you hear voice when you start on the vowel following the 't' in *tip*. To convince yourself that that's what's happening, put your tongue in the position to say *tip* but explode the air without saying the vowel. You will then have heard just the consonant 't'. By contrast, if you get ready to say the 'd' in *dip* and stop before you get to the vowel, you'll hear voice, because voice is one of the features involved in producing the consonant 'd'.

The contrast between voiceless and voiced initial consonants also occurs in such pairs as *pea* and *bee*, *fat* and *vat*, *cot* and *got*, *Sue* and *zoo*, *thin* and *this*. The initial consonants in these pairs would be represented phonetically as [p] and [b], [f] and [v], [k] and [g], [s] and [z], [θ] and [ð]. In each case the first one is the voiceless sound and the second the voiced one. The second one is formed in exactly the same way as the first, except for the addition of voice.

So far I've mentioned vowels only in passing, but they're at least as important as consonants. When we're talking about spelling, we usually say there are five vowels: a, e, i, o, u; but phonetically there are more than that. Consider the variety of medial vowel sounds (sounds in the middle of a word) in *bat*, *men*, *tip*, *key*, *bird*, *caught*, *path* and *hot*. The vowels are what differ most in different dialects. The way Americans say *hot* sounds roughly like the way I say *heart*. But then, the pronunciation of *heart* used by many Americans is different from mine, too, because they pronounce the 'r' in such words, whereas I don't. (Some Americans don't, either.)

In addition to vowels, there are diphthongs, which are vowel-like sounds, in which the tongue begins in the position for one vowel, and then glides towards the position of another vowel. The sound following [b] in *boy* is a diphthong, in which the tongue begins in the position for [ɔ] (the vowel sound in *caught*, in my speech) and then glides towards the position for [ɪ]. The relevant sounds in your dialect may be similar, or they may be somewhat different. If your dialect is similar to mine, you can hear the diphthong if you say the sound [ɔ] followed by the separate sound [ɪ], then gradually reduce the time gap between them, and eventually blend them. Other diphthongs occur in *day*, *night*, *tour*, *here*, *there* and *go*. Sometimes, what's pronounced as a vowel in one dialect will be pronounced as a diphthong in another. *Tea for two* is pronounced [ti fə tu] in the so-called 'cultivated' variety of Australian English, but as [təɪ fə təu] in the so-called 'broad' variety. It's easy to see that diphthongs would seem to complicate life for a baby learning the language.

There's one very important vowel I haven't discussed yet, and that's the first sound in *astonished*. It's often called the 'neutral' vowel, partly because it can take the place of almost any other vowel under certain conditions.

In order to clarify what I mean by that, I must talk about stress. Stress is the amount of emphasis we put on a syllable, and it ranges from very

23

strong to very weak. A strong stress can involve various factors, including loudness, duration and intonation (change of pitch). Compare the words *buck* and *bucket*. There's a strong stress on the word *buck*, as there is on all monosyllables produced in isolation. But when there are two or more syllables, there'll most often be a differentiation in the amount of stress put on the different syllables. If you say *bucket* aloud, you can hear that the first syllable, *buck-*, is more heavily stressed than the second one, *-et*. In consequence, the vowel in *-et* is reduced to the neutral vowel, [ə] – also called 'schwa' – so that the *-et* doesn't rhyme with *bet*.

The way in which we stress words sometimes varies from dialect to dialect, or even from person to person. I have an English friend who pronounces *cricket* as [krɪkɪt], while I pronounce it with a neutral vowel in the second syllable: [krɪkət]. In other words, I reduce the second vowel to a neutral vowel because it's in an unstressed position, while my English friend doesn't always do that. He has pointed out to me that in his speech there is a contrast between *badgers* (where the vowel in the last syllable is reduced to schwa) and *badges*, where it is pronounced [ɪ]. In neither case is there any stress.

I pronounce *exquisite* with the main stress on the first syllable (EXquisite), but most other Australians pronounce it with the main stress on the second syllable (exQUISite). It isn't really a question of being right or wrong. How you pronounce things probably depends more on your family and the environment you grew up in than whether you're a goodie or a baddie. I'm not about to change my pronunciation of *exquisite* to conform to the majority pronunciation, but if I had consistent difficulty in being understood, I would.

There are more than just two degrees of stress in English. In the word *undisturbed*, the strongest stress is on the final syllable, *-turbed*, but there's a difference between the amounts of stress on the first two syllables, the second being weaker than the first. We may talk of primary, secondary and tertiary stress, and perhaps others, as well as weak stress. You might like to amuse yourself by trying to work out the degrees of stress in such words as *internet*, *pizzicato*, *undifferentiated*, *electromagnetism*.

The assignment of stress in words is a complex technical issue, yet little children pick it up very well, on the whole. There are some words in which the stress is different depending on whether the item is a verb or a noun. The noun PERmit has a strong stress on the first syllable, but the verb perMIT has it on the second. The same difference between the stress on the noun and that on the corresponding verb occurs with *export*, *protest*, *progress*, *suspect*, *torment* and numerous other words. (Check these out for yourself.)

What's all this got to do with babies? Obviously, a great deal. I remarked above that how you pronounce things depends a good deal on the family you grew up in, and the process starts when you're a baby, learning your first words. Babies must learn not only the sounds of words, but the stress and intonation that go with them.

It's even more complex than that. Once we put words into phrases and sentences, the stress that they have in isolation frequently changes. If I ask you to pronounce the word *that*, you will put a strong stress on it; but if you use the same word in the sentence *Did I tell you that I went to a party last night?* you'll almost certainly reduce *that* to a weakly stressed syllable and reduce the vowel from its normal quality to that of a neutral vowel. On the other hand, if you say *I think I'll take that one*, indicating a particular shirt or blouse in a shop, you'll be likely to give the vowel in *that* its full quality and stress it strongly. You can also give a strong stress to any word that you want to contrast with some other word. (*I want the GREEN dress, not the yellow one.*) These are some of the skills that children must acquire, and they seem to acquire them very young – an astonishing performance.

One of the more amazing things is that they pick up the sounds of the language from speakers around them who don't all sound the same. Men's voices sound different from women's, and children's voices sound different again, but this doesn't seem to cause a huge problem. Children probably have a head start, since they seem to be born with the ability to use stress and intonation. Their earliest cries exhibit this ability.

The baby, then, is confronted with all this and much more. Reading this chapter, you may find it forbidding enough to be confronted with so many facts about phonetics/phonology, but at least it's being carefully explained to you what (some of) the system consists of. Nobody explains it to the baby; that would be impossible and of course ineffective. Yet (s)he somehow latches on to the system; not all at once, but gradually, over a period. Imagine an English-speaking adult being set down in China and having to pick up the sounds of the language without help – just by listening. But even that wouldn't be as difficult as what the baby has to do, because at least as adults we've heard language sounds before, even if somewhat different ones. The baby starts from a total lack of experience of speech sounds of any kind. (There is some evidence that babies hear their mother's voice even while they are still in the womb, but that just means that's where they start getting experience.)

We could expand the details of the description of English sounds enormously, so that it occupied at least the rest of this book. And with each step, the number of things a baby must absorb would grow. It's certain that the baby doesn't think consciously about these things, but takes them on board unconsciously, since people who haven't studied phonetics aren't conscious of them even in adult life. That raises a question about how the feat is accomplished. We'll face that question further on in the book. See Chapter 13 on bootstrapping.

But even if I set out a fairly extensive description of the phonetic facts of English or any other language, I would still have covered only the surface facts; I would not have dealt with the intricacies of the underlying sound system.

We almost stumbled upon the existence of such a system above, when I was talking about the fact that the 't' at the end of 'pet' is articulated differently from the one at the beginning of 'tea'. If they're different, why do we think of them as being 'the same sound'? (This is what I referred to as a paradox, above.) The spelling moves us in that direction in this case, but that isn't the basic explanation. The fact is, those two kinds of 't' are members of a family of t-sounds which is usually referred to as a 'phoneme'. All the sounds in the language fall into different phonemes. Actual sounds, such as you hear, are called 'phones', whereas the families of sounds into which they cluster are the 'phonemes'. You can't actually hear phonemes, since they are just category labels (family labels). If we wish, instead of making a phonetic transcription (a representation of the actual sounds heard), we can make a phonemic transcription; that is, a representation of the phonemes to which the actual sounds belong. Native speakers of the language regard members of the same phoneme as being 'the same sound' as far as the organization of the language is concerned, even if they're physically somewhat different. It's conventional to place phonemic transcriptions between right-leaning slashes, thus: /ti/; /pɛt/. (You'll recall that phonetic transcriptions, by contrast, are placed in square brackets: [tʰi]; [pʰɛt]. The diacritic 'ʰ' means that the sound immediately preceding is aspirated.)

You might think that a baby wouldn't have to acquire an awareness of phonemes, as long as (s)he gets the sounds right – but you'd be wrong. The groupings of sounds into phonemes differ from one language to another. Although [tʰ] and [t] are thought of by native speakers of English as being 'the same sound' (in the organization of the language), there are other languages in which they're thought of by native speakers as being 'different sounds', which could make a difference to the meanings of words. Even the phones may differ from language to language; for example, French doesn't contain the aspirated stops $[t^h]$, $[p^h]$, $[k^h]$ at all.

By now it must be evident that what babies have to absorb about the sound system of their native language is highly complex. They don't absorb it consciously, but somehow have to come to operate the system. They just seem to 'pick it up', though we will have more to say later in the book about what this means.

As already mentioned, there are two different sounds in English for the spelling 'th'. One is the so-called 'voiced th', which is what you hear at the beginning of *this*, and the other is the so-called 'voiceless th', which is what you hear at the beginning of *thin*. Some people find it difficult to hear the difference. If you go to say 'thin', but stop yourself from going past what is represented by the letters 'th', you will hear that there is no voice, only air escaping between the tongue and the teeth. But if you go to say 'this' and stop yourself from going past the 'th', you will hear voice as part of the 'th' sound. You should also hear the difference if you say the word *thistle*, followed by the phrase *This'll (make you happy)*. Also, as Neil Smith has pointed out to me, 'Some of us have a relevant minimal pair for "your leg": *thy thigh*.' This means that the two words in *thy thigh* differ only in the first sound in each case: the voiced 'th' in the case of *thy*, and the voiceless one in the case of *thigh*. However, I suggest you restrict your usage of the phrase to either amorous or reverential discourse.

These two items are not just different sounds (phones), however; they represent different families of sounds (phonemes). Different phonemes can make a difference to meaning; different phones can't. If someone used $[t^h]$ on the end of 'pet' instead of $[t]$, it would not form a different word; it would simply sound excessively clear. I could actually do this if I had said 'I'll give you a pet', but my listener thought I had said 'I'll give you a pen'. In clarifying the difference, I could use the exploded form of 't'.

Although the two 'th' sounds in English are differentiated by whether voice is present or not, that difference doesn't always make for different phonemes. For instance, 'm' can also sometimes have voice and sometimes not. It is voiced in *make*, but usually isn't voiced in *smoke*. Hence there is only one /m/ phoneme in English, and we can't find cases where two words of different meaning are the same in every respect except that one has 'voiced m' and the other has 'voiceless m'. Yet in some other language, that very difference might constitute a difference of phoneme, and could thus cause a difference of meaning.

You can see, then, that a small child has to get to detect the difference between different phonemes, if (s)he is to understand the language correctly.

There's an important school of linguistics, called generative linguistics, whose adherents don't literally accept the idea of phonemes as I've described them, but the reasons why they don't, and the machinery that they use instead, are too complex for an introductory book like this. And even generative linguists usually admit that for many purposes, phonemes are a good approximation. In a similar way, Newton's picture of the universe will serve quite well for many purposes, even though Einstein's is ultimately a better one. Phonemes are adequate for present purposes.

There are even more complex things that a baby has to master, in relation to the sounds of the language. So far, I've talked as though the word *pet* is made up of three separate sounds, $[p^h]$, $[\varepsilon]$ and $[t]$, constituting three separate segments in the stream of speech; but that isn't really so. Before we've finished articulating $[p^h]$, the tongue and other parts of the speech apparatus have started getting ready to articulate $[\varepsilon]$, so that the two articulations overlap and are not clearly separated. Likewise with $[\varepsilon]$ and $[t]$. To reach the level of mastery of sounds that most children reach by the age of 4, they have to 'catch fire' in this aspect of language, too.

In this chapter I've said a great deal about what babies have to acquire, but very little about how they do it. This is partly because no one knows with absolute certainty. There are various theories about it, however, and in later chapters the different schools of thought about how language is acquired will be described.

Notes

1. It can, however, occur a good deal earlier or a good deal later than that.
2. That is, contextual meaning. It has sometimes been claimed in the past that the context (situation) in which an utterance occurs is entirely responsible for its meaning. It is a factor, but only a factor, and the meanings of the words are also important.
3. The figure of 14,000 words is based on the findings of an earlier study by Mildred Templin (1957).

4. That is, base words like *write*, as opposed to those with endings, like *writing* and *writes*.
5. The work of linguists and of psychologists overlaps closely in this area, and although there are sometimes differences of methodology, we can virtually ignore them for present purposes.
6. Notice, incidentally, that *kick* has one of the varieties of **[k]** at the beginning and the other one at the end.
7. This is somewhat simplified. As Neil Smith and Deirdre Wilson (1979: 126 n. 2) point out: 'In fact, the most important characteristic of "voicing" is *voice onset time*; i.e., the exact point when the vocal cords start vibrating, rather than the simple presence or absence of voice.'

3. Do we *teach* children to speak?

3.1 Some popular ideas

What's difficult to understand about a child acquiring language? Isn't it self-evident? Doesn't everyone know how it happens?

The usual belief goes something like this: one day the mother's leaning over the end of the cot, talking to the baby and perhaps trying to get it to say its first word. 'Say Mum-Mum,' she says, or words to that effect, and after a few gurgles and splutters the baby manages to say something that sounds a bit like 'Mum-Mum'.

Perhaps the baby has just opened its lips and made a natural sound; but no matter. The mother will seize on this performance with delight, smile very warmly and repeat the little game. Her pleasure is infectious, and the baby enjoys the game as much as she does. It smiles, and maybe even laughs.

Pretty soon, the baby is very good at responding with 'Mum-Mum', so the mother introduces another word – perhaps even 'Dad-Dad'. After a number of trials, the baby manages to say something pretty close, and is rewarded with more beaming smiles.

The baby's vocabulary is built up word by word, until it has quite a repertoire of words it can say: probably the names of brothers, sisters and animals, as well as the names of various objects and activities.

Everyone knows that this is so, don't they? And the next part of this procedure is that the mother teaches the baby phrases, one by one, and then sentences, and then longer utterances, until the baby has learnt the language. So what's the problem?

The problem is that that's almost certainly *not* the way the baby acquires language. Well, it possibly *is* the way the baby learns those first dozen or so words, but it can't be the way most of it proceeds, as we'll see a little later.

3.2 The sources of these beliefs

If the account given in the preceding section isn't correct, why do so many people believe it? First of all, because it seems plausible. Everyone has seen mothers go through those steps with a baby, and the baby does, after all, learn to talk. But in spite of this apparent plausibility, it's worth repeating that there's good evidence that those procedures don't teach the baby the language, though they might get it started.

The second reason people believe that this is the way children learn their language is that in the past, it was more or less what scientists believed. It became the standard account, and to most scientists concerned with these questions (i.e. linguists and psychologists) it seemed self-evident, too.

It will help our aims if we have a detailed look at the set of beliefs that those linguists and psychologists had, a set which was collectively known as behaviourism. Although I'll maintain that it was a mistaken set of beliefs, we can learn a lot by seeing why it was mistaken.

The journey we're about to undertake will perhaps seem surprising to the reader. In order to discuss the different views on how children acquire their first language, we're going to look at different attitudes to what happens in the brain/mind when people speak. It may seem that we're straying far from what we set out to do; but I think you'll come to see that all this is relevant, and that it will lead us to considerable illumination about how the different points of view came about, and what different claims their proponents make.

In the preceding paragraph I referred to the brain/mind, and I'd now better discuss what the difference is. When linguists, psychologists and other cognitive scientists think about the physical aspects of the brain, they call it that: the brain. But when they concern themselves with its psychological aspects, they tend to call it the mind. The relationship between the mind and the brain has been a continuing problem at least since Descartes. For a very interesting discussion of this matter, see Chomsky (1995a, 1996b), which is reprinted in Chomsky (1997).

Linguists tend to talk of the mind rather than the brain, because the things that linguists study are abstract, and it isn't clear how they relate to the physical side of the brain. But Chomsky (1980: 31) claims, 'We may think of the study of mental faculties as actually being a study of the body – specifically the brain – conducted at a certain level of abstraction.' As you can see, there's still room for a little mystery.

3.3 Early behaviourism

3.3.1 PAVLOV'S RESEARCH

Ivan Pavlov, a Russian physiologist, showed as early as 1906 that certain behaviour by animals could be described in mechanistic terms and could therefore be predicted and controlled.

Pavlov's first step was to attach some tubes to the saliva ducts in the tongue of a dog, and measure how much saliva came from the tongue when the dog had a plate of meat put in front of it.

After the dog had been trained to expect the meat to be presented in this way, Pavlov added a new element to the procedure: he not only presented the plate of meat to the dog, but also rang a bell at the same time. He estimated that after this procedure had been followed a number of times, the dog would associate the sound of the bell with the presentation of the meat, and that it would salivate even if the meat wasn't presented, as long as the bell was rung. He then showed experimentally that this was indeed the case. The dog had been 'conditioned' to respond to the bell, and the bell was called the 'conditioned stimulus'.

What Pavlov had shown in this remarkable experiment was that one stimulus could be substituted for another, so as to elicit the same response. By using conditioning, it was possible, at least in part, to predict and control animal behaviour.

3.3.2 J. B. WATSON

In 1913 J. B. Watson, an American psychologist, launched a new model of psychology and called it 'behaviourism', or, more accurately, since Watson was an American, 'behaviorism' (with no 'u'). It attempted to make psychology into a rigorous science – every bit as rigorous as the established sciences like physics and chemistry.

3.3.3 THE BEHAVIOURIST CONCEPTION OF SCIENCE

The success of the 'hard' sciences seemed to be in part due to the fact that they followed 'scientific method', a set of procedures which were supposed to be used by all scientists. The only kind of evidence that was scientifically respectable was evidence that could be publicly inspected, was open to scrutiny by other scientists, and was therefore considered to be objective.

Scientific method was adopted wholeheartedly by behaviourist psychologists, who were (quite naturally) intent on making their science as respectable as the very successful physical sciences. They must have become all the more convinced that they were on the right track when they saw the spectacular advances in physics during the 1920s and 1930s.

But as a matter of fact, so-called 'scientific method' wasn't consistently followed in the hard sciences; see Bohm (1983) and Collins and Pinch (1993). At best, scientific method seems to have been an ideal which was constantly breached, even by those who professed to believe in it. It was not a method for making scientific breakthroughs, but a method for writing up the research later (and not always even that).

Just as religious converts are often more zealous than the other adherents of the faith, many psychologists became more 'pure' about scientific method than most scientists. They insist, for instance, more than physicists usually do, that all accounts of the research must be written in an 'impersonal' style, in which passive sentences are favoured over active ones, and it's forbidden to use the pronoun 'I'.

The myth is that the 'scientific method' style is more 'objective'. But that style doesn't guarantee objectivity, and, conversely, the writer can be just as objective without it.

These beliefs about the nature of science raise an important issue for us in our quest to find out how children acquire their first language. If you believe that the only scientific evidence is what can be publicly observed and inspected, it follows that feelings, thoughts, mental pictures, ideas, meanings and a host of other things that are said to take place in the brain are beyond the scope of science. They simply can't be studied scientifically.

To be sure, under such a view, the physical aspects of the brain are not beyond the scope of science. Operations on the brain can be observed, and the neurological structure of the brain studied. The trouble is, no matter how you open a brain and inspect it, you won't find anything like thoughts or mental pictures inside. They may exist, said the behaviourists (though most of them were pretty sceptical about that), but science can't study them, because there's no objective way of examining them.

It followed that any scientific account of how children learnt their first language couldn't make any reference to anything that was going on inside the baby's head, such as thoughts or ideas. It would have to be a description entirely 'from the outside'. That's why this approach was called 'behaviourism', because only behaviour could be studied scientifically. Psychology, in fact, was (and often still is) defined as the study of behaviour.

3.3.4 ARE HUMAN BEINGS JUST COMPLEX MACHINES?

Along with the view described in the preceding section went another: that human beings are basically complex machines. For thousands of years there have been two competing views about how much control human beings have over their own actions. One view is that we're free to decide what actions we'll take. People who accept that are said to believe in 'free will'. The other view is that we have no control at all over our actions, for everything we do is the result of the forces acting on us in our environment. We may think we have freedom to choose which way we'll act, but that's an illusion. People who accept this are said to believe in 'determinism', because they believe that everything is determined by forces acting on the individual.

Suppose someone is tempted to steal some money. According to the determinist view, if the forces acting to make the person steal it are stronger than the ones acting to prevent them from doing so, then they will steal the money; otherwise they won't.

This view has a certain plausibility about it. The machines that we use in everyday life, such as washing machines and vacuum cleaners, act according to what buttons we push. We are the forces manipulating them: they start if we press a certain button, and they stop if we press a certain button (which may be the same one). In the case of a washing machine, all its actions after starting are governed by the settings we make before we start it. It can't do anything that it hasn't been designed and programmed to do. Perhaps human beings are like that, too, only much, much more complex. At least, that's what a determinist thinks, and that's what behaviourists thought, too.

Perhaps you find this idea, that we could all be just complicated machines, a rather repulsive one. But before you rush to embrace the opposite point of view, that human beings are free to choose what they do, you should realize that this view is not without its difficulties, either.

34

What does it mean, to say that we're free to choose? Does it, for instance, mean that our actions are not caused? If so, they must be random, and although this might be a kind of freedom, it isn't a very satisfying one. In what sense, then, are we free?

The discussion so far may seem rather surprising. You opened this book, presumably, wanting to find out how children were able to learn to use their first language, and here we are, discussing whether human beings have free will or not.

The reason is that the use of language is something that is very close to the essence of being human. Our answer to the question of how children acquire their first language will depend on the nature of human beings. If we're just complicated machines, then one kind of answer will suffice; but if we're more than that, if we have some kind of freedom in choosing what we want to say, then a rather different kind of explanation will be necessary.

It isn't altogether clear to what extent the brain is just a complex machine, and to what extent human thinking is somehow 'free'. Although I believe that the behaviourists were wrong in trying to describe people as complex machines, I don't think they were silly for making the claim, in the era in which they first made it.

3.3.5 THE WORK OF LEONARD BLOOMFIELD

Leonard Bloomfield, a linguist, published his ideas on language in his book *Language* (1933). It took a behaviourist stance.[1] He points out (p. 32) that human conduct, including speech, has great variability, and that this has led to the development of two opposing theories about it.

Bloomfield describes the first theory as follows:

> The mentalistic theory, which is by far the older, and still prevails both in the popular view and among men of science, supposes that the variability of human conduct is due to the interference of some non-physical factor ... that is present in every human being. This spirit, according to the mentalistic view, is entirely different from material things, and accordingly follows some other kind of causation or perhaps none at all.

Bloomfield and other behaviourists were at that time causing a swing away from that view to the second kind of theory, which was known as the *materialist* or *mechanistic* theory. This claims that speech is so complex only because the human body is a very complex system. Bloomfield goes on (p. 33):

> We could foretell a person's actions (for instance, whether a certain stimulus would lead him to speak, and, if so, the exact words he will utter), only if we knew the exact structure of his body at the moment, or, what comes to the same thing, if we knew the exact make-up of his organism at some early stage – say at birth or before – and then had a record of every change in that organism, including every stimulus that had ever affected the organism.

Now, Bloomfield was quite aware that the matter was complicated. Even if we know a lot about a speaker and about the stimuli to which he is subject, he wrote, 'we usually cannot predict whether he will speak or what he will say' (p. 32). Nevertheless, he believed that it was possible *in principle* to predict people's actions, including what they say.[2]

We'll be returning later to the conflict between the two theories cited by Bloomfield. In fact, it will play a continuing part in the story that is to be told, though changing as it goes along.

3.4 The work of B. F. Skinner

The work on conditioning done by Pavlov was later to be of considerable interest to B. F. Skinner (1904–90), an American who was one of the most famous psychologists of his day. Skinner too carried out some very impressive conditioning experiments with rats and pigeons.

Pavlov's famous experiment had simply involved a physiological conditioning, in which the change in response took place within the body of the dog. But Skinner wanted to see whether the external behaviour of animals could be changed by conditioning.

He developed the so-called Skinner box, which was set up in such a way that if a rat in the box pressed a lever, a food pellet would be released. The rat did it the first time more or less accidentally, but soon learnt to press the lever at will. More complicated conditions for releasing the food pellet were then introduced; for instance, the rat might have to press a light switch as well as the lever before it would be rewarded.

Skinner did other notable conditioning experiments, too. In one famous one, he taught pigeons to walk in the shape of a figure eight, simply by rewarding them with food pellets every time they happened to walk in the right direction to achieve part of this feat. If a pigeon just by accident walked in a brief arc that conformed to a part of a circle, it was rewarded. Then, bit by bit, Skinner extended the proportion of the circle that would be rewarded, and gradually the pigeons learnt to walk around in a circle, in order to achieve the reward of the food. Finally, Skinner taught them to reverse direction and walk the other way in a circle, so as to complete the figure eight.

This method of rewarding 'correct' behaviour was called *reinforcement*. Skinner's experiments were very successful in showing that certain behaviour in animals could be developed and controlled by conditioning and reinforcement.

Next, Skinner wanted to apply his techniques of conditioning and reinforcement to human behaviour. In everyday talk, we say that people have been 'conditioned', and that's why they act in a particular way. This popular usage will give you a rough idea of the technical meaning of the term, though psychologists use it in a rather more precise way.

Skinner held the two most prominent beliefs of behaviourists, already described: (a) that behaviour must be described entirely in terms of what is observable, without any reference to what goes on in the head; and (b) that human beings are just complex machines.

It's quite possible that some of our habitual behaviour can be accounted for in terms of conditioning and reinforcement; for example, much of our behaviour while driving a car may be of this kind. But Skinner then made a very important leap. He claimed that conditioning could also account for human language learning and language behaviour.

His account of the nature of language and language acquisition was presented in his book *Verbal Behavior* (Skinner, 1957). The book had been in preparation for some twenty years before that.

Skinner felt that his work on animals could be 'extended to human behavior without serious modification' (p. 3). And the behaviour to which it could be so easily extended included language behaviour. 'The basic processes and relations which give verbal behavior its special characteristics are now fairly well understood,' Skinner wrote. 'Much of the experimental work responsible for this advance has been carried out on other species, but the results have proved to be surprisingly free of species restrictions.' Thus Skinner hoped to be able to describe the whole of human behaviour, including language behaviour, in terms of stimulus, response, conditioning and reinforcement.

Suppose someone uttered the word 'chair' in the presence of such a piece of furniture. Skinner would say that certain properties in that piece of furniture were acting as stimuli to elicit that particular verbal response. If it had been a different piece of furniture, say a bed, then the rather different properties of that piece of furniture would have caused a different response: the word 'bed'. Thus, what we say is always a response to some stimulus (or stimuli) in the environment. All behaviour can therefore be explained in terms of the 'building bricks' of *stimulus* and *response*.

I happen to think that Skinner's view of language behaviour is wrong, but it seemed reasonable for him to put it forward at that stage in history. The idea that very complex happenings can be built by multiplying some very simple ones is certainly plausible. This becomes evident when we consider the way in which all matter is built up of atomic particles, or the way in which computers are programmed in very complex ways, simply by using the fact that current in a circuit can be either flowing or not flowing – on or off. These two states can be represented by 1 and 0 respectively, in very intricate arrangements.

Another example of stimulus and response that Skinner mentions is that of a student who's learning to pick the composer of an unfamiliar piece of music, or to name the artist who painted an unfamiliar picture, or the school to which the artist belongs. Certain properties in the music might lead the student to respond with 'Mozart' in the one case or with 'Dutch' in the other. These responses are then reinforced by the community with 'right', or punished with 'wrong'.

Still another example is that of the child who's doing arithmetic and is praised and thus reinforced if (s)he gives the response 'four' to the question 'two and two?'. We will be looking at some crucial criticisms of Skinner's proposal in Chapter 5, but it's perhaps worthwhile commenting here that this account is inadequate for the general case. What about the response 'ninety-two' in response to the stimulus 'thirty-five plus fifty-seven'? Many people are capable of giving this response, perhaps after a hesitation of a second or two. It is surely absurd to claim that such a response is made because of previous reinforcement in giving that answer.

Or, for that matter, what about the answer 'six hundred and twelve' in response to the question 'two hundred and seventy-four plus three hundred and thirty-eight'? Surely anyone who can give this answer engages in some mental computation, but Skinner can't allow such an explanation, since for him anything that goes on in the brain is outside the scope of scientific explanation. So he persists in considering only the externals of behaviour.

The interesting thing is that what Skinner presented as his theory of how children learn language was basically the same as the popular theory described earlier in the chapter – only, of course, Skinner's description was more complex and technical. In fact, the reason that the popular theory is so widely held is possibly because Skinner's work had such a strong influence. But it may also be that the popular theory has been around a lot longer than Skinner's work; I somehow suspect it has.

3.5 Why can't that be the way children acquire language?

Why am I so confident that that couldn't be the way children acquire their native language? Because it implies that the method that the mother uses to teach the baby is simply that of providing a model utterance for it to imitate. We would then have to assume that the baby stores up each utterance in its memory and on later occasions produces one of the utterances from its store, just when it's needed. That's what I call the 'human tape recorder' theory of language acquisition. Well, what's wrong with it?

The answer to that question was expressed very well by George Miller, an American psycholinguist, many years ago (1970: 82–3).

If you interrupt a speaker at some randomly chosen instant, there will be, on the average, about ten words that form grammatical and meaningful continuations.[3] Often only one word is admissible and sometimes there are thousands, but on the average it works out to about ten. (If you think this estimate too low, I will not object: larger estimates strengthen the argument.) A simple English sentence can easily run to a length of twenty words, so elementary arithmetic tells us that there must be at least 10^{20} such sentences that a person who knows English must know how to deal with. It would take 100,000,000,000 centuries (one thousand times the estimated age of the earth) to utter all the admissible twenty-word sentences of English. Thus, the probability that you might have heard any particular twenty-word sentence before is negligible. Unless it is a cliché, every sentence must come to you as a novel combination of morphemes.[4] Yet you can interpret it at once if you know the English language. With these facts in mind, it is impossible to argue that we learn to understand sentences from teachers who have pronounced each one and explained what it meant.

Note that George Miller was talking only of the twenty-word sentences of English. There's good reason to think that if we take all sentences into account, there are an indefinitely large number of sentences and potential sentences in the English language.

Mathematicians have made us familiar with the fact that there's an infinite set of numbers. If anyone told us the highest number they could think of, we could always exceed it by simply adding 1 to it; so there's no end to how many numbers there are. What I'm claiming is that something similar applies to sentences: there's no end to how many there are. If you haven't met that claim before, you might find it incredible, but it's nevertheless true.

It's easy to demonstrate trivially that it must be true. Consider a sentence such as *There were two grains of sand in the box*. It's possible to replace the word *two* by the word(s) for any number up to infinity.[5]

While granting that that gives an infinite number of sentences, you may nevertheless feel that's a pretty uninteresting kind of infinitude. Agreed. But there are several other pieces of evidence that might convince you that there are an infinite number of potential sentences in the English language (or any other language).

Try a simple exercise. Go to the nearest large library – maybe a national or state library, or a university library. Choose a section of the library at random. Point your finger at a random shelf, and then run your hand along the shelf and stop it at a random book. Take the book down and open it at a random page, then run your finger down the page and stop it at a random sentence. And then see if you can find EXACTLY THE SAME SENTENCE anywhere else in the library. You may well spend the rest of your life at the task.

Of course, I know you won't do that, but I think even if you do the exercise for a little while, you'll soon become convinced that there's a great multitude of different sentences – many more than you would have imagined. Remember, it has to be exactly the same sentence, not just one that resembles the first one you put your finger on.

Let's come at the matter another way. Those of you who are native speakers of English (and many who aren't) will be familiar with the rigmarole that's taught to children, which begins with the words 'This is the house that Jack built.' As you know, the formula keeps expanding, bit by bit, until eventually it becomes 'This is the cock that crowed at dawn and woke the priest all shaven and shorn that married the man all tattered and torn that loved the maiden all forlorn that milked the cow with the crumpled horn that tossed the dog that worried the cat that chased the rat that ate the malt that lay in the house that Jack built.'

You'll notice that this is all one very long sentence which has constantly been extended by adding another clause. The question now is, how many more clauses could we add to the rigmarole and still have a grammatical sentence of English? The answer is surely that we could add an indefinitely large number without becoming ungrammatical. We would, of course, become boring after a while, or we would stop because we had run out of breath, or because all the seconds in our lifetime had elapsed. But notice that none of these things would render the sentence ungrammatical. In fact each of those events has nothing to do with grammar.

Since we could have stopped the sentence at the end of any of the clauses, each of these potential stopping-points marks the end of a potential sentence. And since the sentence can be infinitely long, there's an infinite number of potential sentences implied.

To repeat George Miller's point, it is impossible to argue that we learn to understand sentences from teachers who have pronounced each one and explained what it meant.

Let's play just one more game. Get a piece of paper and write down the longest sentence you know. However long a sentence you write, I will then suggest to you that you actually know a longer one, because if I begin with the words 'Jack said that . . .' and then add on your long sentence, you'll almost certainly agree that that's also a sentence of English.

Suppose you've already thought of that, and have started your sentence with 'Jack said . . .' Then I'll suggest to you that if I begin with the words 'Mary claimed that . . .', then carry on with 'Jack said that . . .' and complete your very long sentence, you'll almost certainly agree that that too is a possible sentence of English.

To cut a long story short, I'll always be able to add another clause to the beginning so as to make a longer sentence than the one you suggested. It's similar to always being able to add one number, however high someone counts. Again, the sentence might become boring, but it wouldn't become ungrammatical.

There's another reason why I don't believe children learn the language by imitation from their parents and others. When they make so-called 'mistakes', children often say things that no adult would say, and which are highly unlikely to be failed imitations of what adults would say. I'm thinking of a case where a child says *I goed* instead of *I*

41

went. I goed sounds nothing like *I went*, which is what an adult would say, so it can hardly be a failed imitation. But there's more to it than that. The form that the child produces, *goed*, is exactly what we might predict the past tense of *go* would be, if the language were regular, and all past tenses were formed on the analogy of *walk – walked*; *love – loved*; *start – started*, etc. These three are not phonetically identical in their past-tense endings, but the endings are all forms of the same morpheme; that is, despite their phonetic differences, the words have the same grammatical significance. This means that the child is acting as though (s)he's constructed a rule to which many of the verbs in the language conform, but has over-generalized it so that it's wrongly applied to a verb which is an exception to that rule.

What I've been criticizing in this chapter is behaviourism as a theory which can explain normal language acquisition. I'm told that speech pathologists have applied uses of behaviourism which are said to be helpful in the treatment of both children and adults. That may be an area where conditioning does have a role to play. I'm a great believer in the dictum 'If it works, use it.' Nothing beats that.

Although I've given some reasons above for being suspicious of Skinner's claims about normal language and language acquisition, I haven't yet presented the main criticisms of his theory. This is because Skinner's most trenchant and cogent critic is Noam Chomsky, whose work will be described in Chapters 5 and 6.

Notes

1. Neil Smith points out to me that Bloomfield was actually a behaviourist for only part of his career and that his early mentalist and his late descriptive work ignored his own precepts.
2. I am indebted to Neil Smith for his remark (in a private communication) that 'It's ironic that quantum indeterminacy [Heisenberg] saw the light of day in the hard sciences in 1927.'
3. For example, if you interrupt a speaker after he has said 'The other night, I wanted . . .', it's possible that the utterance could have continued with the words *a drink*; *to visit a friend*; *Sue to see me receiving a prize*, etc. In each case the continuation would be both grammatical and meaningful.

42

4. Morphemes are the smallest meaningful parts of words. So, *unusual* consists of two morphemes, *un-* and *usual*; *hotel* consists of only one morpheme; and *playgrounds* consists of three, *play*, *ground* and *-s* (signifying plurality).

5. This assumes a box of infinite size, as well, but imaginary boxes will do just as well as real ones for the purpose of judging whether the sentence is grammatically possible.

4. Learning through touching and feeling

4.1 Introduction

In this chapter we'll have a look at the work of a famous Swiss psychologist who had a major influence for a large part of the twentieth century. Jean Piaget's main interest was in developing a theory of cognitive growth – that is, of how thinking abilities mature in the growing child. He lived from 1896 to 1980, and his main work was done at the University of Geneva.

He had begun his academic career as a biologist, and always tried to connect his psychological theories to the underlying biological facts. He was also a philosopher, and became active in numerous other fields as well.[1]

Piaget felt that the theory he developed for describing how general cognitive growth occurred was enough to explain language learning, too. The development of language was just one aspect of general cognitive growth. Because Piaget held that view, a fair amount of this chapter is going to deal with what he said about cognitive development. Without some knowledge of that, you wouldn't be able to understand the significance of the things he and his followers said about language.

Piaget himself didn't say very much about language. Fortunately, some of his followers paid much more attention to it than he did, and tried to fill out the details, though (understandably) nearly always with an eye to showing that language fitted in well with the rest of his theory. We'll come back to some of that work later in the chapter.

4.2 Piaget's account of cognitive growth

4.2.1 SENSORI-MOTOR LEARNING

To begin at the beginning: Piaget observed his own three children intensively, starting immediately after their birth (and I mean imme- diately after). He noticed that each baby had an impulse to suck from the very first minutes of life, and he assumed that this was hereditary. He noticed that the sucking reflex seemed to be applied to anything that presented itself, even if some objects were then rejected.

By the way, the word 'reflex' has a special meaning in Piaget's usage, one which is different from the meaning behaviourists sometimes give it. 'A reflex, in the Piagetian sense, is a reaction of the organism that is hereditary and not acquired by experience' (Gruber and Voneche, 1977: 216). For Piaget, sucking was a reflex in just this sense.

Piaget noticed that the sucking reflex seemed to have a need to repeat itself, so that objects other than the nipple came to be sucked: perhaps the bedclothes, or the father's finger, given to the baby as a pacifier.

As a baby grows older, more and more objects are assimilated into the sucking reflex: thumbs, shoes, dolls, etc., and perhaps the odd snail. In fact, Piaget uses the word 'assimilation' as a technical term, to describe the way in which more and more items are absorbed into the set of things to which the particular reflex – in this case, sucking – is applied.

But in those early minutes of his children's lives, Piaget noticed something else. No matter how good the sucking reflex was, it had to adapt itself to the nipple, through repeated attempts. As Piaget puts it, 'it is capable of gradual accommodation to external reality'.

The word 'accommodation' is also, for Piaget, a technical term. He elaborates his remark in this way:

> In order that a useful function may result, that is to say, swallowing, it often suffices to put the nipple in the mouth of the newborn child, but as we know . . . it sometimes happens that the child does not adapt at the first attempt. Only practice will lead to normal functioning. That is the first aspect of accommodation: contact with the object modifies, in a way, the activity of the reflex. (Piaget, 1953: 29–30)

At first, the impulse to suck is stimulated by contact of the lips with any part of the breast, but the sucking stops if there is nothing to swallow.

45

Then the infant starts to search for the nipple, and only when it has found it do the sucking motions settle down to continuous activity. Piaget concludes, 'In all behaviour patterns it seems evident to us that learning is a function of the environment.'

The lips, then, have to make slightly different motions according to what's being sucked. There's obviously a difference between sucking the bedclothes and sucking the nipple, so the sucking reflex 'accommodates' to the particular object it's sucking.

We now have the two terms 'assimilation' and 'accommodation'. If you're feeling a little vague about the difference, don't worry; it's an effect these terms often have on people.[2] Let's just recap. The way in which new objects are made targets of sucking is called assimilation. The way the lips adapt to sucking different objects is called accommodation. The two concepts are just different aspects of a single act. It isn't possible to have one without the other, since assimilating a new object into the reflex inevitably involves adapting the lips to a slightly different action.

These comparatively simple observations by Piaget on his newborn children were the starting-point for a much larger conception: that very young children learn about the world through actions performed on the environment; that they use their muscles and their senses to gain knowledge about the world, long before they're able to talk.

Given a new toy, a very small child will often grab it, lift it up, suck it, then bang it on the floor or push it. The child who explores the universe in these ways is in what Piaget calls the 'sensori-motor' stage – the stage in which children use their senses and muscles to explore the world. In feeling an object and sucking it, the child is learning about its shape and texture and taste, and perhaps exploring its function.

According to Piaget, all perceptions arise from actions. And actions often occur in sequences. Picking up a toy involves (at least) looking, reaching out, grasping, and lifting, and maybe pulling the toy back to the body. But these actions become integrated into a single 'scheme' (or 'schema') of action, which then applies to other picking-up operations as well – say, picking up a shoe or a ball. Each time a new object is involved, it is 'assimilated' into the scheme. In that way, the child builds up a 'practical concept' of this sequence of actions.

Piaget claims that in the beginning babies are profoundly egocentric. When we describe someone in adult life as being 'egocentric' it carries a certain condemnation with it. We don't like people who are totally obsessed with themselves. (They should pay more attention to us!) But, of course, Piaget intends none of those connotations when he says that babies are egocentric. It isn't a judgmental term, but a neutrally descriptive one, since the baby can't help being egocentric in Piaget's sense.

If Piaget is right, babies can't distinguish themselves from the world, which just seems like part of them. Learning to distinguish the world from themselves is an important part of the learning that will take place over the next few years. Only then will they be able to see that there might be other points of view than their own; that other people mightn't see the world from their perspective.

When one of my own children was 3 or 4 years of age, he was learning to count, and his older brother urged him to count the people at the dinner-table. (There were actually five, including a third child.) He counted, 'One, two, three, four', pointing to each person as he counted. Then he stopped, obviously feeling he'd finished, though he hadn't counted himself. 'And what about you?' someone asked. 'Oh,' he said, 'no, I'm counting!' It was a good example of a child at this stage seeing the world only from his own point of view, though he must have been on the threshold of passing out of that stage. Readers who have children of an appropriate age can try this experiment for themselves, and will probably get a similar result. (Piaget had already noted the fact that this is typically the outcome.)

The sensori-motor stage of development lasts from birth to about 18 months or 2 years of age.

4.2.2 THE PRE-OPERATIONAL STAGE

Piaget claims that cognitive development proceeds in four main stages.[3] Each one has a number of internal divisions, but here we'll ignore the internal divisions and concentrate on the main stages.[4]

The second one (after the sensori-motor stage) is the 'pre-operational' stage – that is, the stage before the child can carry out (mathematical and other) operations. It lasts approximately from 18 months to 7 years of age. Incidentally, the ages that are cited as representing the boundaries of a particular stage vary with different children. Piaget was not very concerned about fixing exact ages: he was more interested in claiming that the stages had to occur in a particular order. So the sensori-motor stage has to come before the pre-operational stage (fairly obviously).

We have seen that during the sensori-motor stage, the child is able to carry out 'practical schemes of action' – that is, sequences of actions that combine to make a more complex action. An example is the scheme 'picking up an object', which consists of (at least) reaching out a hand, opening the hand, bringing it into contact with the object, closing the hand, lifting the object and (possibly) drawing the hand containing the object back to the body. There are many other such schemes of action.

According to Piaget, although knowledge of the outside world initially comes in with the aid of such actions, 'no knowledge is based on perceptions alone' (Piattelli-Palmarini, 1980: 23). The mind has to shape the perceptions: anything that is observed has to be 'interpreted'. For example, the observer might notice that one object is larger or smaller than another, or that one object is close to or distant from another. 'Interpreting' observations, then, will often mean noticing relationships among objects; hence, the mind imposes some structure on what is observed. In fact, Piaget called his model of children's cognitive development 'constructivism'. That is the crucial way in which Piaget's system differs from Skinner's, for Skinner didn't allow the idea of mental structures.

But the child (or an adult) cannot make a generalization from a set of separate similar actions without being able to compare them with each other. In order to do that, the child must be able to think of them at times when they're not happening. And that's possible only if the child can form mental representations of the actions. So, says Piaget, it's 'necessary' to make the leap from merely assimilating the actions into a 'practical concept' to representing them mentally.

Piaget seems to imply that because some event is 'necessary' for progress it will therefore happen; but it's difficult to see why. At crucial points in his argumentation, Piaget is often not explicit.

He says it is intelligence that creates cognitive structures through observations. But he has to account for the fact that children arrive at about the same stages of development at roughly the same ages. His answer to this problem is to say that the child's progress to each new stage is 'necessary' (inevitable). He doesn't mean by this that it's biologically necessary (pre-programmed in the child), but rather something more akin to logically necessary (though this comparison is not exact).

We might ask whether a dog 'necessarily' makes the same leap to mental representations as the child does. After all, a dog explores the world by sensori-motor actions, and presumably has 'practical concepts' too. The dog would then 'necessarily' have to develop mental representations in order to be able to compare individual acts when they weren't happening. It's difficult to know how rich a dog's conceptual life is, and Piaget would probably hesitate to make that claim. By way of explanation, he could only point to the difference in intelligence between a dog and a human being. But this is a biological difference, in that, in order to have human intelligence, you must be born human, with a human brain. This goes beyond the idea of a kind of logical 'necessity'.

We won't pursue this question further, but the reader can perhaps see that there are many questions to ask once we start thinking about the details. Piagetians acknowledge the many questions that Piaget's theories raise.[5]

Piaget wrote many books, so if you wish to pursue his ideas further, you should be able to find a number of them in any university library.

It isn't accidental, of course, that the beginning of the pre-operational stage coincides with the onset of language. As we've already seen, prior to the age of 18 months (on average), children acquire individual words, but don't yet put them together into two-word or multi-word utterances, and their vocabulary is restricted to maybe a dozen to twenty words. At about 18 months there's a sudden surge in vocabulary acquisition, and two-word utterances develop.

Piaget believed that before words can be acquired, there must be 'practical concepts' (schemes) to apply them to. Since language has begun to develop by the pre-operational stage, the child can acquire a name for each scheme – for example, 'pick up'. Piaget claims that language develops independently of cognitive structure, but he's always a bit obscure on the subject of how language does develop. He says, though, that like cognitive structure, language is 'the "necessary" result of the constructions of sensori-motor intelligence' (Piattelli-Palmarini, 1980: 31).

At times he talks as though the ability to use sentence structure depends on the prior development of particular types of conceptual structures (mental representations).

49

4.2.3 THE CONCRETE OPERATIONAL STAGE

The concrete operational stage is said to last from about 7 to about 10 or 11. As always, there's considerable variation from one child to another. It's 'concrete' because the child thinks about a particular situation and doesn't generalize or formalize the operation.

The transition to the concrete operational stage is very important, Piaget says, since within a few years the child 'spontaneously reconstructs operations and basic structures of a logico-mathematical nature, without which he would understand nothing of what he will be taught in school' (1953: 26). This is a fairly dramatic claim, but Piaget then goes further (p. 26):

> After a lengthy pre-operative stage during which he still lacks these cognitive instruments, he [the child] reinvents for himself, around his seventh year, the concepts of reversibility, transitivity, recursion, reciprocity of relations, class inclusion, conservation of numerical sets, measurements, organisation of spatial references (coordinates), morphisms, some connectives and so on – in other words, all the foundations of logic and mathematics.

In case you aren't sure what some of these terms refer to, I'm about to provide some explanations. Although Piaget mentions reversibility first, I'll deal with it last, because there's a fair bit to say about it.

Fortunately, you don't have to learn the definitions below. (I can't throw a test at you tomorrow.) So apart from absorbing some information that you may not have known before, all you have to do is to notice the wide scope of the concepts that Piaget says children 'reconstruct' for themselves. I imagine he means 'construct for themselves', and the 're-' comes from the fact that others have done it before (cf. 'reinventing the wheel').

Transitivity

If A is taller than B and B is taller than C, then A is taller than C. If I'm taller than you are and you're taller than Jane, then it follows that I'm taller than Jane, too.

Recursion

Recursion is a process which enables a term in a sequence to be calculated by examining one or more of the earlier terms in the sequence. An example is a Fibonacci sequence, in which each term after the first two is obtained by adding together the two preceding terms; thus: 0, 1, 1, 2, 3, 5, 8, 13, 21, . . . By starting with 6, 9, . . . you can test whether you can make a Fibonacci sequence for yourself. The answer is in this note.[6]

Reciprocity of relations (if A = B then B = A)

If Bill's arm is the same length as mine, then my arm is the same length as Bill's. You have to be careful if you depart from measurement, though. If Sue's boyfriend is a Frenchman, it doesn't necessarily follow that a Frenchman is Sue's boyfriend.

Class inclusion

For example, the class of corgis is included in (is a subset of) the class of dogs.

Conservation of numerical sets

The number of objects in a group doesn't alter if they're spread out over a wider area. (See the fuller account below.)

Measurements

No explanation needed.

Organization of spatial references (coordinates)

Finding a city on a map involves the use of coordinates, but Piaget means three-dimensional coordinates, such as you might use to locate an object in space.

51

Morphisms

A morphism occurs when two groups of items have the same mathematical structure. Piaget may have in mind the idea that a child perceiving, say, six books and six oranges comes to realize that something is the same in the two groups, namely the number of objects. The group of books could be mapped on to the group of oranges, one to one (or vice versa). What does 'mapped' mean? Roughly, that you could link each orange up with a book, without using the same book twice.

Some connectives

Certain conjunctions, such as *and* and *or*.

Piaget's claim that children 'reinvent' the basic concepts of mathematics and logic is a breathtaking one. That isn't to say that it's necessarily wrong, of course. The story is told that Niels Bohr, the great Danish physicist, once had a new theory outlined to him by a colleague, who then asked him what he thought of it. 'Your idea is crazy,' Bohr is reported to have said. 'But not crazy enough to be right.' In other words, correct ideas may seem crazy at first hearing.

Back to Piaget, whose idea may (or may not) have been crazy enough to be right. I promised above that I would come back and discuss reversibility at greater length. It's now time to do so.

Reversibility

The concept that a process can be undone or 'done backwards'. Below, we'll examine some examples of this process.

Many Piagetian investigations of children's cognitive development involve tests to determine the level of sophistication the children have reached in handling reversibility. For instance, a group in New York led by Harry Beilin administered five such tests (Beilin, 1975). The investigators wanted to see how performance on the tests of reversibility correlated with the children's ability to use and comprehend passive sentences. Reminder: pairs of sentences like (a) *The dog bit the postman* and (b) *The postman was bitten by the dog* are related grammatically. Sentence (a) is called an 'active' sentence because the subject of the sentence (*the dog*) is responsible for the action described by the verb *bit*. Conversely, (b) is said to be a 'passive' sentence, because the subject of (b) (*the postman*) is just the 'passive' receiver of the action. (Though of course he might be very active a fraction of a second later!) If we compare the sentences (a) and (b), we see that there's a reversal of the order of the noun phrases *the dog* and *the postman* in (b) as compared with (a), and that's why reversibility tests seemed relevant to these structures.

Figure 4.1 Piaget: simple reversibility test

At the lowest level, a child was required to drive a toy car from one 'garage' (a red card) to another 'garage' (a green card), a distance of about 30 cm, and then to drive it back again to where it had been before (Figure 4.1). A child who could do *only* this had reached only the sensori-motor level in reversibility, and in general was unable to cope with passives.

The other tests described below are more difficult, and in general it was only after children could pass them all that they were able to produce and comprehend passives satisfactorily. This happened for most of the children in the second grade.

First, the child had to pass a test of 'conservation of discontinuous quantity'. All that means is that separable objects remain the same in number, no matter how we shift them around. That won't surprise you too much, but children have to come to realize it. Smaller children tend to think that if there are two rows of objects (say, sweets) and one is longer than the other, the longer one will contain more objects. But they may simply be placed more widely apart, and the longer line may then contain the same number as the shorter one (or even fewer). (See Figures 4.2 and 4.3.)

Figures 4.2 and 4.3 are based on the description given in Beilin's second test, slightly adapted. A line of sweets was placed before each of two dolls, with the same number of sweets in each line, in such a way that the lines were the same length, as in Figure 4.2. The investigator asked each child whether the dolls had the same amount to eat, and, if the answer was 'no', the child was asked which one had more.

53

Figure 4.2 Piaget: test for conservation of discontinuous quantity: lines of same length

Figure 4.3 Piaget: test for conservation of discontinuous quantity: lines of different length

The sweets were then spread out more widely in one of the lines, so that it was longer than the other, as in Figure 4.3. The children had to judge whether the dolls now had the same amount to eat, and many of the younger ones judged that they did not. They were then asked to

anticipate whether the dolls would have the same amount to eat if the sweets were moved back to their original positions. Notice that this involves making a mental representation of what the situation will be then. It therefore involves reversibility.

The third test concerned 'conservation of continuous quantity'. If you have something that doesn't come packaged as objects, but as a mass of some substance (water, milk, etc.), then simply moving it from one container to a different-sized one won't change how much there is. Surprised?

Figure 4.4 Piaget: test for conservation of continuous quantity

The investigator showed each child two glass containers which were of equal size and contained equal amounts of water. The child was then asked whether there was the same amount of water in each jar. If not, the levels were adjusted until the answer was 'yes'. The child was then asked to anticipate what would happen if the water from one container was poured into a taller, narrower container which was also present (Figure 4.4). If the reply was that there would be a different amount, the child was asked to point to the place on the new container where the water would reach. The investigator then poured the water and asked the child whether the two containers had the same amount in them.

The next instruction was to point to the spot on the original container where the water would reach if it was poured back again, and to say whether the amounts would be the same or not. Reversibility is again involved, and demands a mental representation. Only a child who

55

has the concept that the process is reversible will predict that it will reach the same height as it did before it was poured out of the wider beaker.

The fourth test concerned seriation (that is, placing things in a series). There was a sequence of lines or sticks of different lengths, with one item in the series missing (Figure 4.5). The child had to draw in the missing one or choose from a pool of other sticks in order to put the missing one in place. In another example, there were four beds of different lengths and four dolls of different lengths, and the problem was to place the dolls in their right beds.

The fifth test asked the child to carry out various classifications of toy animals according to colour and kind, by putting different groups into different containers. In general, the questions were designed to assess the child's ability to classify, add and subtract classes, and to deal with whole–part class relations.

Each such task tested the child's knowledge of reversibility (as did all five main types of test). If the child classified the animals into horses, cows, etc. and was later asked to reclassify them into brown ones, black ones, etc., then the first classification had to be 'reversed' in order to carry out the second one.

The overall conclusion drawn from these tests was, then, that we should not expect children to be able to handle the passive until about the age of 6 or 7, which is about when they should be able to do these tests of reversibility.

The experiments on the passive provide a good demonstration of what I said earlier: that it's necessary to know some of what Piaget said about cognitive development before you can understand his account of the development of language.

These concepts don't arrive suddenly, but are the result of cognitive growth. George E. Forman (1982) gives a very interesting account of an experiment in which children were filmed while they engaged in spontaneous play with small geometric blocks. Forman says that while children are putting blocks on top of each other, removing them again and recombining them, they are 'both expressing their knowledge of objects in space and inventing new relations as they turn their thoughts to what they have done' (p. 98).

The constructions children build with blocks are rule governed, and 'block play can be studied as an early system of logic'. Forman focuses on the equivalence relation (A = A' but is not A'); for instance, two blocks of the same size are equivalent in that sense, but different in that they

Figure 4.5 Piaget: test of seriation

(a) The child is given a set of sticks of ascending size, but out of sequence, and is asked to arrange them according to size.

(b) The child is given a drawing of a series of upright lines ascending in size. There is a double space between the third and fifth lines. The child must draw in the missing line.

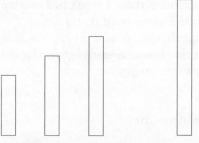

(c) The child is given a card with sticks pasted on it, with a double space between the third and fifth sticks. (S)he is instructed to choose the missing stick from four remaining sticks.

are separate objects. Forman claims that the notion (A = A' but is not A') originates in the manipulation of blocks.

The child has two hands, which function in symmetry with each other and might serve as the elementary basis of the logical notion of equivalence. Furthermore, elementary addition and subtraction follow fairly naturally from the actions of putting a block on top of another block (or a pile of other blocks) and of removing one or more blocks. Piagetian investigations of logico-mathematical relations are frequently thorough, insightful and persuasive.

Now consider reversibility again. Piaget says that at the sensori-motor stage the child can reverse PHYSICAL actions, but has not yet developed the CONCEPT that an operation can be reversed ('done backwards'). That ability doesn't arrive until the onset of the third stage: the so-called 'concrete operational stage'.

4.2.4 THE FORMAL OPERATIONAL STAGE

At about the age of 11 or 12, according to Piaget, the child moves to the fourth and final main stage, which Piaget calls the formal operational stage. (S)he is now able to follow complex rules and logic, and can do algebra or play games like chess.

Having been humiliated at chess by a friend's 10-year-old child many years ago, I feel that Piaget's threshold for this stage must be quite variable. (The child had been playing for years and was champion of south-east England for his age group; I have still not graduated from the 'beginners' class. My defence is that I haven't had much practice. In fact, I don't think I've played a game since then.)

The formal operational stage is said to last until about 16. Many Piagetians believe that that is not the end of cognitive development, and that there are further, adult, stages.

4.3 Language development

4.3.1 SOME EXPERIMENTS

I've already remarked that for much of his long career, Piaget had little to say about language or children's acquisition of it, being more interested in other aspects of mental development. He did little himself

LEARNING THROUGH TOUCHING AND FEELING

to establish the claim that language could be explained by the workings of 'sensori-motor intelligence', but other Piagetians at the University of Geneva and elsewhere tried to give substance to his claim in their research on language.

Ferreiro (1971) and Ferreiro and Sinclair (1971) provide good examples. Ferreiro made a study of temporal relations in children's language. She tested children's understanding of sentences in which two events were described as taking place without there being any causal connection between them. The events could be either simultaneous or one after the other.

Ferreiro's book was written in French, but an English example would be *His wife greeted him and he went upstairs*, in which there is (normally) no causal connection between the two events. The same events could also be described by the sentences:

1   After his wife greeted him he went upstairs.
2   Before he went upstairs his wife greeted him.

In (1), the order of mention is the same as the order in which the events happened, but in (2), the order of mention is the reverse of the order of events. It is natural to assume that this is because of the difference in meaning between *before* and *after*; but matters are more complicated than that. The implications of the two words with respect to the order of mention and the order of events become exactly the opposite if they are put between two clauses, instead of at the beginning of the whole sentence:

3   He went upstairs after his wife greeted him.
4   His wife greeted him before he went upstairs.

A different comparison is provided if we put (1) and (3) alongside each other:

1   After his wife greeted him he went upstairs.
3   He went upstairs after his wife greeted him.

Although (1) and (3) both contain *after*, in (1) the order of mention and the order of events are the same, but in (3) they are the reverse of each other.

Likewise, compare (2) and (4):

2   Before he went upstairs his wife greeted him.
4   His wife greeted him before he went upstairs.

Although (2) and (4) both contain *before*, they are opposite in the relations they display between the order of mention and the order of events.[7]

Other researchers carried out similar investigations at the beginning of the 1970s. All concluded that sentences where the order of mention is the same as the order of events are easier for children to process than ones where that isn't so. Furthermore, children acquire them earlier.

Now, why should these results be of interest to followers of Piaget? Because some of the sentences in question involve a reversal of the order of events and the order of mention, and it isn't until children reach the concrete operational stage that they're able to handle cases of conceptual reversibility. For that reason, such investigations are frequently accompanied by tests of the children's 'reversibility level', of the kind we saw earlier.

Piaget claimed that the first conception of time arises in the sensori-motor stage (before the age of 2). Understanding temporal events requires a knowledge of duration and of the way in which events can occur in a certain order. The infant becomes aware of duration as (s)he cries and then has to wait to be fed. Later, as children develop 'schemes of action', they become aware of the fact that events occur in a certain order. By definition, schemes of action involve a series of simple events which have to occur in a particular sequence.

Another step forward occurs when language develops (say, before the age of 4). By then the child has progressed from 'practical schemes of action' to mental concepts of action, but is still not ready to do 'operations' on these mental concepts. That ability arrives at the age of about 6 or 7. Ferreiro's results were in accord with that, though she was more concerned with the operational level the children had reached (i.e. their ability to handle reversibility conceptually) than with their exact ages.

The claim, then, is that children can't handle such grammatical structures as the passive and the *before* and *after* sentences discussed above until they're able to cope with the cognitive concept of reversibility, and the related abilities of seriation and conservation, such as we met earlier in the tests described by Beilin.

If you wish to read about further Piagetian experiments, Beilin (1975) describes some.

There will be more about Piaget towards the end of the next chapter, where there will be an account of the important debate he had with Chomsky.

Notes

1. For a more extensive account, see Boden (1979).
2. Chomsky once said that such terms as *assimilation* and *accommodation* seemed to him 'semimystical' (in Otero, 1988: 384–5). But there are many who do not find them so.
3. Strictly speaking, three main stages, but the second one is divided into two movements, consisting of (a) preparation for formal operations, and (b) achievement of the ability to handle them. These are frequently regarded as separate stages.
4. What I am here calling 'stages' have sometimes been called 'periods', the term 'stages' then being reserved for the internal divisions. 'Stages' seems the better term for the main divisions, because it does not carry as strong a connotation of a fixed time-span.
5. They discuss them in some detail on the Piagetian e-mail list on the Internet, and in much greater detail in a continuing output of scholarly books and articles.
6. The sequence is 6, 9, 15, 24, 39, 63, . . . (you can keep going as long as you like).
7. On the other hand, (1) and (4) are the same with respect to order of mention and order of events, though (1) contains *after* and (4) contains *before*. It is the same in (2), which contains *before* and (3), which contains *after*.

5 What goes on in the mind?

5.1 Mentalism

The main aim of this book is to examine how children come to know their native language, but already we've found it necessary to look at the nature of *adult* language. Linguists who have different views on that are also likely to have different views on how children get to know their first language. As we've seen, if someone regards human beings as complex machines, their account of both language and language acquisition is likely to make reference to automatic responses to stimuli. The account will pay attention to what happens to the child from outside, since such events will provide the necessary stimuli for the child to respond to.

But there's another school of thought, called mentalism, that takes a completely different approach. It's concerned with what goes on inside the child's head as language develops.

The split between behaviourists and mentalists goes right through the social sciences: linguistics, psychology, philosophy, sociology, education, etc. It's therefore a pretty basic division.

In 1959 Noam Chomsky, who was almost unknown at that stage, wrote a review of Skinner's *Verbal Behavior* (Chomsky, 1959, reprinted as Chomsky, 1964a), which still seems one of the best of his many outstanding papers. Near the beginning of the review, Chomsky says that he and Skinner can agree on one thing: anyone investigating language will have to be concerned with (a) the language the person hears, and (b) the responses the person makes. Furthermore, the investigator will have to try to account for the responses in terms of the inputs. This is just to state the definition of the problem, he said.

So what's the difference between Skinner and Chomsky? It is that Chomsky believes that the organism (in this case a human being) makes a complex contribution to the process, but Skinner takes little or no account of it. Chomsky says about Skinner (Chomsky, 1964a: 549):

> He confidently and repeatedly voices his claim to have demonstrated that the contribution of the speaker is quite trivial and elementary, and that precise prediction of verbal behavior involves only specification of the few external factors that he has isolated experimentally with lower organisms.
>
> Careful study of this book (and of the research on which it draws) reveals, however, that these astonishing claims are far from justified.

Chomsky doesn't deny that the research on stimulus and response and reinforcement that had been carried out in the laboratory on animals had achieved genuine insights, but he asserts that they 'can be applied to complex human behavior only in the most gross and superficial way' (p. 549).

Getting down to details, Chomsky attacks the notion that a person's actions are completely controlled by stimuli. He picks up Skinner's example of someone standing in front of a picture and saying 'Dutch' as they look at it. For Skinner, the man's response would be brought about by certain (extremely subtle) stimuli in the picture. Chomsky comments (p. 552):

> Suppose instead of saying *Dutch* we had said *Clashes with the wallpaper, I thought you liked abstract work, Never saw it before, Tilted, Hanging too low, Beautiful, Hideous, Remember our camping trip last summer?*, or whatever else might come into our minds when looking at a picture.

In other words, there is a virtually infinite set of responses that could be made. Skinner would be forced to say that in each case, a different set of stimuli would be acting to produce the response. But Skinner doesn't name the stimuli; he just says that when we say 'Dutch' we must be responding to properties of 'Dutchness' in the picture. As Chomsky says, nothing is being said about any real, physical properties at all. Once you know what the response is, you can say that the stimuli must have been appropriate ones to produce that response, but without specifying what they are. Such a process doesn't account for anything.

Chomsky systematically attacks the other main concepts in Skinner's account: reinforcement, conditioning, verbal operant, response strength, and so on. The demolition is systematic, efficient and devastating. Finally, Chomsky claims that the facts about how children learn language are almost completely unknown. 'It is clear that what is necessary in such a case is research, not dogmatic and perfectly arbitrary claims.'

Chomsky has an interesting prefatory note to the reprint of his review (1967: 142–3). He explains that when he wrote the review, his intention was not so much specifically to criticize Skinner's 'speculations regarding language' as to make a more general criticism of behaviourist 'speculation as to the nature of higher mental processes'. He goes on:

> My reason for discussing Skinner's book in such detail was that it was the most careful and thoroughgoing presentation of such speculations ... Therefore, if the conclusions I attempted to substantiate are correct, as I believe they are, then Skinner's work can be regarded as, in effect, a reductio ad absurdum of behaviorist assumptions. My personal view is that it is a definite merit, not a defect, of Skinner's work that it can be used for this purpose, and it was for this reason that I tried to deal with it fairly exhaustively. I do not see how his proposals can be improved upon ... within the framework of the general assumptions that he accepts.

This might seem fairly complimentary to Skinner, though the last sentence is ominous. But the next sentence says that the general point of view behind Skinner's work 'is largely mythology, and that its widespread acceptance is not the result of empirical support, persuasive reasoning, or the absence of a plausible alternative'.

It probably isn't too much to say that this review acted as the watershed between the behaviourist era in linguistics and the Chomskyan one. The revolution that Chomsky was to bring about in linguistics was enormous. The whole way of thinking about language and language acquisition was to become dramatically different. In fact, it was also to have a huge impact on psychology and philosophy.

That isn't to say that everyone was convinced about the need for change. Behaviourism continued to be practised, and continues to be to the present day. And many people who would now reject the pure form of behaviourism nevertheless stop short of fully embracing mentalism.

Chomsky's theories about language are by no means universally accepted, but it's important to know what they say, even if you come to reject them.

As you may already have come to suspect, my own preference is for mentalism. However, my aim is not to indoctrinate you in any particular view, but to raise interesting and relevant issues for you to consider. If this book succeeds in doing that, it will have achieved its purpose.

5.2 Descartes' contribution to mentalism

The mentalist tradition goes back as far as Plato, but there's a very close link between the mentalism of Descartes, the seventeenth-century French philosopher, and that of the most important mentalist of the twentieth century, Noam Chomsky.

Descartes (Haldane and Ross, 1931: 115–18) was very much concerned with the question of whether human beings are complex machines, and his answer was that they are not. He thought it wouldn't be possible to make a robot which would resemble a human being in all ways. A doll might be made to say various things, like 'I'm hungry' and 'I want to go to sleep now', depending on where you touched it, but there would be two things which would allow us to detect the difference between a robot or a doll and a real human being.

In the first place, robots could only act in accordance with 'the disposition of their organs' – that is, what they could do and say would depend on the way they were built. They would never act in accordance with knowledge, as human beings do. In the second place, they wouldn't be able to make their replies appropriate to virtually any situation, 'as even the lowest type of man can do'.

Even with the advances made in computer technology in recent years, Descartes' answer is still correct, though various claims are made about the possibility that computers will one day be able to adapt appropriately to any situation. It would probably be wise for us not to expect computers to rival humans in this capacity very soon, but of course it's dangerous to predict what computers may or may not do in the future.

One of the big deficits in computers is their lack of emotions and emotional experience; in other words, they aren't human, or even animate. Those who use computers constantly refer to them as being able to 'read files', 'understand instructions', and so on. It's well to remember that these are only metaphors at present, though quite sophisticated people are often oblivious of the fact. I was once talking to the head of a university computing department and mentioned the fact that talk of computers 'reading' and 'understanding' was metaphorical. He vigorously denied it, and seemed to have difficulty even conceiving of the possibility. I'm not advocating that we stop using such useful terms, of course. Mostly it doesn't matter; but when we come to considering the differences between people and machines, then it does matter.

Descartes thought that the same facts that would enable us to tell the difference between robots and human beings would also help us to recognize the difference between people and animals. He pointed out (Haldane and Ross, 1931: 116–17) that

> it is a very remarkable fact that there are none so depraved and stupid, without even excepting idiots, that they cannot arrange different words together, forming of them a statement by which they make known their thoughts; while, on the other hand, there is no other animal, however perfect and fortunately circumstanced it may be, which can do the same.

The latter part is a matter that's still sometimes disputed, and many dog-owners are convinced that their dogs understand a great deal of English, even if they don't speak it. We'll postpone the discussion of that question, since animal communication will be discussed at length later (see Chapter 12).

Descartes argued that the reason for this difference between animals and human beings couldn't be simply that the animals lacked the right organs to speak, because 'magpies and parrots are able to utter words just like ourselves, and yet they cannot speak as we do, i.e., so as to give evidence that they think of what they say' (Haldane and Ross, 1931: 117).

By contrast, in deaf people the appropriate organs for listening are not functioning, yet they use signs and other methods of making themselves understood. Such sign languages have the same expressive power as spoken ones. Descartes was suggesting that language is a human capacity, and one which survives even quite adverse physical difficulties.

In the twentieth century, Ursula Bellugi and others who work with the deaf have attested that the various sign languages that are used by deaf people are real languages which have grammars of their own, and which change and evolve just like other languages. Thus the human brain finds ways to use language, even if the body is sometimes deficient for normal communication. (See Chapter 11.)

5.3 Chomsky's contribution to mentalism

5.3.1 SCIENTIFIC METHOD

Just as Skinner's book represents a classical behaviourist position, so Chomsky's remarks on it represent a classical mentalist position. According to mentalists, the mind plays an enormous role in language behaviour, and consequently they believe it's all-important in language acquisition, too. They're willing to try to examine what processes go on in the mind, as far as language is concerned.

But how can that be done? What about scientific method, which says that the only things that can be scientifically studied are ones that can be examined publicly and objectively? Weren't the behaviourists right when they said that it's impossible to do that with mental phenomena such as ideas, meanings, mental representations and so on? (See the remarks in Chapter 3 on scientific method.)

Well, in order to depart from behaviourism, Chomsky found it necessary to depart from the scientific method that had been used, at least nominally, in the physical sciences, and that had been adopted by behaviourists unchanged. Chomsky's departure from standard scientific method was one of the most fundamental changes that came about in what is sometimes called the Chomskyan revolution (and sometimes the cognitive revolution).

Chomsky thought that the scientific method that was needed to study human behaviour was inevitably somewhat different from the one that had often been pursued in studying physics and chemistry.[1] The difference is that the human mind is part of what is being studied in the human sciences, whereas it isn't in the physical sciences. (Though in fact, the mind is relevant to the way in which observations are made in the physical sciences.)

Chomsky began by rejecting the idea that it was scientifically improper to try to examine what was going on in the mind. For if that were true, the study of language would be virtually impossible for someone who believed, as he did, that most of the important action concerning language occurs in the mind.

He took the bold step of proclaiming that he was willing to allow introspection (examining one's own thoughts) as a permissible procedure in the study of language. This was not the first time in the history of linguistics that that had been done, so it was not altogether new, but it was the first time for many decades that it had been heard of.

It was quite contrary to behaviourist beliefs. Behaviourist linguists had only one way in which they could collect data about language, and that was to tape-record (or, equivalently, write in notebooks) samples of actual speech used in the community. They would then develop methods of analysing those samples in order to see how language worked – for example, by finding recurring patterns.

The samples of language in the collection were together called a 'corpus'. There are still linguists who believe that that's the only way to proceed scientifically, but they're far fewer than they once were.

Suppose you were such a linguist, who knew that a certain sentence structure was part of the English language, but wanted to demonstrate objectively that it was indeed part of it. You'd have to take tape recordings until one of the speakers happened to use that structure. But that might take a very long time; in fact you might record for years (or for the rest of your life) without happening upon it. In order to speed things up, linguists tried 'eliciting' the answers they wanted – that is, they administered tests or engaged in conversation to induce the subject to use the desired construction.

Chomsky felt that this was a very time-wasting and unnecessary procedure to find out something you already knew. If a linguist is a native speaker of English, (s)he knows pretty well what are normal sentences of the language and what are not. That is what knowing the language means. So it was legitimate for linguists to probe the linguistic intuitions of native speakers about their language, or even to search their own minds for their own intuitions.

Chomsky explains his point of view very well (1965: 20). He asks whether linguistics is excluded from the domain of science if we allow introspective evidence and use the intuitive knowledge of a native speaker. His answer to this is that it's just a terminological question – that is, it's just a question of labels, which 'seems to have no bearing at all on any serious issue'. Then he goes on:

> However, this terminological question actually does relate to a different issue of some interest, namely whether the important feature of the successful sciences has been their search for insight or their concern for objectivity. The social and behavioral sciences provide ample evidence that objectivity can be pursued with little consequent gain in insight and understanding. On the other hand, a good case can be made for the view that the natural sciences have, by and large, sought objectivity primarily insofar as it is a tool for gaining insight.

Scientific revolutions often occur when the basic assumptions of one generation of scientists are rejected by the next. Chomsky's stance on scientific method amounted to such a revolution.

Like the behaviourists, the reader might still feel some disquiet about this change in the rules of scientific method. After all, if linguists can just say whatever they find in their own minds, how is anyone to know they're not cheating? Or even if the cheating isn't intentional, mightn't they find the answers that they need, to confirm their theories?

There are several safeguards against this. In the first place, if linguists publish their 'intuitions' about some aspect of language, the rest of the world's linguists will see whether the observations are verified by their own intuitions, and if not, the suggestions won't persuade many people.

In the second place, more evidence than that is usually required, in the shape of predictions that arise out of the observations. If the predictions turn out to be true as attested by other evidence, that gives the claims greater credence. An excellent example of this is given in the next chapter, where there will be an account of Chomsky's principle that all linguistic rules are structure dependent (see pp. 96–100). Evidence is just as necessary for mentalist linguists as for behaviourist ones, but what counts as evidence is different.

There's another fact that ought to be mentioned. Having so-called objectivity as part of scientific method is no insurance against cheating. There have been several notorious cases of behaviourist psychologists who faked their results and later admitted it. In fact, with the less 'objective' method, there may actually be a greater safeguard against cheating, if everyone has equal access to the data. It's actually quite difficult to imagine how a mentalist would go about cheating.

5.3.2 THE IDEAL SPEAKER–LISTENER

Chomsky's position on scientific method, then, was a revolutionary one. But that wasn't all that was involved. His aims were different from those of previous linguists. He wrote (1965: 3):

Linguistic theory is concerned primarily with an ideal speaker–listener, in a completely homogeneous speech-community, who knows its language perfectly and is unaffected by such grammatically irrelevant conditions as memory limitations, distractions, shifts of attention and interest, and errors (random or characteristic) in applying his knowledge of the language in actual performance.

This statement contains a lot of ideas in fairly condensed form, so it will be worth our while to examine what's meant. First, what's meant by 'an ideal speaker–listener'? In our daily use of language, we're all both speakers and listeners – that is, we're speaker–listeners. In referring to 'an ideal speaker–listener', however, Chomsky was not referring to any actual speaker, but to a scientific idealization.

In physics, people sometimes talk hypothetically of rolling a ball down 'a frictionless inclined plane'. Now of course, in the real world, no such thing exists. Any surface in the real world will involve friction if an object moves along it. But it is a useful scientific fiction: if we can work out what would happen under these ideal (but fictitious) circumstances, we may discover principles which will later form a basis for a description that includes real-world conditions such as friction.

Similarly, Chomsky is saying: Let's adopt a scientific idealization. Let's imagine a world in which there is an ideal speaker–hearer, who knows the language perfectly, etc. Such a speaker doesn't exist, any more than a frictionless inclined plane, but it's useful to consider this ideal case, which will possibly lead to principles that will also be relevant to any study of real-world conditions.

This ideal speaker–hearer is to be 'unaffected by such grammatically irrelevant conditions as memory limitations, distractions, shifts of attention and interest, and errors'. In other words, if someone says *I gave the book Mary* instead of *I gave the book to Mary* because (s)he is dog-tired, that doesn't reveal anything about that person's grammar. Likewise, if someone stutters and sometimes says *the-the-the man*, sometimes *the-the man* and sometimes *the man*, that doesn't mean that the person thinks there are three different noun phrases in the language corresponding to those three utterances. As Chomsky says, those things are 'grammatically irrelevant'.

5.3.3 COMPETENCE AND PERFORMANCE

Chomsky has made a further important distinction which is relevant here. He uses the term 'competence' to refer to the knowledge that a speaker has about his/her language. Notice that this is not the usual meaning of *competence*, which has to do with ability to do something.

So in Chomsky's sense of the word, all of us have a linguistic 'competence', in that we have knowledge of our native language. This is to be distinguished from what Chomsky calls *performance*, by which he means what actually occurs in real utterances.

Performance, then, happens in real time, whereas competence doesn't 'happen' at all; it's knowledge that lies dormant in a person's mind. It might be compared with your knowledge of, say, the six times table, which is in your (usually unconscious) memory (as competence), but which is sometimes brought out and used in an actual calculation (in performance).

Chomsky was interested in writing a grammar of competence – a grammar of what an ideal speaker–listener would know about his/her language. Presumably if this could be done, then the grammars in the brains of speakers in a particular speech community could best be described as departures from this ideal grammar.

And what about performance? Well, it wasn't that Chomsky wasn't interested in it, but he believed that in the present state of knowledge that would be a much tougher project, one not likely to be fulfilled soon. So he put his effort where he expected research results were available. In any case, he thought that any account of performance would have to be based on a grammar of competence. And he expected a grammar of competence to be much more revealing about human beings than a 'grammar' of performance would be.

Chomsky's attempt to describe the grammar of an ideal speaker–listener brought much criticism, especially at first. People complained that what linguists ought to be doing was studying real language, used by real people, not some abstraction which didn't exist. But Chomsky replied that this was normal scientific practice. Nobody complained to physicists that they should be studying real objects in the world around them, instead of theorizing about subatomic particles. He was also criticized greatly for making the distinction between competence and performance, for of course that was an integral part of the same idealization.

As in all disciplines, there are different schools of thought – and that's a healthy state of affairs. Those who find Chomsky's arguments convincing have no difficulty with the objections that were raised; but those who don't find them convincing feel that these objections are weighty. Having declared that my own convictions are mentalist, I must also repeat that my aim is not to indoctrinate the reader into that way of thinking, but to raise the questions on which the main issues

71

turn. On important questions, I believe, you shouldn't accept what I say or what anyone else says without thinking about it for yourself.

5.3.4 UNCONSCIOUS KNOWLEDGE

Chomsky claims that the knowledge that we have about our language is largely unconscious. We can sometimes summon up small parts of it to our consciousness, but that's just the tip of the iceberg. There's very good reason to believe that most of it is unconscious.

There may be philosophical difficulties about the phrase 'unconscious knowledge', and Chomsky admits that 'knowledge' may not be an altogether appropriate word; but it's *as if* we had knowledge that we're not conscious of.

In order to get closer to this problem, let's consider what we do every day of our lives. We get involved in conversations or other situations that require us to use language, and we just open our mouths and out come sentences.

Usually we don't consciously think about how we do that. We probably think about the meaning of what we're saying, but surely we give no attention at all to the grammatical construction of the sentence. We don't think to ourselves, 'Now, I must start with a pronoun, then I must put a verb, then I must put a noun phrase ...' If we did this consciously, we wouldn't get through utterances fast enough to make the conversation interesting, or to get anything achieved. And people who didn't know much about grammar (that is, most people) wouldn't be able to say anything at all.

But *something* must be working away in your brain producing those sentences. They surely don't get into your mouth by accident. What you do when you speak is nothing short of a miracle.[2] It's an extraordinary mystery how you do it – a mystery of considerable interest to science. Fortunately, thanks to the work of linguists and psychologists (the scientists who are concerned with language), it isn't a complete mystery, but there are many aspects of the process that aren't understood yet.

Now, it isn't only you and I who can perform this miracle of constructing sentences without consciously thinking about it; 4-year-old children can do it, as well. Most of them can talk very fluently. They may make some 'mistakes' in grammar, but those are comparatively trivial. What's remarkable is how much they can do. And they haven't even heard about grammar consciously, so they can't be working out the construction of the sentences in a conscious way, either. But again, something must be working away in their brains to produce this result.

I hope you're beginning to see that there *are* problems here that scientists might be interested in. How language is processed in the brain, and how little children acquire their first language, are problems of central importance to studies of the human brain. The study of 'inner space' is surely just as exciting and important as the study of 'outer space'.

But you may still not be convinced that it's all that miraculous. Is it such a puzzling matter? Isn't it just a matter of people using their intelligence, even if they're not fully conscious of how they form sentences?

The reader who isn't used to the idea that we all unconsciously 'know' things about our language might have only the vaguest idea at this point of what's involved. In order to try to get rid of the vagueness, let me draw your attention to some things that you probably never think about consciously.

The first example involves the sentences in (1)–(3) below. (Remember, sentences marked with an asterisk aren't grammatically well formed.)

1a   Kylie is small.
1b   *Kylie is much small.
1c   Kylie is very small.

2a   Kylie is smaller than Michael.
2b   Kylie is much smaller than Michael.
2c   *Kylie is very smaller than Michael.

3a   Kylie is too small.
3b   Kylie is much too small.
3c   *Kylie is very too small.

These sentences present a reasonably complex set of facts about English. Imagine how much difficulty you would have if you undertook to explain to a foreign learner of English what was going on here. Yet I'm prepared to bet that if you're a native speaker of English, you've never made a mistake in any sentences of those kinds. (If you aren't a native speaker of English, there are sure to be complex things in your native language in which you never make mistakes.)

I'm willing to make another bet, too. Unless you've taken a linguistics course, or read books about linguistics, you've never consciously thought about these facts. But you act as though you know them, even though you weren't previously conscious of them. That's the sort of thing that Chomsky means by 'unconscious knowledge'.

Let's take another example. If you're a native speaker of English, you know that the following pattern is correct, even though you've probably never thought about it:

4a   John intends to go to London.
4b   John hopes to go to London.[3]
4c   John wants to go to London.

5a   *John thinks to go to London.
5b   *John believes to go to London.
5c   *John dreams to go to London.

Again, if you're a native speaker, you'll agree that the sentences in (4) are normal sentences of English and that the ones in (5) aren't. You almost certainly never make mistakes in this area, either, even though you've probably never thought about it.

You may think that this pattern is a matter of the differences in meaning among the verbs, but it isn't solely a matter of that, since in French it's permissible to say the equivalent of (5a) (*Jean pense aller à Londres*). So again, it's as if you had this structural knowledge unconsciously.

One final example, because the point is of crucial importance:

6a   John is too stupid to talk to.
6b   John is too stupid to talk to Sue.

Both of these are perfectly good sentences of English, but they're interpreted in very different ways. Take the phrase *to talk to*, in (6a). We interpret this to mean 'for anyone to talk to John', so that we're discussing the possibility of John being the receiver of the speech, not the speaker. On the other hand, in (6b) the phrase *to talk to Sue* means 'for John to talk to Sue', so this time we're discussing the possibility of John doing the talking.

How do we know that in (6a) John's the imagined receiver, and in (6b) he's the imagined speaker? More to the point, how do children learn to work that out, as sooner or later they must? Linguists can explain what's going on here, but only by recourse to very complex grammatical theory – theory that is too advanced to be presented here. If you nevertheless feel able to tackle advanced linguistics, you will find this particular matter discussed by Chomsky (1986: 105), among others.

And once again, the same point has been demonstrated: you have unconscious knowledge of this matter, so you don't make mistakes in it, as either a speaker or a listener.

It should be obvious that nobody ever taught you these facts, since most people just aren't aware of them, and certainly couldn't explain how they work. Chomsky goes further and claims that not only did no one teach you these facts, but you didn't ever learn them, either.

5.3.5 Language capacities are innate

That brings us in a natural way to Chomsky's next major claim: that certain aspects of language knowledge are innate – inborn in every child.

When Chomsky first made this claim, many linguists reacted strongly against it and refused to accept it. There are still many who don't accept it, so it remains a controversial claim. But acceptance of it has grown strongly over the past few decades.

It's important to notice that when Chomsky says that language is innate, he doesn't mean that any particular language like English is innate. If it were, everyone in the world would speak that one language. He means that certain principles about language are innate, and that those principles help infants to learn whatever language they're exposed to.

What kinds of things are meant by innate 'principles'? Well, some of them might be comparatively simple, such as the principle that all languages have sentences, or that they all have nouns. But there are also more complex and interesting 'principles'. We'll have a closer look at some of them in the next chapter.

Chomsky maintains, then, that as well as general intelligence, human beings have special linguistic capacities including the principles to which I made reference above. Of course, that doesn't *have* to be true. Many people believe that all human mental accomplishments are achieved by the same kind of intelligence; so whether we're doing mathematics, writing a novel or painting a picture, we'll be using the same general intelligence. Likewise, such people say, when children learn to use language, they learn by using their general intelligence. Chomsky disagrees with that. There's a special faculty of the mind, he says, which deals only with language matters.

How does he know? Well, he points to numerous pieces of evidence that suggest that. Most children have virtually acquired the essentials of the language by the age of 4 or 5. Yes, they sometimes make mistakes, but these are of a fairly trivial kind. A child of 4 can usually speak very fluently. This feat is achieved by virtually all children, not just a few gifted ones. Children who don't acquire language usually have some pathological condition that interferes with acquisition. Almost all children do acquire a language – the one that's spoken by the people around them.

This means that the capacity to learn a language isn't correlated with intelligence, since children at all levels of intelligence do it. There is no doubt a correlation between intelligence and the later ability to use language with expertise and finesse, but that's not the same thing; here we're talking only of the ability to learn to communicate by language, and to make the kind of judgements illustrated in (1)–(3) on p. 73.

Chomsky points to the fact that at the same age, children are not achieving spectacularly in any other mental activity. The average 4-year-old can't do mathematics, compose music or write a novel. Of course, there are geniuses like Mozart, who do compose music and do other marvellous things at a very tender age. But remember we're saying that virtually *all* children acquire language at a tender age.

This means that they seem to learn with astonishing rapidity. Since they didn't start to speak until they were, on average, about 1 year old, they've achieved this feat in three years. Most adults trying to learn a second or subsequent language, even if they live in a country where it's spoken, will be much slower to master the language, and they'll probably never speak it as well as a child who learnt it early.

The claim that children learn language very quickly has been rather controversial. Some linguists have argued that three years isn't such a short time for the children, since they spend a good many of their waking hours listening to the language and then later speaking it. Also, they have very strong motivation to learn, since their survival more or less depends on it. In any case, the argument runs, they've probably been learning for four years rather than three, since they're probably listening and absorbing during that first year before they start speaking. This actually appears to be true. There's excellent evidence that the child has quite a bit of knowledge by the end of that first year (see Mehler and Dupoux, 1994; also Chapter 13 of this book). But to agree with that is not to agree with the claim that the child takes a long or longish time to acquire the language. If anything, it strengthens the argument, since study of this phenomenon makes it clear how much the child learns.

Another piece of evidence that Chomsky points to as indicating the likelihood of language capacities being innate is the fact that children will learn any language to which they're exposed at the right age. There are some 5,500 to 6,000 languages on earth, and the child will learn *any one of them* to which it's exposed at the right time. A Vietnamese baby who is brought up as part of an English-speaking Australian family in Australia will learn to speak English with an Australian accent, and will sound indistinguishable from any other Australian child. (There have been many such cases in recent times.) And the reverse would be true, of course, if an Australian child were brought up in a Vietnamese family in Vietnam.

5.3.6 THE BIOLOGICAL CLOCK

If the propensity for language is innate in babies, why can't they speak soon after birth? An equally good question is why they don't learn to walk soon after birth. Foals and some other animals do.

The reason why some species take longer to walk than others isn't altogether clear, but it seems that each species has a biological 'clock', so that members of the species keep to a fairly uniform schedule.

Other events in our development also seem to be biologically programmed; for example, puberty occurs at around the same time in most people, though of course there are individual differences and differences between the sexes. And, as Chomsky comments, maybe even death is biologically programmed, too. People die at different ages because there are a lot of variables, but the maximum age to which humans live has been fairly constant for a long time.

It seems, then, that language develops in accordance with a biological programme for the human species. Later we'll have more to say about the course it follows.

5.4 The debate between Piaget and Chomsky

In 1975 an intellectual event of extraordinary importance took place at the Abbey of Royaumont, close to Paris. It was a debate between Noam Chomsky, who was regarded by many linguists as the greatest living linguist, and Jean Piaget, who was regarded by many psychologists as the greatest living psychologist. Both were also regarded as notable philosophers.

The debate at Royaumont didn't involve only Piaget and Chomsky. Many other outstanding researchers participated in the discussion, drawn from disciplines such as linguistics, psychology, philosophy, anthropology, biology, education, mathematics and sociology. At the beginning of the debate, Piaget and Chomsky (in that order) gave 'position papers' setting out their views, and then a more general discussion began, involving all the scholars.

An account of the proceedings was published under the title *Language and Learning: The Debate between Jean Piaget and Noam Chomsky*. The French-language edition of this report was published in Paris in 1979 (Piattelli-Palmarini, 1979), and the English-language version in the United States in 1980 (Piattelli-Palmarini, 1980). More than a couple of decades on, the debate still stands as one of the richest stores of ideas about language acquisition, the functioning of language and the philosophy of language. But be warned that the level of difficulty is far above that of the present book.

5.4.1 A HIGHLIGHT OF THE DEBATE

The most important difference between Chomsky's views and Piaget's was that Chomsky believed that the child was born with innate linguistic principles, whereas Piaget explicitly denied that.

In his position paper, Piaget made two interesting challenges to Chomsky's claim that language acquisition involved innate principles. Piaget attributed his first argument to Konrad Lorenz, a famous Austrian zoologist. It was this: if language is innate, we would have to make one of two assumptions about how it came to be innate, and the assumptions seem equally improbable.

For instance, we could assume that the innate principles of language had been passed on from generation to generation throughout the history of evolution. But in that case, we'd have to assume that even the most primitive animals, very near the beginning of the evolutionary cycle (e.g. the single-celled protozoa), must have had innate propensities for language. We would have to agree with Piaget that this is 'a fairly incredible assumption'.

The only other assumption we could make, said Piaget, is that the innate propensities for language only arrived with *Homo sapiens* (humankind). But this means it arrived suddenly, in which case it must have been due to a mutation. But that, says Piaget, would be 'biologically inexplicable'. He adds:

> It is already very difficult to see why the randomness of mutations renders a human being able to 'learn' an articulate language, and if in addition one had to attribute to it the innateness of a rational linguistic structure, then this structure would itself be subject to a random origin. (Piattelli-Palmarini, 1980: 31)

Again, the position Piaget advances seems very persuasive. It does seem implausible that such events could be random.

It might seem, then, that Piaget had put forward an unanswerable argument. However, Chomsky made a brilliant response to it. He said he agreed only in part; that is, he agreed that the evolutionary development was 'biologically unexplained', but didn't accept the stronger claim that it was 'biologically inexplicable'. He went on (Piattelli-Palmarini, 1980: 36):

> Exactly the same can be said with regard to the physical organs of the body. Their evolutionary development is 'biologically unexplained' in exactly the same sense ... Although it is quite true that we have no idea how or why random mutations have endowed humans with the specific capacity to learn a human language, it is also true that we have no better idea how or why random mutations have led to the development of the particular structures of the mammalian eye or the cerebral cortex.

Piaget's second reason for rejecting Chomsky's claims about innateness was that all the alleged properties of 'innate' language principles would still be operative if they were not in fact innate, but were the 'necessary' result of the constructions of sensori-motor intelligence. Chomsky commented that this second argument 'seems to me a more important one'. However, if Piaget felt encouraged by that remark, he must have been extremely discouraged by Chomsky's follow-on:

However, I see no basis for Piaget's conclusion. There are, to my knowledge, no substantive proposals involving 'constructions of sensorimotor intelligence' that offer any hope of accounting for the phenomena of language that demand explanation. Nor is there any initial plausibility to the suggestion, as far as I can see (p. 36).

In order to give substance to these claims, Chomsky outlined the details of some of the universal principles which he thought must be innate. They included the principle that linguistic rules are structure dependent, which will be described in Chapter 6, as well as the argumentation cited there as evidence for it. 'As in the case of physical organs,' Chomsky concludes, 'there seems to be no possibility of accounting for the character and origin of basic mental structures in terms of organism–environment interaction' (pp. 51–2).

Chomsky elaborated his position in an interview (Otero, 1988: 414–15):

Consider the properties that determine the reference of pronouns ... Once you ferret out these rules for pronouns, they seem to have nothing in common with the logical operations that Piagetians single out as being typical of the early stages of the child's mental development.

Interviewer: In other words, a four-year-old who may not realise that the amount of water stays the same when you pour the contents of a low, wide glass into a tall, thin container nevertheless displays sophisticated logical abilities in his grasp of the complex rules of English grammar?

Yes. And these abilities are independent of the logical capacities measured by tests. There's just no resemblance between what a child does with blocks and the kind of knowledge that he displays of English grammar at the same age.

Who won the debate at Royaumont? Well, that depends on whether the person you ask is a Piagetian or a Chomskyan. That's not too surprising, of course.

Massimo Piattelli-Palmarini, the editor of the published versions of the debate, is in no doubt that Chomsky and his supporters (such as Jerry Fodor) won. More recently (Piattelli-Palmarini, 1995) he looks back across twenty years to the debate and tries to assess it with the benefit of that perspective. Piattelli-Palmarini says that while he was editing the book that reported the debate, he felt he had to observe 'a self-imposed neutrality'; but now he feels free to comment. He strongly supports the arguments put forward in the debate by Chomsky and

Fodor, and is very critical of those put forward by Piaget and his supporters.

Since he says these are things that he 'studiously avoided' saying at the time of the debate, we may assume that he subscribed to them even then. In principle, of course, this could mean no more than that he was partisan then and remains so now, especially since the people he thanks for their help include Chomsky, Fodor and various supporters of their views. Certainly, Piattelli-Palmarini's paper is regarded with disdain by many Piagetians.

If you really want to make up your own mind, you should read the report of the debate (Piattelli-Palmarini, 1980), or at least sections of it, and Piattelli-Palmarini (1995). Then, to balance the picture, you should read Campbell and Bickhard (1987) and Loreno and Machado (1996). But be warned, all these papers are at an advanced level. There is not the space here to go into the detailed arguments, and the level of difficulty that it would entail goes far beyond the limits of this book.

5.5 Was the debate the end of Piaget's model?

It shouldn't be thought that the only criticism of Piaget's model has come from people not working in that paradigm, such as Chomsky. A great deal of criticism has come from within the ranks of people who would call themselves Piagetians. But as a later chapter (Chapter 15) will be partly concerned with just such criticisms, they haven't been included here.

A discussion on the Piagetian e-mail list during February 1997 showed that there were not only fairly 'classical' Piagetians, but also neo-Piagetians (who were described by one writer as scholars who had worked either with Piaget or in his paradigm, but had now moved on to a modified model) and, more recently, what were referred to in the discussion as 'new Piagetians' (people who had never worked with Piaget or even at Geneva, but who had made departures from his theory that were sometimes quite radical). One of the latter group said privately that he would like to hold a round-table discussion on just what it means to be a Piagetian at the present time. It obviously means different things to different people.

The biggest outstanding difference between the Piagetian school and the generative (Chomskyan) school, as far as language is concerned, is over the question of whether there are innate linguistic principles. For a

Piagetian to embrace the notion that *some* linguistic tendencies are innate would by no means necessarily involve accepting the rest of Chomsky's model. Nor would it necessarily involve jettisoning everything Piaget did. In Chapter 15 we will see how such a step has been taken in recent years.

Notes

1. This didn't mean, of course, that Chomsky thought there were two different sets of scientific methods, but he believed that the scope of scientific method had to be widened.
2. In using the word *miracle*, of course, I don't mean to imply that it's a phenomenon that can't in principle have a scientific explanation.
3. I am grateful to Peter Peterson for drawing my attention to the fact that further evidence that semantics is no help here comes from the fact that 'hope' patterns with the verbs in (5) in accepting *that*-clause complements.

6. A close look at Chomsky's theories

6.1 Innate principles

Suppose we take seriously the idea that a child is born with innate principles of language which give him/her a 'head start' in acquiring the language that is in the immediate environment. How could we find out what those principles are? At present, it's impossible to demonstrate physically what's going on in the child's brain as far as language is concerned, so what conceivable means could be used to get at the problem?

The seventeenth-century German philosopher and mathematician Gottfried Leibniz (1646–1716) wrote that 'languages are the best mirror of the human mind'. This idea was picked up by Chomsky in the twentieth century and taken seriously. In fact, it became the basis of his method of trying to discover what was going on in the mind. He claims that there's a special faculty in the mind for language, and he's tried to deduce how it works by studying the structure and operation of language itself.

Chomsky claims that the child is born with some innate principles about language 'wired in' to the brain. We may say, therefore, that the child has a kind of 'knowledge' about language at birth, though it's largely unconscious. Obviously (s)he doesn't know any particular language at birth, but exposure to the language in the immediate environment leads to the baby soon beginning to act as if (s)he knew something of the grammar of the language.

The child goes through a number of mental states as (s)he acquires more and more of the language. Eventually, after a few years, (s)he arrives at a 'steady state', when (s)he has adult-like competence in the language. After that, there'll be no more major developments, though each individual will go on learning some vocabulary and perhaps occasional new sentence structures throughout life.

Notice how this view of language learning contrasts with Skinner's view, described in Chapter 3. Skinner thought that the important things all happened externally to the child. It was what the mother and other people did that caused the child to learn language, and there was virtually no contribution from the child itself. Nothing was assumed to go on in the child's head – or at least nothing that could be described scientifically. By contrast, Chomsky believes the most important part of language acquisition is what goes on in the mind, and he's committed to trying to deduce what it's like. He's devised some ingenious methods of doing so.

A key question for Chomsky is what kind of 'knowledge' about language doesn't have to be learnt by the child, because it's already there at birth. You might think that this would be an impossible question to answer, but Chomsky has found ways of making progress with it. His main tool for probing the mind is grammar. Before we can get down to describing how he uses it, we need to make clear what sort of grammar we're talking about. The next few sections will be devoted to that matter.

6.2 Socially based views on grammar

Since the term 'grammar' here means something rather different from what most people might understand by it, I'll take a little space to make clear what the difference is.

In the past, grammar, especially in schools, was often concerned with questions of correct usage. Sometimes this took the form of rules, such as 'Never end a sentence with a preposition', 'Never use a double negative' or 'Never use a split infinitive'. They were designed to make people use language in a certain way which was said to be 'correct', and very frequently this meant trying to make people conform to one dialect rather than another.

Linguists talk of two kinds of 'dialect': regional and social. A regional dialect is the way people speak in a certain region; but even within the same region, there are different ways of speaking according to socioeconomic factors: level of income, level of education, type of work, and so on. These are the social dialects.

The 'prestigious' dialects which schoolchildren were taught (usually ineffectively) all over the English-speaking world in the fairly recent past were nearly always the social dialects used by the well educated, the rich and the powerful, and the dialects that were said to be 'incorrect' were the ones that were frequently spoken by the less well educated, the poor and the powerless. That's an oversimplification, but there's a good deal of truth in it.

This approach to teaching grammar was usually based on the idea that the English language was constantly in danger of deteriorating, because people made so many grammatical 'errors', used slang, and so on. Virtually all change was regarded as deterioration, but linguists today regard change as a regular feature of language, which has been going on for centuries and is still going on.

Language that departed from what was regarded as the most prestigious dialect was frequently regarded as 'shoddy' or 'slovenly' – something that needed to be changed. It seems clear that some people use language more skilfully than others, and with more elegance and artistry. But speakers of any dialect may fall into that category, and using language well is not the same as conforming to a particular (prestigious) dialect.

Many people, though, have come to believe that grammar is about what's 'right' and 'wrong'. That's the idea of grammar that I invite you to discard. It has nothing to do with the scientific study of language, whatever it may have to do with social judgements.[1] From a linguistic point of view, all dialects are equally legitimate and equally interesting. Yes, even the dialects in which people say 'I seen it', 'I done it', 'I ain't', 'them books', and so on. All English dialects have a long history, and the prestigious ones are no better *linguistically* than the less prestigious ones.

The science of linguistics, in any case, isn't interested in making judgements of these kinds about the variety of language people use. It's interested in the scientific question of how people are able to acquire and use language so fluently, whatever dialect they talk.

6.3 Scientific grammar

I mentioned in Chapter 3 that it isn't feasible that children learn a list of sentences which they later use, because there's a potentially infinite number of sentences that every child gains control of. Chomsky suggested that it isn't sentences that we all have in our memories, but words and a set of principles by which sentences are formed from those words.

The store of words is called a lexicon, which is a fancy name for a dictionary. But this one isn't like the dictionaries on our bookshelves; it's a purely theoretical one, an attempt to characterize the 'lexicon' which it is thought your brain must have compiled from the words it has acquired, perhaps with the aid of some innate principles. Nobody's ever seen such a lexicon, but linguists sometimes make reasoned estimates as to what it might contain.

The grammar that Chomsky assumes is in our heads is a set of principles for constructing[2] sentences. In a rough way, we can call them 'rules' for making up sentences, but they have nothing to do with those rules of usage we've already referred to. The rules we're talking about here will vary a little according to what dialect we speak, but only a little. The differences are fairly trivial from the linguistic point of view.

Now let's look at a few details.

6.4 Enough scraps of grammar to keep you alive

This is not a grammar book, and many readers who are attracted by the subject of children's acquisition of language won't be very anxious to learn a lot of grammar. Still, there are a few basics that we have to confront, if you're to understand the message of the rest of the book, and especially the rest of this chapter. All I can do is promise to keep it to a minimum and to try to make it clear.

6.4.1 WORD CLASSES

Words in any language belong to various classes, which have different roles to play in sentence structure. At least two classes, nouns and verbs, seem to occur in all languages, and that probably means these concepts are innate (though unconscious).

There are about nine[3] word classes in English, depending on who's counting. The labels that are commonly employed are noun, verb, adjective, preposition, auxiliary, adverb, intensifier, determiner and conjunction. Pronouns are regarded as a special kind of noun.[4]

There are strict constraints on the ways in which representatives of the various word classes can combine to make a satisfactory sentence. For instance, although (1) contains genuine English words, belonging to proper word classes, it isn't a well-formed sentence of English, as everyone will agree:

1   *ran the up by for and a

It won't help if we shift the words around into a different order. There's no order we can give to those words which will make them into a normal English sentence.

The problem is that we don't have the right selection of word classes to make a satisfactory sentence. The classes that occur in (1) are[5] verb (*ran*), determiner (*the*), preposition (*up*), preposition (*by*), preposition (*for*),[6] conjunction (*and*), determiner (*a*). So the first thing about well-formed sentences is that they have to have the right selection of word classes.

But that isn't enough. Even though the sequence in (2) contains all the right word classes to make a well-formed sentence of English, it isn't one.

2   *stuck bottle his has finger Paul a in

But if we change the order of the words, we have a perfectly well-formed sentence:

3   Paul has his finger stuck in a bottle.

So now we know two requirements that must be fulfilled before we have a satisfactory sentence of English: we must have the right selection of word classes, and we must have them in a certain order. The study of syntax attempts (among other things) to describe how these two requirements are met.

6.4.2 NOUNS AND VERBS: GETTING TO KNOW THEM

I've mentioned nouns and verbs, and hinted that they're pretty important. You'd better get to know one when you see one, then. How can I best help you to be able to do that? Well, you might think that I could give you a definition, and then you'd remember it and that would be that. Uh-uh; we can't go down that track. I'd only have two choices:

either I'd have to give you the conventional definitions, which are full of holes, or I'd have to give you a year's course in linguistics. After that, I could show you a couple of better definitions for nouns and verbs than the conventional ones, but I assume most of you haven't got a year to spare. And even then, the mystery of what nouns and verbs are would still remain to some extent.

So what I've got to do is let you see the conventional definitions, show you some of the holes, and then hope that you'll 'catch on' to what's meant anyway.

First, an observation about definitions. Dr Johnson wrote the first great dictionary of English, which was published in 1755. He defined *cat* as 'a familiar domestic animal'. Now, that isn't really an adequate definition of *cat*, since it would also apply to *dog*. But Johnson apparently thought that any further words wouldn't tell a person what a cat was if (s)he didn't recognize it from that description. His aim, then, seems to have been, not to provide a watertight definition of *cat*, but to meet the reader at the point where (s)he would say, 'Oh yes, of course. I know what it is.'

And, really, modern dictionaries can't do a lot better. The first entry for *cat* in my *Chambers 20th Century Dictionary*, for instance, says it is 'a carnivore of genus *Felis*, esp. the domesticated kind or any of the smaller wild species'. The only thing that has been added to Dr Johnson's definition is the information that another name for it is the Latin word *felis*. So if you don't recognize this Latin word – if that doesn't make you cry 'Ah, yes, I know what it is!' – you still won't understand what's being referred to.

I'm going to adopt a similar course of action to Johnson, with my treatment of nouns, verbs and other word classes. I'm not going to try to provide watertight definitions (because that's impossible), but I'll try to meet you at the point where you'll say, 'Oh, yes, I know what it means.' Probably many readers will already be at that stage.

Let's start with (4):

4   The actor wrote a book.

In (4), *actor* and *book* are nouns. Nouns are 'names' or 'labels'; but when we try to define them more closely, difficulties arise. The traditional definition of nouns that used to be given to schoolchildren is: 'a noun is the name of a person, place or thing'. Since *actor* refers to a person and *book* to a thing, all might seem to be well.

But in fact the definition isn't very good, since there are words which everybody agrees are nouns but which are not covered by it. For instance, we'd want to say that *meeting* and *hour* in (5), and *happiness* and *blessing* in (6), are nouns.

5   The *meeting* lasted an *hour*.

6   *Happiness* is a great *blessing*.

Yet if we're strict about it, none of these words seems to refer to 'a person', 'a place' or 'a thing'. And there are many more examples which cause similar problems.

Perhaps the definition could be improved if we added a couple more labels, so that a noun would be 'a word that describes a person, place, thing, event, unit of time, or emotion'. Then *meeting* would be covered because it's an event, and *hour* because it's a unit of time, and *happiness* because it's an emotion. But what about *blessing*? And we could add many more nouns which would not correspond with any of those descriptive words – for example, *length*, *beauty*, *delay*, *weight*. The list could go on and on.

Let's cut through this problem. The fact is, we're unlikely ever to arrive at a satisfactory definition by adding more items. Sixty years or so ago, most of the world's linguists played this game for a long time, and nobody ever succeeded in coming up with a watertight definition. And no one has succeeded in achieving that sort of definition since, either.

There are other ways of trying to capture what nouns are. For instance, they tend to be able to fill certain positions in sentences. The matter is complex to describe, and I won't do that here, but in fact we apparently all unconsciously recognize what classes words belong to, since we use them successfully all the time. And since I've given a number of examples of nouns above, I'll assume that readers will have no great difficulty in getting the idea of what they are, even if we can't define them. You've got through life so far without having a watertight definition of 'noun' (or of 'love' or of 'beauty'); surely you can survive a bit longer.

Let's have another look at (4):

4   The actor wrote a book.

Wrote is a verb. Verbs are said to express actions, events or states (or, in the version of the schoolroom of the past, a 'doing, being or having word'). But there are further mysteries about what that means. For instance, *action*, *event* and *state* are themselves nouns, not verbs, as are also many words that refer to actions (*fight*, *race*, *climb*), events (*disaster*, *earthquake*, *flood*) or states (*contentment*, *anger*, *love*). Incidentally, you'll notice that some of these, namely *fight*, *race*, *climb*, *flood*, *anger* and *love*, can be used as either verbs or nouns, so words can be paid-up members of more than one word class.

We won't go along the confusing track of trying to define verbs, either. My aim is solely to get you to the point where you can recognize a verb when you see one. Some verbs are: *run*, *eat*, *talk*, *like*, *make*, *give*, *sing*, *find*, *receive*, *play*, *resign*.

Verbs are usually capable of being used with different forms for present tense and past tense; for example, *walk/walked*, *run/ran*, etc. Are you ready now to say 'Oh, yes, I know what they are'? If not, keep going. There are more verbs to come, and at some stage I'm sure you'll get the idea of what they are. And again, you do know unconsciously what they are, because you use them successfully all the time.

It remains to be said that in (4), *The actor wrote a book*, *the* and *a* are determiners. There are only a few determiners, so we'll get to know them as individuals as we go along. The words *a* and *the* used to be called 'articles'. The class 'determiners' now includes them as well as a few other items, such as *this*, *these*, *that*, *those*.[7]

6.4.3 PHRASE STRUCTURE

Consider the short sentence in (7):

> 7   Vicki laughed.

We're now able to label the words with their category names:

> 8   [N Vicki] [V laughed]

where 'N' stands for 'noun' and 'V' for 'verb'. We could just as easily say the sentence in (9) in the same circumstances, if Vicki is a woman, not a young girl:

> 9   The woman laughed.

Again, we know how to label the words with their categories.

10   [DET the] [N woman] [V laughed]

where 'DET' stands for 'determiner'.

Earlier, we saw that two conditions must be met before we have a satisfactory sentence of English:

- there has to be an appropriate selection of word classes; and
- they have to be in the right order.

We can now add a third condition:

- the words must be arranged in phrases.

A phrase is either a single word or a group of words. If you have ever studied algebra, you will know that expressions can be grouped together by putting them in brackets, thus: (a − b) + c; a − (b + c). The brackets make these two expressions different in value. If $a = 5, b = 3$ and $c = 1$, the value of the first expression is 3, but the value of the second one is 1. Brackets can be used similarly in representing the structure of sentences, to show which words are grouped with which. The bracketing can make an important difference to meaning, as (10a) and (10b) show:

10a   [drunken lecturers'] wives
10b   drunken [lecturers' wives]

If we group together *drunken* and *lecturers*, as in (10a), it is the lecturers who are drunken; but if we group together *lecturers* and *wives*, as in (10b), it is the lecturers' wives who are drunken.

It's by no means always the case that there are ambiguous sequences like this; in fact, it happens comparatively infrequently. But it's still necessary to bracket words that belong together, in order to show what the structure of the sentence is, and to be able to talk usefully about it.

Now consider (11):

11   The woman laughed.

There are three possible ways to group the words:

11a   [the] [woman] [laughed]
11b   [the woman] [laughed]
11c   [the] [woman laughed]

91

The bracketing in (a) makes the claim that there are no internal groupings of words: they are all separate. On the other hand, (b) makes the claim that *the* and *woman* are grouped together to make a phrase, and that *laughed* is not a member of that phrase. Finally, (c) makes the claim that *woman laughed* is a phrase, but that *the* is not a part of that phrase.

Which one seems intuitively right to you? We can dismiss (c) straight away, since it simply isn't true that *woman* is more closely associated with *laughed* than it is with *the*. In fact, the best analysis is (b). If you didn't intuitively decide that, let's help your intuitions a little.

12   Vicki laughed.

Sentence (12) can be a description of the same event as (11) describes, if Vicki is a woman and not a young girl. So *the woman*, in (11), is equivalent, in some way, to *Vicki* in (12). In the case I described, they're equivalent in that they refer to the same person, but more importantly, they're equivalent in the role they play in the sentence.

Each of the sentences (11) and (12) consists of two parts: a phrase which nominates the person who did the action of laughing, and a verb, which names what the action is. Traditionally, these two parts are called the 'subject' and the 'predicate' of the sentence. The subject can be a single noun, like *Vicki*, or it can be a phrase which contains a noun (*woman*), but also contains a determiner (*the*) as a kind of satellite. Both subjects, then, contain a noun, and for this reason they're called 'noun phrases'. A noun phrase MUST contain a noun, and the noun is therefore said to be the 'head' of the noun phrase. It MAY also contain certain other items, such as the determiner that occurs here.

The words and phrases in these sentences can be labelled in the way depicted in (13):

13a   [NP [DET the] [N woman]] [v laughed]
13b   [NP [N Vicki]] [v laughed]

In (13a), *the* is labelled as a determiner and *woman* as a noun, but there is also a larger bracket around the sequence *the woman*, labelled 'noun phrase'. In (13b) there's no determiner, but *Vicki* is labelled as a noun, and also has larger brackets around it labelled 'noun phrase', showing that it belongs to both classifications at once.

The bracketing is not yet complete in these two sentences. Just as *Vicki* is both a noun and a noun phrase, so *laughed* is both a verb and a verb phrase. And just as a noun phrase MUST contain a noun and MAY also contain other items, so a verb phrase MUST contain a verb and MAY also contain other items.

We may complete the bracketing of these sentences as shown in (14):

14a   [NP [DET the] [N woman]] [VP [V laughed]]
14b   [NP [N Vicki]] [VP [V laughed]]

Let me now turn to something that I said earlier that may have puzzled some readers. At one point I said that *the woman* and *Vicki* are the 'subjects' of their respective sentences. But I have also said they are noun phrases. How do these two characterizations relate to each other?

'Noun phrase' is the category name of this kind of phrase. 'Subject' is the relationship that exists between the phrase and the sentence as a whole. The subject is the subject OF the sentence, but the noun phrase is not 'the noun phrase OF the sentence'. A one-clause sentence, such as these two are, can have only one subject, but can have more than one noun phrase, as in *The woman took her lunch from her bag*, where there is only one subject, *the woman*, but there are three noun phrases, *the woman*, *her lunch* and *her bag*.

Similarly, I've said that the rest of the sentence after the subject is called the predicate, but I've also said that *laughed* is a verb phrase. The difference is parallel to the one described in preceding paragraph for 'subject' and 'noun phrase': 'Verb phrase' is the category label for this kind of phrase, whereas 'predicate' (in the sense in which I'm using it) is a relationship between the phrase and the sentence. It is the predicate OF the sentence, but it is not 'the verb phrase OF the sentence'; just a verb phrase.

Strictly speaking, in the sentences shown in (14) we should have another set of large brackets, labelled 'S' (for 'sentence') around the whole sequence.

15a   [S [NP [DET the] [N woman]] [VP [V laughed]]]
15b   [S [NP [N Vicki]] [VP [V laughed]]]

When sentences are longer and syntactically more complex than these, bracketings can become visually complex. You may be coping all right up to this point, but as we talk about more complex sentences, full bracketing can be perplexing and may interfere with your concentration on the points I'm making. To overcome that, I plan not to include all the brackets, much of the time. So, for instance, if I am talking about the sentence in (15a), but am not concerned about the internal structure of the noun phrase, I might represent it like this:

16   [NP the woman] [VP[v laughed]]

Depending on what I'm discussing at the time, I might even strip off more brackets:

17   [NP the woman] laughed

In other words, I'll include just the number of brackets necessary to explain what I want to explain. But you should remember that it's always shorthand for a full bracketing, which could be provided.

Let me use these principles straight away. I want to explain that there are more complicated noun phrases than have occurred yet. For instance,

18   [NP [NP a woman] [Cl who lives near me]]
       (won a big prize)

The point I want to make is that there's a noun phrase here that contains a clause, labelled 'cl', within it. A clause is like a sentence, only often slightly different. The clause here, for instance, resembles the sentence *The woman lives near me*, but contains *who* instead of *the woman*. I won't pursue that any further here. All I want to make clear is that there's a sentence-like sequence called a clause within the large noun phrase *a woman who lives near me*. There is also a smaller noun phrase, *a woman*, within that larger one. The first set of inner brackets surrounds the small one; the outer brackets surround the large one.

Why am I telling you all this? Because I need you to be acquainted with these ideas so that presently I can tell you a bit more about the claims that Chomsky makes about how children acquire their first language.

We can all make up sentences and speak them without stopping to think how we're doing it. Obviously, most of it's done unconsciously, but somewhere in our brains there must be a 'program' for putting words and phrases together to make sentences of whatever language we speak. If it helps to get the idea, you can think of it as a little like a program in a computer. But having used that analogy to help give you some idea of what I'm talking about, I want to repeat that it's only an analogy. I do *not* think human beings are much like computers. However, we do seem to have some sort of program by which we make up sentences unconsciously.

Let's suppose that we have innate knowledge of what the main word classes are, and that, furthermore, we know that some of them are 'major' classes and some of them are 'minor'. The ones that are usually thought of as the major ones are nouns, verbs, adjectives and prepositions. The others, such as determiners, conjunctions, and so on, are like bits of grammatical cement that stick the major classes together into a structure. That was a way of putting it, not very satisfactory; but I hope it might be useful in giving you the broad idea.

Let's go a little further and imagine that among the notions that are innate in our brains is the knowledge that the four major classes are always heads of phrases, to which we give related names. In other words, we know that a noun is always the head of a noun phrase, a verb of a verb phrase, an adjective of an adjective phrase and a preposition of a preposition phrase.

We've already seen examples of noun phrases and verb phrases. In *The cat is very fat*, *very fat* is an adjective phrase, of which the adjective *fat* is the head word. (*Very* is an intensifier, which can be the satellite (modifier) of an adjective in an adjective phrase.) In *The cat is on the roof*, *on the roof* is a preposition phrase, and its head word is the preposition *on*.[8]

Now, just wait a minute, I hear you protesting. Didn't you say Chomsky claimed that this is knowledge that the baby's born with? And at first, the baby hasn't yet learnt any words, so how can he/she label items as 'nouns', 'noun phrases', 'head of a phrase', etc.? Just so. You're absolutely right. But Chomsky doesn't assume that knowledge in the mind is expressed in words. Nor does he profess to be able to say how it's laid down physically in the brain. It's just that I'm forced to describe in words the knowledge that the child seems to have. There are unsolved mysteries here. See Elman *et al*. (1996: chapter 7) for a penetrating discussion of claims about innateness.

It may be arrangements of cells, or electrical patterns, or, for all I know, bits of Blu-Tack arranged in patterns, though I wouldn't put too much money on that one. But there's strong evidence that there's some sort of representation of what I've expressed in words.

Katz *et al*. (1974) did an interesting experiment in which they showed that girls of only 17 months of age acted as though they knew the difference between proper nouns and common nouns. (Proper nouns are those that are always spelt with a capital letter: Karen, Michael, Chicago, England, etc. Common nouns are all the others.) The girls were divided into two groups. The ones in the first group were each shown a new doll and told 'This is Dax.' There was also another, similar doll lying on the table. The word 'Dax' was therefore presented to these girls as a proper noun.

The girls in the second group were also shown a new doll, but were told 'This is a dax.' So 'dax' was presented to them as a common noun. Again, there was another doll lying on the table nearby.

Later, each girl from the first group was told, 'Show Dax to Mummy'. They each picked up the doll that had been shown to them in the first place. The girls from the second group were told 'Show a dax to Mummy.' These girls chose either of the dolls, seemingly at random.

Other questions were asked, and the girls showed they could use the two dolls interchangeably. But the ones from the first group always used the same doll they had been shown. This suggests that the girls could tell the difference between a common noun and a proper noun, even if they hadn't heard that particular one before.

Furthermore, when the experiment was repeated using boxes instead of dolls, that difference didn't occur; each group used either box indiscriminately. This suggests that they knew that dolls were the kinds of objects that might have personal names, but that boxes weren't.

Now, it's certain that no one had consciously taught these 17-month-old girls what nouns are, let alone the difference between proper and common nouns; yet they acted as if they unconsciously 'knew' about these matters. There have been numerous other experiments which have shown that children at extraordinarily young ages have 'knowledge' that no one has ever taught them. We'll look at some of those experiments in Chapter 13.

Recall that in the last half of Chapter 5 I gave various examples of grammatical matters that we all act as though we 'know', even though we may never have consciously thought about them in our lives.

6.5 One way of deducing something about the mind

Chomsky has argued persuasively that underlying our sentences there are abstract mental structures which are probably much the same for every language. But they have to undergo various computations before emerging as sentences of a particular language. These computations are the hidden grammar – the engine that drives our language operations.

There are constraints on what kinds of computations these can be, imposed by the nature of the human brain. Since this is not the place to go deeply into linguistics, I can only give the reader hints of the kind of thing that's meant.

Let's begin with two sentences of English which are generally regarded as related to each other.

19a   The baby is eating a snail.
19b   Is the baby eating a snail?

And let's assume that, roughly, the question (19b) is formed by carrying out a change on the statement (19a). That's something of a simplification, and we're ignoring a lot of things that would be involved in a technical linguistic account, but for present purposes we won't do too much violence to the truth if we talk in these terms.

Suppose I ask you what change is carried out. You might answer, 'Take the word *is* and move it to the left-hand end of the sentence.' That, of course, would get the right answer in this case. But there are also examples like these which seem to work very similarly:

20a   Dad will come home soon.
20b   Will Dad come home soon?

21a   Sally could play in the team.
21b   Could Sally play in the team?

There are a small number of other words that can be moved to form a question in the same way as *is*, *will* and *could*. They include *shall*, *can*, *would*, *must*, *may*, *might*, *has*, etc. Let's just refer to them here as '*is*, *will*, etc.'.

One rule we could invent in order to form questions like these from statements like the ones given above would be Rule A:

A   Run your eye along the sentence from left to right. When you come to the first example of *is*, *will*, etc., move it to the left-hand end of the sentence.[9]

But, although this rule works successfully in these cases, there's very good evidence that it isn't the one we use, even in principle. And it isn't the one children use, either.

In order to see this, let's take a minute to examine this sentence:

22   The girl who is chasing Peter is his friend.

We've already encountered a sentence of this general construction, namely item (18). The subject of the sentence is *The girl who is chasing Peter*. As you can see, it's a large noun phrase which contains a smaller noun phrase (*the girl*) within it. Adjoined to that smaller noun phrase, and constituting the rest of the larger noun phrase, is a clause (cl).

Now let's try Rule A on this one, to see if we can form a question. We scan along the sentence from left to right until we find the first example of *is*, *will*, etc. The first one we come to is the verb *is*, in the sequence *is chasing*. The rule tells us to move it to the left-hand end of the sentence. But the result is (23):

23   *Is the girl who chasing Peter is his friend?

Something has clearly gone wrong, since (23) is not a well-formed English question. But if we adjust Rule A so that it becomes Rule B, we'll be able to arrive at the correct answer:

B   Run your eye along the sentence from left to right. When you come to the first example of *is*, *will*, etc. following the noun phrase that is the subject of the sentence, move it to the left-hand end of the sentence.[10]

Whereas Rule A tells you to scan until you find 'the first example of *is*, *will*, etc.', Rule B tells you to look for the first one 'following the noun phrase that is the subject of the sentence'. In (22), the subject noun phrase is *The girl who is chasing Peter*, so we look for the first example of *is*, *will*, etc. after that. It is the second *is*, so we move *is* to the left-hand end of the sentence and make the correctly formed question (24):

24   Is the girl who is chasing Peter his friend?

Rule B will also get the right answer in the cases we looked at earlier, *The baby is eating a snail*, *Dad will come home soon*, and *Sally could play in the team*, as you can easily verify. By contrast, Rule A gets the right answers in those earlier cases, but the wrong answer in the case of (22). Rule B is therefore the better rule.

Now, A and B are two very different types of rules. Rule B refers to the grammatical concepts 'noun phrase' and 'subject', but Rule A contains no references to grammatical concepts. Rule B is said to be a 'structure-dependent' rule, but Rule A is not. For this reason, A is a much simpler type of rule: it doesn't involve any knowledge of grammatical structure. But it's wrong.

Now reflect on the fact that when anyone speaks a sentence, there's nothing in the sound that signals which bits are noun phrases, which bit is the subject, etc. Nothing at all. These are completely abstract notions, and apparently must be supplied by something in our minds. On the other hand, if you had to listen for a particular word, like *is* or *has*, you would be listening for something that can actually be perceived in the spoken sentence.

So you'd think that children would naturally tend to listen to actual words when they were trying to learn how to form questions, and not worry about such abstractions as noun phrases or subjects. With short sentences of the kind we looked at in (19), (20) and (21), they'd get the right answers by using Rule A, but then they'd run into difficulties when they later heard longer sentences like (22).

It might seem plausible, then, that children would at first arrive at Rule A while they were only hearing shorter sentences, and then be forced to change to Rule B when they heard more complex sentences like (22). But if so, you'd expect that they would at first make mistakes with the longer sentences and produce wrong sequences like (23). But apparently they never do. Chomsky (1976: 30–3) concludes from these facts that from the very beginning, children leap to the rule that involves an unconscious knowledge of grammatical structure. In order to do so, they must have an inborn knowledge that linguistic rules are always structure dependent; that is, that they always make reference to grammatical structure.

The argument of Chomsky's I've just been presenting perhaps seems complicated, but I think it will prove very illuminating if you try to follow it. It might be a good idea at this point to see if you can recall the main points, and if not, to read back over the section.

The logic of this argument of Chomsky's is very elegant. Whether it's right or wrong, it's a very good example of how properties of the language can be used to formulate hypotheses about inborn principles. Of course, this principle needs further confirmation, and it isn't presented here because it *must* be right – nothing falls into that category – but because it shows that hypotheses about what is in the mind are certainly available, with a bit of ingenuity.

Evidence is also available. If Chomsky's claim that children never make 'mistakes' like the one in (23) continues to hold without being successfully challenged, then it adds weight to the likelihood that the reasoning is correct. And the principle that linguistic rules are structure dependent will hold not just for English, but for all human languages, since it will be evident that the principle is innate. On the other hand, if that particular piece of evidence proves not to be true, then the argument breaks down. That would not necessarily mean, of course, that the whole theory had been negated.

6.6 Parameters

I said above that Chomsky claims that certain linguistic principles are innate in the brain. In recent years he has claimed additionally that certain 'parameters' are innate too. For present purposes, 'parameters' is another word for 'variables'. In case you're not clear what that means, recall that in algebra, the letters that are used in expressions are called 'variables', because they can be given different values. And 'parameters' here has a similar meaning.

To give you an idea of what Chomsky means, we'll use an analogy (which he used first). It's as if the brain's equipped with some dials which can be tuned to different settings. (This is only an analogy, of course; we don't really have dials in the brain.) And it is as if the baby, when it becomes conscious, starts asking 'What kind of a language are these people around me speaking?' (Again, it's just an analogy, of course.) And after a while, the baby recognizes that the dials have to be put on to certain settings for that particular language. Or, more likely, the dials set themselves, in accordance with what comes into the child's ears. These 'dials' are the parameters, or variables, which have to be given values for a particular language. When they're set, only one language is possible.

But what kinds of things am I talking about? Most of the parameters that have been proposed so far involve fairly technical linguistic theory, so it isn't easy to select an example because most of my readers have probably not studied linguistics. But I'll take just one example, which might serve to give some inkling as to what's meant.

In English, we can say (25a), which is matched in Italian by (25b):

25a John is eating (eats) a pear.
25b Giovanni mangia una pera.
[John eats a pear]

100

If we have already used John's name in a previous sentence, and we want to refer to him again, in English we can say:

26   He is eating (eats) a pear.

In Italian, however, the equivalent sentence does not use the pronoun, but leaves it out. Thus, the equivalent to (26) is:

27   Mangia una pera.
      [eats   a pear]

But this is understood exactly as (26) is in English. These facts have been reported in the linguistic literature by Italian linguists. They also say that it is possible to include the pronoun in (27), but only if you want to give special emphasis to it. There are other languages, like Spanish, which work the same way. Such languages are known as 'pro-drop' languages, because they drop the pronoun from subject position.

Now, it turns out that if you know that a language is a pro-drop language, you can predict a number of other things about it. For example, you can predict that in Italian it will be possible to say:

28   Mangia una pera Giovanni.

That prediction is correct. But if you know that English is not a pro-drop language, you can predict that it will not have a sentence equivalent to (28). And that prediction is correct, too:

29   *Is eating (eats) a pear John.

This is a very powerful mechanism, namely that if you know one thing about sentence structure in a particular language, you can often predict others.

Research is still continuing concerning pro-drop, and the facts are much more complex than I have just described. (See, for example, Hyams, 1986, 1992; Weissenborn, 1992.)

Suppose there are some facts about the language that allow you to predict numerous others. And suppose a baby, in the process of acquiring the language, registers the fact that the first kind of fact is true of the language that people speak around him/her. (Say, that it drops subject pronouns like *he*.)

Finally, suppose the baby's innate knowledge of general language principles allows him/her to leap to numerous other facts that follow as

101

a natural consequence. That would help to explain how babies learn their native language so quickly – because they don't have to learn it all. They just learn selected facts, and the rest is filled out by inborn knowledge of the principles of language.

In other words, for every parameter that is set, many other things fall into place. Given a certain array of parameter settings, you will have one particular language. Given different settings, another language will be defined.

A very interesting question is what happens in the case of bilinguals. A crucial case is someone who is bilingual in one pro-drop language and one non-pro-drop language – say, Italian and English. Various answers have been suggested, but they are rather too technical to go into here.

Now, all this is only a theory at this stage, though a great deal of research is being done on it. But it's a very imaginative theory, and one that's full of exciting possible consequences if research tends to confirm it. As with any endeavour in science, it could prove to be wrong.

Notes

1. A word of warning is in order, however. People make judgements about you on the basis of the language you speak, and if you don't speak some approved form of the language, you may be assessed as 'unintelligent' or 'poorly educated', and you may not be able to get certain jobs. That's unfair, but it's as well to acknowledge that the attitude exists. It's purely a social matter, about as important as judgements about clothes, though probably more damaging.
2. Or, more accurately, 'generating' sentences. Constructing sentences is what happens in performance, but the generation of sentences is part of our competence. To discuss this difference further here would take us too far afield from the purposes of this book, but those who are interested and feel able to pursue it should read, for example, the relevant entries for 'competence' and 'performance' in Chomsky's book *Aspects of the Theory of Syntax* (1965). It should be remembered, however, that many other parts of that book have now been superseded by more recent work by Chomsky and others.
3. Some languages have many more than this.
4. Strictly speaking, a special kind of noun phrase. A description of what a noun phrase is will come shortly.
5. These words can also belong to other classes in certain contexts. Strictly, since (1) is not a sentence and has no structure, it is difficult to tell with certainty that the classes to which I have assigned the words are the correct

ones. The labels used here represent the classes to which these items most frequently belong.

6. What I have called prepositions here might be called adverbs by some linguists, depending on the context they were in.

7. Words like *his*, *her*, *my*, *your*, *our* and *their*, which were once called 'possessive pronouns', are sometimes included in the class of determiners too, though this seems arguable.

8. In the view of most present-day grammarians, all adjective phrases must contain an adjective. In conventional grammar the notion of adjective phrases was somewhat different, being defined on meaning, and many prepositional phrases which did not contain an adjective were then called 'adjectival' phrases.

9. Things are actually a little more complex, because we would also have to form *Did Jane break her arm?* from the statement *Jane broke her arm.* As you can see, it involves a special process for putting in a 'dummy auxiliary' (a form of the verb *do*) whenever there isn't another auxiliary present. We will ignore this difficulty, because it won't make any essential difference to what is about to be claimed.

10. Further adjustment would be necessary to cope with other sentences. Instead of saying 'move the item to the left-hand end of the sentence', we would need to say 'move it to the left-hand side of the subject noun phrase'. You will see why this is so if you try to carry out the rule on a sentence like *John, your sister is running late.*

7. Do we help children to speak?

7.1 Introduction

The world seems to be about equally divided between people who cheerfully use 'baby-talk' to their small children and those who regard it as a kind of moral fault to do so. Those in the second group no doubt feel that the practice is likely to anchor their child in an infantile state well into the future, and they probably also feel that it's just as easy (if not easier) to teach a child to say *dog* and *lamb* as to teach them to say *doggy* and *baa-lamb*. And there's something about the term 'baby-talk' that seems like a put-down – as if it's babyish for an adult (or even a child) to use it.

No doubt many of the parents who use baby-talk don't analyse their reasons for doing so; they just do it. But there are also some linguists who believe that it serves a useful educational purpose, namely that it makes it easier for the baby to pick up the language that the members of the family speak. But that has turned out to be a controversial claim.

Linguists who discuss 'baby-talk' usually prefer not to call it that, because they feel that the label carries adverse connotations of triviality, and they frequently want to claim that it has a very positive purpose. So what do they call it? 'Motherese'[1] is one term that has frequently been used, but many people reject this, too, since it's used not only by mothers but also by fathers, aunts, uncles and assorted strangers. For that reason various alternative terms have been invented, such as *child-directed speech* (CDS for short), *infant-directed speech, parentese, caretaker speech, nursery talk, nursery language* and *caregiver register*.

Most often I'm going to use the term *motherese*[1] in this book, in spite of the fact that 'infant-directed speech' is more accurate. My reason is

that 'infant-directed speech' has an over-formal flavour, and I'm prepared to sacrifice purist correctness in favour of a more user-friendly
term, provided it's understood that 'motherese' shouldn't be taken too
literally. We get along with the term 'mother tongue' quite well, even
though it isn't literally just that.

7.2 Ferguson on baby-talk

Ferguson (1977) used the now shunned term 'baby-talk', and described
it as a 'simplified register'; a style of speech that's simpler than normal
adult speech. He says it belongs to a whole set of simplified registers,
including the way we talk to people who are hard of hearing, to
foreigners, to retarded people and to children. Also, he claims that
lovers talk to each other in a simplified register – something like baby-
talk. Once, when I reported this to a class of students, they all denied
that they would talk like that with their lovers, but a number of them
said their sisters, brothers, cousins or friends did it! ('Dear Dorothy Dix:
A friend of mine has a problem . . .')

Many of those who have written about motherese have claimed that
it occurs in many if not all languages, and that it exhibits the same
characteristics everywhere. Various writers including Roger Brown
(1977) have claimed there are more than 100 characteristics that mark
out baby-talk from normal adult-to-adult speech. Ferguson (1977)
attempts to group them into classes. He says that a number of them
could be described as *simplifying processes*, others as *clarifying processes*, and
still others as *expressive processes*.

7.2.1 SIMPLIFYING PROCESSES

One example of a simplifying process is the use of simplified sentence
forms, as in *Daddy go work*. Notice that, in comparison with adult-to-
adult English, the auxiliary verb *is* has been omitted, the verb *go* has lost
its *-ing* inflection, and the preposition *to* has been omitted. Or, alterna-
tively, that *go* serves instead of the past tense form *went*, or that it serves
instead of the perfect participle *gone*, and the auxiliary *has* is missing.
You can see the advantage to the child of using the unchanged form *go*:
it will serve for three other different verb-forms in different contexts,
and leave it to others to add the missing ingredients.

105

It's quite general in baby-talk that there are fewer verbs than in adult-to-adult speech, and certain 'support verbs', such as *go* and *do* are worked hard: *go bye-bye, go walkie, do wee-wee*, etc. There are also fewer modifiers (adjectives, adverbs, etc.).

Another simplifying feature of baby-talk is the use of names instead of pronouns: 'Baby want apple' instead of 'I want (an) apple' or 'Baby want apple?' instead of 'Do you want (an) apple?' Many words are made simpler phonetically: *stomach* becomes *tummy*, *Grandma* becomes *Nanna*, *brother* becomes *bra*, and so on.

There is a limited vocabulary, and the words cluster around a few topic areas: (a) BODILY PARTS: handy-pandy, tootsy(-wootsy), toothy-peg, nosy-posy, botty(-wotty); (b) ANIMALS: moo-cow, baa-lamb, bow-wow, piggy-wiggy, birdie, bunny, horsie, gee-gee; (c) FOOD: nana (banana), googie (egg), bicky (biscuit), veggie (vegetable), mato (tomato); (d) NAMES FOR PEOPLE (and animals, dolls, etc.) in the environment: Mummy, Daddy, Nanna, Grand-dad (or Pop), Bubby.

It can be seen that among the body parts there are a good many rhyming ones, and that in the lists overall there are many terms that end in '-y' (phonemically /i/). For some reason, this ending seems to convey affectionate connotations, which could be why we use it to babies. Or maybe that's the wrong way around, and it's the fact that words of this kind are used to babies, to whom most people feel warm, that makes this ending sound affectionate.[2]

7.2.2 CLARIFYING PROCESSES

Among the 'clarifying processes', Ferguson lists repetition, which occurs more frequently than in adult-to-adult talk, a slower rate of speech, and exaggerated intonational contours. (Try saying 'You're a nice little boy, aren't you?' as if to a young child, while imitating your aunt, and you'll probably hear it.)

7.2.3 EXPRESSIVE PROCESSES

The remaining category, 'expressive processes', includes (among other things) the use of a higher pitch when talking to children, and the occasional use of a conspiratorial whisper. These are attempts to get close to the child.

7.2.4 DISCUSSION

There's been a good deal of debate about Ferguson's list of features of 'baby-talk'. To start with, the notion of 'simplicity' in language that is used to small children isn't straightforward. What seems simple from the point of view of a linguist of one theoretical persuasion may not seem so to one working in a different model.

Furthermore, as various writers have pointed out, if children are to acquire the full linguistic system, they must meet fairly complex structures as well as simple ones; otherwise they're likely to draw false conclusions about what the system is. (See Gleitman *et al.*, 1984, for a discussion of the issue.) At times, the language used to children will seem simple in some ways and complex in others. It often contains more questions than adult-to-adult speech, and this might be considered syntactically more complex; but at the same time it may consist of short utterances, which will make it easier to process (Newport *et al.*, 1977).

Richards and Gallaway (1994: 262) say:

> it is now widely accepted that one helpful form of simplification is the reduction of processing demands on the learner. This may be achieved by features such as repetition, routine, memory priming, provision of scaffolding, transparency of meaning, pauses and rate of delivery, 'decomposition' of task (see Wesche).[3]

What about Ferguson's claim that clarification is one of the functions of baby-talk? It has also been controversial. Roger Brown (1977) claimed that simplifying and clarifying processes are really so similar to each other that it would be better to have just a single classification, 'simplifying/clarifying'. Later, Richards and Gallaway (1994: 262) suggested that 'Specific forms of clarification can be subsumed under the general heading of intelligibility; for example, increasing the salience of features which would be otherwise unstressed, contracted or phonologically reduced.'

Finally, what about *expressive* features? Apart from the fact that they provide a warm and friendly environment for the child to experience language in, they do not so obviously lend themselves to claims that they assist in teaching specific features of the language.

Richards and Gallaway (1994: 263) suggest some additional functions to be added to the three broad ones proposed by Ferguson: *attention factors, feedback, modelling* (providing examples of correct utterances and of conversational structures), *conversational participation* and *the teaching of routines*.

Brown (1977: 20) also made the following interesting claim, which was to generate yet more argument (BT = baby-talk):

> The by-now overwhelming evidence of BT [in various languages] refutes overwhelmingly the rather off-hand assertions of Chomsky and his followers that the preschool child could not learn language from the complex but syntactically degenerate sample his parents provide without the aid of an elaborate innate component.

There's a fairly broad consensus that Chomsky's statement about the poverty-stricken sample of the language that small children are exposed to was something of an exaggeration; however, Brown's next statement is more contentious.

> But it has turned out that parental speech is well-formed and finely tuned to the child's psycholinguistic capacity. The corollary would seem to be that there is less need for an elaborate innate component than there at first seemed to be.

But things aren't as simple as that, as we'll see.

7.3 The early work of Catherine Snow

So far, I've simply described what motherese is. It seems a calm, trouble-free area, you might think, with baa-lambs and moo-cows filling the scene.

But the sound of drums can be heard in the distance. Some of the researchers in this field have undertaken a very serious project – namely, to prove that one of the main claims made by Noam Chomsky is wrong.

As we saw in Chapter 6, the claim was that babies come into the world already 'knowing' some things about language. Not about a particular language, like English or Chinese, but about what a baby can expect to find in human languages.

So far, I've cited discussions of motherese which were based on observation, but not on fully fledged experimentation. Snow (1972) presented an account of some controlled experiments which aroused a great deal of controversy. The main question she wanted to answer was whether mothers change their way of speaking when they talk to young children, in such a way as to try to make it easier for the children to learn the language.

In order to try to find out, Snow studied 24 mothers and their children. Twelve of the mothers had children aged roughly from $9\frac{1}{2}$ to $12\frac{1}{2}$ years, and twelve mothers had children aged roughly from 2 to $3\frac{1}{2}$ years. For simplicity, she referred to these groups as the 10-year-olds and the 2-year-olds respectively.[4]

There was another question she wanted to answer, too. Would it make any difference whether it was her own child the mother was talking to or someone else's? After all, a mother may only 'switch on' to this special way of speaking if it's her own child she's speaking to. Her instincts as a mother may be what drives the process.

So she scheduled sessions at her laboratory so that a 2-year-old and a 10-year-old, together with their mothers, came to the laboratory at the same time. There were three tasks for the mothers to do, and each one did them both with her own child and with the other child.[5] The experimenter was not present during the testing.

The three tasks were:

- making up and telling a story based on a picture that was provided by the experimenter;
- telling the child how to sort a number of small plastic toys in several ways;
- explaining a physical phenomenon to the child.

In the last case, no examples are given, but I imagine things like a flood, a storm, or a bushfire are intended. The speech that each mother used during these tasks was recorded on tape, then transcribed into a typescript. A scoring system was worked out so that the degree of difficulty of the utterances used could be assessed.

Of course, it isn't an easy matter to decide whether one lot of language is more complex than another. But Snow assumed:

- that utterances that use more words are more complex than ones that use fewer words;
- that long utterances are more complex than short ones;
- that compound verbs make an utterance more complex than simple verbs do;[6]
- that utterances that contain subordinate clauses are more complex than ones that don't have them;[7]

109

- that the more words that occur before the main verb in an utterance, the more complex the utterance is;
- that the more third-person pronouns there are in an utterance, the more complex it is.[8] Third-person pronouns are difficult for children because there are two ways in which they can be interpreted:
  1. they can refer to another noun phrase in the sentence – and the rules for determining which one it is are quite complex; and
  2. they can be interpreted as 'deictic' items – that is, items which can refer to people or objects in the situational context. The person or object they refer to changes with the situation.

Snow also assumed that repetitions of utterances or parts of utterances would make understanding easier. They could be repetitions of either complete utterances or partial ones. They could be repetitions of a syntactic structure or just of the meaning, even if that meaning was expressed differently. To be counted as repetitions, in all these cases they had to occur within three utterances of the original, and had to contain a subject and a verb.

Now, every linguist would probably have a different method of assessing the degree of difficulty in utterances, but most would probably agree that the features that Snow looked for would be reasonable candidates for consideration.

Snow also wanted to see if it made any difference whether the mothers spoke directly to the child, or recorded some talk which the child would listen to later. The idea was that something about the actual presence of the child might make a difference to how the mother spoke. (Motherese might only be 'turned on' in the presence of a child.)

The mothers weren't told the real purpose of the experiment, but were told that the aim was to study 'how children learn to talk'. This, of course, raises an ethical question. Should you lie to people whose co-operation you are seeking? If so, are you infringing their 'civil rights'? The trouble is, if you tell them the truth (that their own way of speaking is under scrutiny), it might affect the way they speak, and consequently distort the results. There's no completely satisfactory solution to this dilemma, but Snow acted as ethically as it's possible to act while still doing the experiment. She told the mothers the truth after the experiment and then asked their permission to use the data she had recorded from them. All of them agreed. If any of them hadn't agreed, of course, she would have been obliged to delete their data.

Snow carried out a second and a third experiment, too. The second one simply tightened some of the fine detail in the first experiment, and the third one used subjects who were not mothers, and had no regular contact with children. These women made stimulus tapes for the children, but they did no experiments in which the children were present. The tasks and the scoring system were the same as for the women who were mothers. Clearly, Snow wanted to find out whether being a mother gave women a special affinity with children which might affect the result.

Snow reports that the mothers' speech to the children was simpler and more redundant than their normal speech to adults. By every measure of complexity, the speech was more complex when mothers were speaking into a tape-recorder than when they were face to face with a child. Furthermore, it was more complex when they were talking to 10-year-olds than when they were talking to 2-year-olds. There were no significant differences between mothers and non-mothers.

A notable feature of the mothers' speech when face to face with the children was that their utterances were reduced in length.

The reader won't be surprised that the mothers made more repetitions of all three kinds when talking to the 2-year-olds than they did when talking to the 10-year-olds. Snow says that the value of this kind of repetition for guiding the child's behaviour is obvious. Furthermore, she thinks it may have another value, that of giving information about where the boundaries of structural units (phrases, clauses) occur within utterances.

The modifications that mothers use when talking to children may be valuable in two ways, according to Snow:

1. They keep the speech simple, interesting and comprehensible to young children.
2. They are 'admirably designed to aid children in learning language', though this is not intended.

Chomsky had claimed (1968: 23)[9] that the native speaker of a language 'has acquired a grammar on the basis of very restricted and degenerate evidence'. Furthermore, he had said (Chomsky, 1965: 4), 'A record of natural speech will show numerous false starts, deviations from rules, changes of plans in mid-course, and so on.' It is apparently with these comments in mind that Snow writes (p. 561):

111

The present findings strongly suggest that middle-class children such as those included in this study do not learn language on the basis of a confusing corpus full of mistakes, garbles and complexities. They hear, in fact, a relatively consistent, organized, simplified, and redundant set of utterances which in many ways seems quite well designed as a set of 'language lessons'.

7.4 The work of Newport and colleagues

Snow (1972) was almost immediately challenged by a number of other scholars. A very important response was contained in a paper by Newport *et al.* (1977). They reported on an experiment that they had done which was broadly comparable with Snow's experiment, except that certain factors had been changed. Like Snow, they used mothers and their children, but as well as recording the mothers' talk to the children, they recorded the mothers' talk to one of the investigators (Elissa Newport). A detailed comparison was made between the two samples of talk. Each of these was also compared with the speech of the children.

Another important difference between this experiment and Snow's was that the conversations were unstructured; Newport just chatted naturally with the mothers, who were told to have natural conversations with their children.

Another difference was that Newport *et al.* concentrated on younger children and didn't use older ones for comparison. (But they did use adults, which may not have been very different.) They had three groups of younger children, who fell into the age groups 12–15 months, 18–21 months and 24–27 months. The last of these groups was more or less equivalent to Snow's '2-year-old' group.

Fifteen mothers and their daughters were visited in two two-hour sessions, held six months apart. All of the families were middle class. Although the mothers were initially given to understand that it was the children's speech that was being studied, they were told after the second session that it was their own speech that was in focus. They were asked for their approval to use the results, and this was granted.

All the talk was transcribed and analysed to see how many of the sentences were well formed, what the average lengths of the sentences were and how structurally complex they were. Two measures of structural complexity were used:

- the number of sentence-nodes per utterance – that is, how many clauses there were in each utterance; and
- the derivational length of each sentence.

Syntactic theory has changed so much since 1977 that the notion of 'derivational length' as a measure of complexity no longer exists. In a rough way, however, what the authors meant here was that, say, a sentence which is both a question and a passive (e.g. *Was Kim arrested by the police yesterday?*) is more complex than one which is just passive (e.g. *Kim was arrested by the police yesterday*), while one that is a question, a passive and a negative (e.g. *Wasn't Kim arrested by the police yesterday?*) is more complex than either.

Now let's have a look at the results obtained by Newport *et al.*[10] They reported that the speech of mothers to children was, at least at first sight, simpler than that to adults. The sentences were shorter, more phonetically coherent (fewer mumbles and slurs) and 'unswervingly well-formed'. The majority of utterances to both children and adults were fully grammatical (60 per cent to the children and 58 per cent to the adults). The rest consisted of well-formed isolated phrases, such as 'the ball'; 'under the table'; 'OK'; 'thank you'. This result seemed to refute Chomsky's claim that children had to learn from a degenerate sample of the language.

So it might seem that motherese is well qualified to be a simplified teaching language. But, say the authors, if that's correct, motherese has a number of puzzling characteristics. In the first place, in an ideal teaching language you'd expect to find a preponderance of simple, active, declarative sentences, with subject–verb–object order. But, by this criterion, motherese is more complex than ordinary adult-to-adult talk. Only 30 per cent of the utterances to children were declaratives, but 80 per cent of those to adults were.

Second, you would expect that an ideal teaching language would introduce one new construction at a time. One of the most important principles of teaching is to introduce only one difficulty at a time. But by this criterion, motherese is again more complex than speech to adults; there's a wider range of sentence types and more inconsistency. Questions and imperatives (commands) scarcely occur in the speech to adults, whereas 18 per cent of the motherese utterances are imperatives and 44 per cent are questions. Only one finding fitted the idea that motherese is syntactically simpler: there were fewer clauses than in adult-directed speech.

113

A third principle that you would expect an ideal teaching language to obey is to move from the simple to the more complex as the child made progress. But this doesn't turn out to be so. Newport *et al.* could find no significant correlations between the brevity, intelligibility or grammaticality of a particular mother's speech and that of the particular children she spoke to.

According to these authors, there are certain extremely limited aspects of the mothers' speech that do affect correspondingly limited aspects of the children's language. This seems to happen only with certain language-specific properties such as grammatical morphemes and parts of grammar that vary in different languages.

Grammatical morphemes are word endings which carry grammatical information – for example, plural endings on nouns in English.[11] These endings are used in speech only by English; other languages generally use different ones.[12] It is those kinds of features that Newport *et al.* are referring to when they say that the mothers' speech models affected only language-specific items.

They also refer to 'parts of grammar that vary in different languages'. What's the difference between that and the language-specific grammatical morphemes like the plural endings on nouns? Well, although most languages don't have the same plural morphemes as English, there are many languages that do have plural morphemes.

By contrast, the English use of verbal auxiliaries is highly unusual. Take as an instance a sentence like *Sue is eating her lunch*. Here, the auxiliary verb *is* is combined with the main verb *eating* to express the idea of continuous or progressive action. In many other languages, such a notion would be expressed by just the main verb, without any auxiliary. For example, in French, German and Italian, the equivalent of *Sue eats her lunch* is used to express continuous or progressive action, as well as to express what we mean by *Sue eats her lunch*.

Back to English, where *Sue is eating her lunch* can be turned into the question *Is Sue eating her lunch?* When questions are asked in that way, the auxiliary goes to the front of the sentence, and is therefore in a very prominent position. Thus, auxiliaries are probably brought to children's attention.

In negative imperatives, too, such as *Don't eat until I tell you*, the (negated) auxiliary is taken to the front of the sentence, and so is in a prominent position and is probably noticed. This doesn't happen with ordinary statements like *You can eat your lunch now*, where the auxiliary *can* is not at the beginning.

114

Now, when Chomsky claimed that a good deal of knowledge about grammar was innate, that implied that a good deal of grammar is universal, in the sense of occurring in all languages. Inborn knowledge will be expressed in all languages. On the other hand, any aspects of grammar that are not universal won't be innate.

So what Newport *et al.* are getting at here is that motherese doesn't rule out Chomsky's claim about innate knowledge since, according to the results of their study, motherese doesn't have any influence on the universal, innate parts of grammar (for which it isn't necessary, of course), but only on the non-universal parts that are specific to certain languages. This evidence therefore has the effect of weakening the claim of Catherine Snow and others that Chomsky's claim was wrong.

Finally, they say, there are three aspects of mothers' speech that could serve a teaching function.

1. DEICTIC TERMS (in which what is referred to varies according to circumstances). Examples are *there* ('There is a ball'), *here* ('Here's your giraffe') and *that's* ('That's your nose'). Sixteen per cent of the motherese utterances involved deixis, compared with only 2 per cent of adult-directed language. Deictic expressions might help with the learning of vocabulary.
2. EXPANSIONS. For instance, if the child says 'Milk allgone', the mother might answer with 'Yes, the milk is all gone'. Some 6 per cent of mothers' utterances were expansions and, of course, none of the utterances to adults were. Expansions might conceivably help the learning of syntax.
3. REPETITIONS. Twenty-three per cent of the mothers' utterances involved some repetition. This might conceivably help by allowing rehearsal or comparison of different forms.

But, comment the authors, these features do not allow us, in themselves, to distinguish between cause and effect. That is, the fact that a mother is speaking to a small child might cause her to do these things because she *thinks* they might help.

The overall message from Newport *et al.* (1977), then, is that Snow's claim that motherese is an ideal teaching language has not been verified.

115

7.5 Wexler and Culicover

Wexler and Culicover's *Formal Principles of Language Acquisition* (1980) is a highly technical book which is not recommended for beginners in linguistics. But there is one part, beginning on p. 66, that's fairly straightforward and discusses motherese.

The authors discuss the claims of writers like Roger Brown and Catherine Snow that presenting sentences in some special way to children will feed them information that will make it easier to learn the language. They cite Brown's claim that 'parental speech is well-formed and finely tuned' to the child's needs.

They comment that people who make such claims rarely explain why simplicity or fine-tuning should be useful for the child learning the language. Even if it could be shown that they were useful, that wouldn't necessarily mean that a less elaborate innate component would be needed.

Wexler and Culicover are saying that in order to show that simplified language would help a child to learn the language, proponents of motherese would have to show exactly how simplified sentences could help overcome the gap between the data and the grammar of the language. But this question is rarely discussed.

The reason Wexler and Culicover think that the use of simple sentences won't make it possible for a child to learn the grammar of the language is that there's no way that children could deduce the grammar of any language from being exposed to simple sentences. However, there is an obvious reply that can be made to this, namely, that children do pick up the grammar of their language just from exposure to it, as Chomsky claims and as Wexler and Culicover themselves admit.

Newport *et al.* (1977) commented that claims about there being innate linguistic principles are neither validated nor invalidated by the claims of motherese, and that seems correct. Besides, a prior question to 'How does motherese help?' is 'Does motherese help?', and that is the question that Snow was exploring.

Horning (1969) proposed that children should be presented with a limited subset of the vocabulary and syntax of the language, which could be expanded as their competence grew. But Wexler and Culicover say that limiting the language in that way won't help solve the language-learning problem. It will simply mean that the learner is given less information, which will increase the problem of how the child learns. And that would make the case for an innate component even stronger.

They say that some knowledge does exist about the kind of speech adults present to children, and it does seem to have special characteristics. But these characteristics don't code information in any way that could help with the language-learning problem.

They stress several times that they are not claiming that special features of mothers' language to children have *no* effect on *any* aspect of language development. But they are claiming that what is known about motherese (baby-talk) can in no way remove the need for an innate language component.

7.6 Discovery procedures

The reason Wexler and Culicover say that it's necessary to postulate an innate language component in the brain is that it's impossible to work out the grammar of any language by directly examining its sentences. The child needs a 'head start' in order to do it. In a somewhat comparable way, atomic structure can't be deduced by examining the surfaces of physical objects.

You may still feel convinced that you could work out the grammar of English by examining English sentences in the form in which we hear them or see them. That process would be what linguists call a 'discovery procedure'. An army of linguists who were also convinced it ought to be possible spent many decades trying to find a discovery procedure, but without success.

So that you'll know what's involved, let's have a look at a failed attempt to provide a discovery procedure by which children could acquire a knowledge of the structure of English. In Chapter 1 I gave an account of the so-called 'pivot grammar' proposed by Martin Braine to show the structure of two-word utterances (see pp. 9–10). He also suggested extending his pivot grammar to cover multiple-word utterances as well (Braine, 1963b).

He thought that children learned the positions that certain classes of words occupy in multiple-word utterances. For instance, the first position is occupied by a noun or a noun phrase, and the second position by a verb or a verb phrase. This is no doubt true, in utterances like

1   Mummy drink Coke.
2   Teddy sleep now.

If we use a nonsense-word in second position, says Braine, children will identify it as a verb. (They won't know that label, but unconsciously they will tag it as a word of that class.) Example:

3   People kivil.

They then learn that the same nouns or noun phrases that can occur in first position can also occur in other positions, in different sentences:

4   <u>Teddy</u> kiss <u>Mummy</u>.
5   *<u>Mummy</u> kiss <u>Teddy</u>*.

6   <u>Teddy</u> kivil <u>Mummy</u>.
7   <u>Mummy</u> kivil <u>Teddy</u>.

There is one other thing. It was pointed out in Chapter 6 that nouns that are not accompanied by any 'satellites' (modifiers) are also noun phrases, as well as being nouns. Now there are noun phrases in first (phrasal) position in all the examples (1) to (7). Furthermore, in every case, a verb occurs in the second position, following the noun phrase.

It is also obvious that positions will change in certain structures. For instance, the question corresponding to (8) is (9):

8   Scott is a baby.
9   Is Scott a baby?

Sentence (8) conforms to Braine's extended pivot-grammar description in that *Scott* is a noun phrase and is in first position, while *is* is a verb (phrase) and is in second position. But these positions are reversed in (9). For this reason, Braine claimed that his theory was adequate only for simple, grammatical, declarative sentences; but he said that these are basic and account for most speech. His analysis involves a good many complications which I've omitted from this simplified account, but I believe I have correctly characterized the essence of what he claimed.

Bever *et al.* (1965) presented a critique of Braine's theory. They denied his claim that most sentences of English were simple, grammatical and declarative. They made an analysis of the speech of mothers conversing with their children, who were from 6 months to 30 months old. Out of a total of 432 utterances, only 258 were fully grammatical, and only 48 were simple declaratives.

They also denied that once you know one position in which noun phrases occur, you can predict others. On the contrary, the types of expressions that can occur in a given position in a simple declarative sentence are extremely varied, and cannot be predicted. Bever *et al*. drew attention to examples like the following:

10   The book weighed one kilogram.
11   *One kilogram was weighed by the book.

Likewise, we have:

12   The book cost fifty dollars.
13   *Fifty dollars were cost by the book.

There are other positions that can't be predicted, either. Both (14) and (15) are grammatical:

14   Meg sent the book away.
15   Meg sent away the book.

But if we substitute the pronoun *it* for *the book*, only a sentence like (16) is grammatical; not one like (17).

16   Meg sent it away.
17   *Meg sent away it.

So it isn't true that the positions of noun phrases can be generalized from one type of sentence to the other. Bever, *et al*. concluded that the types of expressions that can occur in a simple declarative sentence are extremely varied, and cannot be predicted by the positions they can occupy.

Meanwhile, generative linguists have tried to show why a discovery procedure is impossible. They've postulated underlying abstract structures which control the grammar of the surface structures of sentences. Not all linguists are generative linguists, of course, but even those who aren't have run into a brick wall trying to find a discovery procedure.

In order to accept the main point being made here, you don't necessarily have to accept the principles of generative grammar; you only have to believe the claim that no one has ever succeeded in finding a satisfactory discovery procedure. If you can prove that that claim's wrong, then you'll have proven that I'm wrong, and what's more, you'll have shown that Bever and his colleagues, Chomsky, and thousands of other linguists of all persuasions have been misled.

7.7 A Snow drift

In Snow's later work (1986) there is quite a change of position in comparison with her 1972 paper. Some readers might think that this is something for which she should be adversely criticized, but that isn't by any means the case. It's honourable, and not shameful, for a researcher to make changes to her theory if she becomes convinced that certain aspects of what she has previously claimed aren't correct. That's the way progress is made in theories: through continued research and revision.

Snow admits that there were a couple of 'oversimplifications' in earlier claims about motherese. The first, which she attributes to Levelt (1975), was that motherese represented a set of ideal 'language lessons' for children. She says, 'such an interpretation was, of course, an unwarranted extrapolation from the findings' (p. 72). But Snow herself had made a similar claim, although she did not use the word 'ideal'. To repeat a paragraph that was quoted earlier, what Snow (1972: 561) said was:

> The present findings strongly suggest that middle-class children such as those included in this study do not learn language on the basis of a confusing corpus full of mistakes, garbles and complexities. They hear, in fact, a relatively consistent, organized, simplified, and redundant set of utterances which in many ways seems quite well designed as a set of 'language lessons'.

The second 'oversimplification' involved in the earlier claims was that there was no innate component to language ability. Snow comments (1986: 72–3):

> It is, of course, absurd to argue that any complex behaviour is entirely innate or entirely learned. Innate and environmental factors always interact in the development of complex abilities, and both are of crucial importance. It is not, however, absurd to ask what proportion of the developmental variation in some complex ability like language is attributable to innate as opposed to environmental factors, for it is certainly the case that environmental factors can be relatively more important in determining an individual's achievements for one type of ability (e.g. solving arithmetic problems) than for

another type (e.g. singing on key). . . . The correct conclusion to be drawn from the Stage 1 studies was that Chomsky's position regarding the unimportance of the linguistic input was unproven.

Having admitted that earlier work was mistaken in some ways, Snow sets about revising her claims. She cites the claims of Gleitman *et al.* (1984) that the simplest child-directed speech is not necessarily the best for the purpose of learning language.

Gleitman *et al.* subscribe to the belief expressed by Wexler and Culicover (1980) that the child doesn't have the benefit of negative evidence; that is, no one ever tells the child that a certain structure is wrong. If a child arrives at a rule which generates some correct sentences, but also some incorrect ones, (s)he will never be able to revise the rule, because there is no evidence as to what is wrong with it. The point that Gleitman *et al.* make is that a child who is not exposed to the full range of complexity in the language will be likely to make such errors in formulating rules.

However, says Snow, even if children don't receive overt correction of grammatical errors, they may well interpret other kinds of responses from adults as negative feedback. 'Any response that reflects a need to negotiate about the exact meaning of the child's utterance is negative feedback' (p. 77). Snow adds that no data are available on the frequency with which such responses occur.

In other words, if the adult makes it clear that she doesn't understand what the child said, that amounts to telling the child that there was something about the utterance that wasn't satisfactory. That doesn't tell her/him *what* was unsatisfactory, but it might lead the child to experiment in saying things like the unsatisfactory utterance in different ways.

Snow claims (following MacNamara, 1972; Pinker, 1979; Schlesinger, 1971; Wexler and Culicover, 1980) that children work out the rules that generate syntactic structure by taking account of the meanings of adult utterances. This involves understanding the important lexical items and guessing what the adult is likely to be saying in the given situation. The process will be aided if the adult says the kinds of things the child expects from the situation. And then, 'after many thousands of chances to observe that the word referring to the agent precedes the word referring to the action in adult sentences, the child can start to induce a rule about the order of those semantic elements' (p. 78). This over-simplistic rule will later have to be revised as the child

121

hears more and more complex sentences. Notice that this is an attempt to find a kind of discovery procedure.

Snow (1986) says that an examination of mothers' speech to young children reveals that they restrict the contents of their sentences to 'the present tense, to concrete nouns, to comments on what the child is doing and on what is happening around the child' (p. 78). She refers to the controversy that has surrounded earlier claims that child-directed speech is 'finely tuned' to the child's language level. Although research tended to show that that wasn't true, more recent accounts of more detailed research have revealed evidence of fine-tuning. But fine-tuning seems more sensitive to the child's level of understanding than to the level of language production (s)he has reached. It's also stronger for word choice and meaning than for syntax.

Snow's next question is this: assuming that mothers' speech is, in fact, finely adjusted to children's linguistic ability, how do the mothers achieve that? How do they strike the right level? Her answer is that a large proportion of the mothers' utterances are responses to children's utterances. Very often the child raises a topic and the mother either comments on it or expands the utterance.

The fact that children are 'relatively incompetent conversational partners' (p. 81) accounts for the fact that the mothers' speech is full of questions: they represent attempts to pass the conversational ball to the child. The expansions are attempts to make the child perform better. And because the mothers are following up topics suggested by the child, they are liable to use speech that's semantically relevant and easy for the child to interpret.

This sort of speech begins long before the child begins to talk, which shows that mothers don't just do it in response to utterances by the child. But Snow is cautious. She says (1986: 84):

> The intuitive attractiveness of the finding that semantic contingency promotes language development has somewhat obscured the absence of any hypothesis concerning exactly how it might work to promote language development. ... Thus, the importance of the findings concerning the facilitative effects of semantic contingency has not yet been fully exploited.

Snow's change of position is part of the reason I think a change occurred in the directions of research in motherese around about 1980 and a little before. Also, some researchers set out in new directions. The experiment described in the next section is amusing, but its purpose is serious, and the points it makes are quite telling.

7.8 Doggerel

Hirsch-Pasek and Treiman (1982) examined the language used by people talking to their dogs, which, at the suggestion of Henry Gleitman, they called 'doggerel'. They had noticed that doggerel had many of the characteristics that have been attributed to motherese; for example, short utterances, many repetitions and few grammatical errors. They set out to examine the matter more closely, and used as subjects four women and their dogs. The women were aged between 25 and 32. (The ages of the dogs are not given, but I assume none of them were in the process of acquiring language.) Two of the women had children and two did not.

The women were told that the purpose of the experiment was to give their dogs an intelligence test. The dogs had to carry out tasks like finding a bone that was hidden under a paper cup and getting a ball out of a shoe-box through a small opening.

The subjects were run in pairs. While one woman and her dog were in the testing room, the other woman and her dog stayed in a waiting room. The two subjects then reversed roles. The experimenters recorded the spontaneous speech of the woman in the waiting room (only), both to the dog and to the experimenter. When the experimenter left the room, she suggested that the woman 'prepare' her dog for the test. This was to encourage her to speak to her dog. Further samples of the women's speech were collected on subsequent occasions.

The average length of utterances to children in motherese has been said to be about 4 words, while the average length of utterances to the dogs in this experiment was 3.59 words. Utterances to adults averaged 9.36 words.

Motherese is said to contain relatively few declarative sentences and many imperatives and questions. Doggerel proved similar in these details. Present-tense verbs predominate in both motherese and dog-gerel.

Just as mothers often repeat their own utterances when they're talking to children, so the dog-owners repeated the utterances they addressed to dogs. They also repeated noises that the dogs made, just as mothers sometimes repeat the sounds their babies make.

123

The language used to both children and dogs is more grammatical than that used to adults, as well as being simpler. It also contains a good many tag questions. One difference between motherese and doggerel, however, is that motherese includes a fairly large number of deictic utterances, whereas doggerel doesn't include any more of them than would normally be used to adult human beings.

The implications of these findings are quite interesting. There is evidence that well-formedness of utterances occurs because they're short, not because the language being used is designed to be grammatically well formed. If the sentences used to dogs and other adults are made longer, ungrammaticality increases. The authors comment that the same would probably hold for motherese.

They quote Levelt (1975) as saying that motherese is used in response to the child's linguistic level. But the fact that the language used to dogs is so similar to that used to children casts doubt on that idea, since dogs don't use language at all. The authors also reject the suggestion of Newport *et al.* (1977) that it's the intellectual level of the child that evokes the use of motherese, since dogs surely operate at a lower intellectual level than children.

But although motherese and doggerel seem alike in syntax, Hirsch-Pasek and Treiman comment that they may differ in other respects; for example, motherese, but not doggerel, uses deictic expressions. Following Snow (1977), they also comment that dogs are never asked some of the questions that are used to children, such as 'What colour is this?'

7.9 The work of Anne Fernald

Anne Fernald has also suggested new directions of research. In an impressive series of papers, culminating with Fernald (1993), she has put forward a view about mothers' vocalizations to very young children, and what they achieve. (See also Fernald, 1992.) What she has to say is rather persuasive, in my view.

When mothers, fathers and even other adults talk to children, they adopt a special way of speaking. They speak more slowly than they would to other adults, and often use higher pitch, as if trying to meet the child half-way with regard to pitch. The intonation patterns are smooth and exaggerated; 'quite unlike the choppy and rapid-fire speech patterns used when addressing adults' (Fernald, 1993). None of this is new, of course.

The speech has different characteristics according to what the mother's purpose is. If she wants to soothe the child, she will tend to use 'long, smooth, falling pitch contours, in marked contrast to the short, sharp intonation patterns used in warning or disapproval' (p. 51). These characteristics of mothers' speech to infants are observed across many cultures and many languages – not only English and numerous European languages, but such different languages as Japanese, Mandarin Chinese and the South African language Xhosa. Fernald comments that the range of pitch expansion in Japanese and Mandarin Chinese is narrower than in English and other European languages. The most expansive intonation movements are made by American mothers, and these differences are probably caused by cultural factors. 'While in middle-class American culture, emotional expressiveness is not only tolerated but expected, in Asian cultures exaggerated facial and vocal displays are considered less acceptable' (p. 61).

Interestingly, Fernald points out that early investigations of mothers' speech to children concentrated on the question of whether mothers were teaching their children syntax and semantics by the way they interacted with them, but in fact mothers use simplified speech and exaggerated intonation contours even to newborns, long before the child starts to speak. Fernald says that this suggests that 'the modifications in infant-directed speech serve prelinguistic functions as well' (p. 65).

The functions that are served by the mothers' vocalizations change during the first year of the baby's life. At first they function as stimuli in alerting, soothing, pleasing and alarming the infant. Then they come to be used to direct the child's attention and to modulate infant arousal and emotion. Later, at about 5 months, vocal and facial expressions help to give the child access to the feelings and intentions of the mother, and ultimately of others.

Fernald makes clear the difference between the second and third stages (p. 72):

When the five-month-old infant smiles to an Approval or startles to a Prohibition, the prosody of the mother's voice influences the infant directly. The infant's differential responses in no way presuppose an ability to decode the emotions expressed by the mother. Rather, the infant listens with pleasure to pleasant sounds and with displeasure to unpleasant sounds, without necessarily understanding anything about the affective states motivating the production of these vocalizations.

125

But round about 8 months, children seek out and appropriately interpret emotional signals from adults. Being unsure whether a particular
object is to be enjoyed or feared, the child will often look at the mother
for a signal. And it's a sign of the trust that has built up through the
bonding of mother and child that if the mother gives exaggerated facial
and vocal signals of pleasure and approval, the baby will seize the object,
but if she gives signals of fear, the child will usually abandon it
(p. 72).

Fernald thinks that the exaggerated vocal and facial expressions could
provide the baby with clues about the mother's emotional state. The
exaggerated intonational 'tunes' of infant-directed speech seem to be
better than those in adult-directed speech at conveying emotion and
communicative intent.

In Fernald (1989) she reported on an experiment in which adult
subjects were exposed to utterances from which the content had been
filtered out, leaving only the prosodic information (intonation, etc.).
They were asked to guess what the speaker's communicative intent was.
It was found they could do this more accurately if the utterances were
child-directed speech (and therefore had exaggerated intonation patterns) than if they were adult-directed. Fernald (1993: 73) comments
that this study 'provides indirect support for the hypothesis that
information about emotion and communicative intent is conveyed with
special clarity through the exaggerated intonation of ID [infant-
directed] speech.'

Finally, towards the end of the first year, stress and intonation are
used to help the child perceive words and other linguistic units within
the stream of speech. In infant-directed speech, words that the mother
was trying to highlight were found to occur most often on exaggerated
pitch peaks in final position in phrases. By contrast, in adult-directed
speech there was much more variety in the acoustic devices used to
impose lexical stress on words.

Fernald goes on to argue for the very strong claim that 'this special
vocal behaviour has been selected for in evolution' (p. 65). This is a
reference to the theory of natural selection, first enunciated by Darwin
and later developed in various ways by others.

Suppose there is a particular kind of insect that feeds on certain
green plants. Those whose colour most closely resembles the green of
the plants will be best camouflaged and may escape being eaten by
birds; but those who are not such a good match will soon be eaten. In
this way, the 'good matches' are selected for survival and breeding,

passing on to their offspring the same characteristics which helped them to survive.

When Fernald claims that the mother's vocal behaviour is 'selected for' by evolution, then, she is claiming that it helps the child survive, and later breed. This is a big claim, as she realizes, and it is by no means certain to be true, but she argues very interestingly and cleverly for it. And by limiting the scope of her linguistic claims, she makes it more plausible than a claim that the mother is directly teaching syntax.

The biological arguments she advances are very interesting and fairly persuasive, but I won't pursue them here. Readers who want to know more about them should read Fernald (1993) for themselves.

The questions raised by motherese are still open. In my opinion the contention that mothers teach their babies syntax through motherese seems dubious; but the different kind of claim made by Fernald seems much more plausible.

Notes

1. Some people make a distinction between 'baby-talk' and 'motherese', but it's a fairly fine distinction.
2. The same sound occurs on the end of some words that are used as contractions among adults, at least in Australia. Thus 'postie' is a shortening for *postman*, 'cabbie' for *cab-driver*, and so on, and people would be unlikely to use these friendly shortenings if they were feeling angry against the individual concerned. On the other hand, 'polly' for *politician*, the now-obsolete 'chalkie' for a schoolteacher and 'clippie' for a female bus conductor have a mildly contemptuous flavour.
3. The reference is to Wesche's chapter in the same volume – that is, Gallaway and Richards (1994).
4. Actually, she referred to them as representing the 'ten-year-old condition' and the 'two-year-old condition', but we'll avoid psychological jargon here.
5. All this was randomized so that half the mothers did the tasks first with their own child and then with the other child, and the other half did the reverse. Also, half did the tasks first with a 2-year-old and half with a 10-year-old.
6. A compound verb is one that is accompanied by one or more auxiliaries: *have seen*; *is studying*; *might have been*; *will be going*, etc.
7. A subordinate clause is any clause other than the main one: *My father was still up when I got home; When I got home, my father was still up; Jane said (that) she would score a goal; Ask the boy where he lives.*

8. Remember: third-person pronouns are *he*, *she*, *it*, *they*, *his*, *her*, *hers*, *its*, *their*, *theirs*, *him*, *them*.
9. In the enlarged edition of 1972, the page number is 27.
10. Readers who are interested in the details of the coding and scoring used on the transcripts should have a look at the original paper.
11. Although we're accustomed to thinking about regular plurals as being signalled by the addition of '-s' or '-es' to the spelling of the singular (*book–books*; *box–boxes*), the phonetic facts are a bit more complex. Some plurals end in /s/ (*books*), some in /z/ (*apples*) and some in /əz/ (*boxes*).
12. Even though French plurals end in -s in the spelling, phonetically they are usually silent.

8. Learning how to mean

8.1 Introduction

M. A. K. Halliday's account of the development of language in children is markedly different from any of the others we've considered. In particular, his approach is totally different from Chomsky's. Chomsky, for instance, has never shown much interest in studying the social aspects of language; in fact, he doesn't think they can be studied scientifically. (See, for instance, Chomsky, 1979: 56–7.) Halliday, on the other hand, is unashamedly interested in the social aspects of language, and in the social influences on language development.

Halliday acknowledges Chomsky's contribution to linguistics, but he defends the right of others to proceed differently:

> The great thing Chomsky achieved was that he was the first to show that natural language could be brought within the scope of formalisation; that you could in fact study natural language as a formal system. The cost of this was a very high degree of idealisation; obviously, he had to leave out of consideration a great many of those variations and those distinctions that precisely interest those of us who are concerned with the sociological study of language. (Halliday, 1974: 84)

Halliday seems to imply that if there's a requirement that he must work within a formal system, then he can't study what he's interested in. Many (though not all) sociolinguists would probably say the same.

The fact that Halliday rejects the idea of working entirely within a formal system doesn't mean that he doesn't use pieces of formalism. The diagram in Halliday (1979: 179) which is reproduced later in this chapter as Figure 8.1 (p. 140) has a quite formal character, though it still isn't part of a formal system such as Chomsky uses. This means that Halliday uses formalism when it suits him, and when he feels that it's useful to do so, but doesn't try to spell out a unified formal system which would embrace every part of his account of child language development.

Halliday shouldn't be neatly pigeonholed as a 'sociolinguist' without qualification. In Halliday (1974: 81) he describes himself as being oriented towards sociolinguistics, but immediately adds that he would prefer to drop the 'socio' part of the word if he could. He has to include it because of the shift in meaning of linguistics in the preceding ten or fifteen years (i.e. prior to 1974).

Halliday frequently pays tribute to the British linguist J. R. Firth (1890–1960), who had a strong influence on him, and from whom he drew his interest in a meaning-based, socially oriented approach to linguistic analysis.

When Halliday was a student, he says, 'linguistics was the study of language in society; it was assumed that one took into account social factors'. But all that had changed, so that he was forced to use the term 'sociolinguistics' to distinguish what he was doing from what the term 'linguistics' had come to mean.

He makes it clear that he's referring to the change induced by Chomsky's influence. Here and elsewhere (e.g. Halliday, 1978: 89–90; 1979: 181; 1991: 417–30) he is intent on marking the difference between Chomsky's approach and his own, and this is certainly justified: their approaches are vastly different.

Halliday is more interested in what he calls the 'inter-organism perspective, language as what goes on between people (language as interaction, or simply as behaviour)', whereas Chomsky has an 'intra-organism perspective, language as what goes on inside the head (language as knowledge)' (Halliday, 1974: 81). These two perspectives, however, are 'complementary and not contradictory'. People will adopt one viewpoint or another according to their orientation in linguistics (which, in the final analysis, depends on what interests them), and they will frequently dismiss the other perspective as irrelevant, or virtually so. This is not unknown in other branches of study, either.

I remarked earlier that Halliday's approach is very different from that of the others we've considered in earlier chapters – not just from that of Chomsky. Skinner could perhaps be called an 'environmentalist', in that he was mainly interested in the world outside the child. But although Halliday is very strongly interested in the role of the environment (especially the environment consisting of other people), he isn't *only* interested in that. Unlike Skinner, he isn't a behaviourist: he acknowledges that language is a product of human consciousness.[1]

130

That last statement might also be made of Piaget, but there is a marked difference between Piaget and Halliday, too. Piaget is strongly oriented towards the contact between the child and the outside world, but has comparatively little to say about the social setting in which the child lives. For Halliday the latter has crucial importance. And since Karmiloff-Smith's approach (which we will look at later, in Chapter 15) takes its inspiration from both Piaget and Chomsky (and Fodor), it too is obviously very different from Halliday's approach.

8.2 Learning how to mean

8.2.1 INTRODUCTION

If we wanted a phrase that would best encapsulate Michael Halliday's account of what the development of language in children involves, we couldn't do better than *Learning How to Mean*, the felicitous title of the book he published in 1975. It implies looking at child language development in semantic terms, which Halliday asserts is valid. He hastens to add that a full description will also involve grammar and phonology, and he covers those matters too. But the semantic perspective is a particularly satisfactory one for explaining a lot of what he holds most important in language development. See, for example, Halliday (1975, 1978, 1979, 1991).

8.2.2 WHAT 'MEAN' MEANS

It's worth pausing here to ask what Halliday means by 'mean'. Notice that, in using a phrase like *learning how to mean*, he's implying that to mean is to engage in an activity and a skill. Hence, it's different from the same verb in 'What does this sentence mean?' and different too from meaning as a function of knowledge, in accordance with Chomsky's views.

We can bring out the nature of this difference by considering an example that Halliday discusses (1973: 25). The example concerns the very restricted kind of language used in some games, for example contract bridge. The bidding system presents a range of options, but each option is associated with a set of conditions of appropriateness. So, 'four hearts' is meaningful in the game following 'three no trumps' or 'four diamonds', but not following 'four spades'.

Halliday says we can describe this (admittedly rather special) use of language in terms of a set of alternatives which includes not only the mere ability to say 'four hearts', but also the specification of when it's appropriate. Such a system is related not to the knowledge (competence) of a speaker, he says, but to what the speaker–hearer can mean within the set of choices that the language offers.

Halliday comments that the ability to say 'four hearts' appropriately in the game,

> is sometimes thought of as if it was something quite separate from the ability to say 'four hearts' at all; but this is an artificial distinction: there are merely different contexts, and the meaning of four hearts within the context of the bidding stage of a game of contract bridge is different from its meaning elsewhere.

For a generative linguist, the knowledge that the bid 'four hearts' is appropriate only in certain contexts within the game would be a part of real-world knowledge, which is not part of the linguistic system at all. But Halliday doesn't accept that distinction. He says (private communication):

> To me what is called 'pragmatics' is just the semantics of (classes of) instances; in principle of course you can call the enterprise what you like – but I think a fair amount of harm has been done (both to pragmatics itself and to linguistics) by setting up pragmatics as a separate discipline.

Halliday sees society as providing a range of possible meanings, from which choices are made. He refers to this as a 'meaning potential':

> The child's task is to construct the system of meanings that represents his own model of social reality. This process takes place inside his own head; it is a cognitive process. But it takes place in contexts of social interaction, and there is no way it can take place except in these contexts. (Halliday, 1975: 139)

8.2.3 THE CHILD AS ACTIVE PARTICIPANT

Halliday stresses that the child isn't just a passive recipient of language, but an active participant in the processes that develop it. Thus from birth the child interacts with his/her mother and others in a cooperative attempt to communicate. Newborn babies have an awareness of people that is different from their awareness of objects.[2] They show clear signs of awareness when someone tries to communicate with them, and they respond in various ways.

This process has been intensively studied by Trevarthen at the University of Edinburgh. A few years ago a programme called *Language and the Brain* was shown on television. In it there was a small excerpt showing Trevarthen at work studying the interplay (or 'dance', as he called it) between a mother and her baby. The mother initiated the activity by taking the baby's arms and working them in various movements back and forth, up and down, while simultaneously looking deeply into the baby's eyes, talking, smiling and bobbing her head up and down. Almost from the beginning, it was not a solo by the mother, but a duet which included the baby; or, to pick up Trevarthen's term, a 'dance' between the two of them. Sometimes the baby initiated the action, and on one occasion, when the mother was moving her hands together and apart in a very slow clapping action, the baby rested his hands on the backs of his mother's and followed her actions, using his own muscles. If you were not fortunate enough to see that programme, you can get a very similar performance by watching almost any mother playing with her baby. Actually, it doesn't have to be the mother; it can be the father or any regular carer of the baby; but it's usually the mother. Halliday cites Trevarthen's work with approval.

Any reasonable observer will have no doubt that the baby is responding to the mother and joining in 'communicative interaction' with her (Halliday's term, 1978: 90). So the baby is communicating long before language proper emerges; in fact, even a few weeks after birth. Halliday believes that the ability to interact and to be aware of being addressed are innate (1978: 91), but he doesn't believe, as Chomsky does, that any specifically linguistic capacities are innate.

Following Trevarthen, Halliday calls these activities 'prespeech'. They involve 'expression' (sounds and gestures) but no semantic component.

8.3 Protolanguage (Phase 1)

Halliday says it's important to distinguish between prespeech and protolanguage, which doesn't begin until about 9 months of age. The difference is that protolanguage has both expression (sounds and gestures) and semantic content.

133

Between about 9 and 18 months,[3] then, the baby builds a proto-language – that is, a kind of forerunner-language from which the child's later language will derive. During this period the child is engaged in figuring out the surrounding world: discovering what things there are, how they relate to each other and what their properties are. There is now a good deal of evidence, gathered during the late 1980s and the 1990s, that these processes are begun a good deal earlier than this, in the first few months – and in some cases the first few weeks – of life. Some of this evidence will be described in Chapter 13.

But Halliday claims, 'Reality is created through the exchange of meanings – in other words, through conversation' (1978: 90). This claim, however, needs to be accommodated to the discoveries just referred to. Halliday agrees that meaningful acts occur before 8 or 9 months (the beginning of protolanguage) but says that they are construed into semantic *systems* only at 8 to 9 months. He adds (private communication):

> I have no problem with the notion that meaning begins at birth . . . but I don't think that conflicts with saying that reality is constructed through the *exchange* of meanings. In other words, if you choose to define 'meaning' in such a way that the exchange of attention between neonate and mother is meaningful behaviour, it is still the sharing – the *exchanging* – that is critical.

In any case, mention of the 'conversations' in which the baby engages implies that the baby is involved in both production and reception. Although Halliday refers to the two processes, he doesn't say a great deal about how they differ. He says that the 'conversations' in which the child builds a picture of reality are an important part of what (s)he is doing, but there's more to it than that: the child is constructing a 'social semiotic'.[4]

'Social semiotic' is a technical term, and Halliday (1975: 139) describes it as 'the system of meanings that defines or constitutes the culture'. But it isn't self-evident that a culture consists of a system of meanings;[5] in fact, if we take the statement literally, it seems dubious. But if we were to substitute 'is derived from the culture' for 'defines or constitutes', it would seem more persuasive. In other work, Halliday elaborates a little more on 'social semiotic'. It is:

> a reality in which things are because people are, and people construe them in certain ways . . . He [the child] is not taking over a meaning potential, or

a reality, that is ready made for him 'out there'; on the contrary ... a child is *creating* meanings, not imitating those he finds around him. (Halliday, 1978: 92)

The meanings that make up the social semiotic are realized through the linguistic system, as well as in other ways (Halliday, 1975: 139).

The idea of the child creating meanings, in concert with the mother or some 'significant other', is a crucial part of Halliday's conception of how language is learnt.[6] The exchange between the child and the 'significant others' 'takes place in the context of, and in interpenetration with, the reality that is "out there", but what is "out there" is a social construct – not a pile of sticks and stones, but a house.'

Before the arrival of language proper, then, the child 'learns how to mean' – that is, learns how to perform acts of meaning. 'Acts of meaning' are more than just acts in which communication takes place. If the baby cries because it has a safety-pin sticking into it, that's a communicative act, sending a message that it's in pain;[7] but something more is necessary before we have an act of meaning, in Halliday's sense. The 'something more' is for the act to be SYMBOLIC, and the cry evoked by the safety pin is not symbolic.

Notice too that there is no logical reason why, for example, *want* should mean 'want'. In some other language, the word for 'want' might be *zunk*. Likewise, there is no logical reason why *biscuit*, and not *blog-blog*, should mean 'biscuit', or why any of the other words should mean what they do. This can all be summed up by saying that the relationship between the form of a word and its meaning is arbitrary; and that is an important part of what we mean when we say that words act as symbols for meanings. But that isn't true of the scream elicited by the safety pin. The scream would be the same in any language; it doesn't symbolize a meaning, but directly communicates the fact that the baby is in pain. So the use of words can be an act of meaning, in the sense in which Halliday uses that term, but letting out a scream (or a sneeze or a hiccup) normally can't.[8]

But words aren't the only things that can be used symbolically. The child's ability to use symbolic communication is, according to Halliday, the result of development during a transitional period of several months, beginning at about 4 or 5 months of age.

Halliday (1975) gives an account of an extensive study of the progress that his son, Nigel, made towards language. Many of the claims about children's language development that he has made in the literature are based on those detailed observations. For example, he claims (Halliday, 1991: 419) that the first time the child reaches out to grasp some object (s)he can see, it represents 'the first symbolic encounter with the environment'. Since that was written, however, there has been a great deal of research carried out (mainly in the late 1980s and the 1990s) which shows that very young babies can process much more than was previously thought. We'll review some of that research in Chapter 13. Some experiments reported by Mehler and Dupoux (1994: 106) show that babies recognize their mothers' faces at less than a week old. That would seem to represent a 'symbolic encounter with the environment' occurring much earlier than the type that Halliday refers to here, so the claim that reaching out to grasp some object is the first symbolic encounter with the environment would seem to need revision.

In any case, Halliday says that the interpretation that can be given to this act is something like 'That's interesting! – What is it?' Of course, he doesn't mean that the child says these words; only that this is the meaning implicit in the action. Hence, the action is an act of meaning.

Not everyone may agree with that interpretation of this event. After all, it's the observer who's thinking, 'Ah! It looks as if the baby wants to express the idea that an adult might express with the words, "That's interesting! – What is it?"' It's impossible to prove that this surmise is correct. The method is that of a sensitive and imaginative projection into the mind of the baby. Halliday comments (private communication):

> But the evidence I would cite (for my opinion that the meaning is not the invention of the adult) is that the infant makes it very clear when the adult has got it wrong (as not infrequently happens!); together with the fact that my interpretations are always made in context – and since the same signs are used very often, the meanings become progressively clearer . . . Also, I could add, the infant makes it clear when the response is to its satisfaction!

Halliday would also probably want to say that there's a progression along a continuum and that as the child moves closer and closer to adult performance with language, the later developments are explained by the fact that the earlier ones occurred.

Let's pursue the idea that when the child reaches out to grab something, it represents an act of meaning equivalent to 'That's interesting! – what is it?' The act of meaning can take any form that's available. Halliday's son Nigel produced a high-pitched squeak, but it can be 'anything which can engage the child and the other in shared attention to some third party'.

Notice that this squeak is not involuntary, as the scream was. The third party is normally not a person or an object, but an event – for example, a sudden noise or bright light. 'But the act of meaning is clearly addressed; the meaning is jointly constructed, and the material phenomenon is construed as experience only through the shared act of exchanging a symbol' (Halliday, 1991: 419).

Gradually the child develops systems of meaning, which are appropriate in different contexts. When new events occur, they have an impact on the system, causing it to change.

About the age of 9 months, Nigel had a system consisting of five meanings. It gave him a 'meaning potential' – that is, a set of meanings to choose from. Three of the meanings were expressed through gestures and two with the voice. The ones that were expressed with gestures were demands for action of some kind, and were interpreted as 'I want that', 'I don't want that' and 'Do that (again)'. The ones that were expressed with the voice were more like assertions of passive reflection: 'Let's be together' and 'Look – that's interesting.'

The gestures were 'iconic' – that is, the nature of the gestures suggested the intended meanings. Iconic gestures contrast with arbitrary symbols, in which there is no essential connection between the symbol and its meaning. As we have seen, that is the nature of most linguistic expressions. But, as Halliday comments (1979: 173):

> There is reason for thinking ... that in fact Nigel had actually got further than this, and that he used iconic gestures not because he could not conceive of an arbitrary symbol but because he did not know how to construct one that would be understood.

The development of a protolanguage is something that may or may not occur universally, Halliday says. And even among those children who do develop one, there will be many individual and social differences. But these children will all have a range of functions along a continuum from 'action' to 'reflection'. That is, they will all have a difference between 'language as doing' and 'language as thinking' (Halliday, 1979: 178), with a range of functions in between.

Halliday (1975: 5) explains that he means 'functions' in two senses. The first is the role that an item plays in sentence structure; for example, in the sentence *Cats eat mice*, the word *cats* has the role of 'actor', because it is the cats that perform the action. *Mice*, on the other hand, has the role of 'goal', for obvious reasons. And *eat* represents the 'process' (in this case, the action) that is involved. In generative grammar there is a rather similar notion, but no role is given to the verb, since the meaning of the verb is considered to be the source of the other roles (actor, goal, etc.).[9]

The second sense in which the word 'functions' is used is that of functions of language, such as those described below. This is the more important meaning of 'function', for present purposes. We can think of a function in this sense as a 'use' that the child makes of language, though that is strictly accurate only in the beginning. Later the concept will mature and change.

Halliday says that between 9 and 12 months, Nigel had four distinct semantic functions, which he calls (a) 'Instrumental', (b) 'Regulatory', (c) 'Interactional' and (d) 'Personal'. In each of these, he was developing a potential for meaning (Halliday, 1979: 177).

As these functions will play a prominent role in what is to come, it will be as well to make quite clear what each one refers to. Halliday (1975: 19f) gives informal 'house-names' for the child's functions, and these are quite useful for remembering what the more formal names mean. For example, his informal name for the Instrumental function is the 'I want' function. When he used language with this function, Nigel was trying to get something that he wanted: either 'goods or services'. In the beginning, these were mainly objects which he could see but couldn't get at. It was a matter of using a second person to be his agent in getting them.

The Regulatory function (whose informal name is the 'do as I tell you' function) is somewhat similar to the Instrumental function, but has the aim of getting control over one or more people, rather than objects. This function, however expressed, means something like 'You do this', and is addressed to a particular person (or to particular people). If someone other than the person addressed were to do the requested action, it probably wouldn't satisfy the child.

The third function, Interactional, is called informally the 'me and you' function. It is towards the 'language as thinking/reflection' end of the spectrum and not the 'language as doing' end. It was used when Nigel wanted to be together with someone – frequently his mother. He would often show her a picture to get her attention, prior to sharing attention with her. His action meant 'Let's look at this together', or something similar.

138

The fourth function, 'Personal', relates to the child's development and self-assertion, and its informal name is the 'Here I come' function:

> The orientation is outward, towards the environment; but the mode is that of reflection, not action, so it is the environment as it impinges on the child, as a focus of his own thoughts and feelings. The meanings are of the kind of 'I like' and 'I wonder'. (Halliday, 1979: 178)

At the age of 12 months, while he was still in the protolinguistic stage, Nigel had developed a semantic system involving these four functions. A semantic system, in Halliday's sense, takes the form of a set of choices, together with a condition of entry to the system. The system at this stage had the form shown in Figure 8.1, which is taken from Halliday (1979: 179). The four functions are shown on the left-hand side, under the heading 'Function', and they represent the four initial choices in the system. They act as entry conditions for the next paths – that is, the first choice you make determines what choices then confront you. These next choices are the ones that are shown in the column headed 'Content systems' (semantic systems).[10] Suppose we select the first function, 'Instrumental'. Then we're confronted with another set of choices, consisting of two members: 'demand, general' and 'demand, specific'. Suppose we now select 'demand, specific'. Then we are confronted with a further set of choices, of which the two shown here ('toy bird', 'powder') are just representative of a host of possibilities. We satisfied the entry condition for this set of choices when we selected 'demand, specific'. The sequence of paths in the system defines one meaning, and the expression that Nigel used for it is shown after it in the column headed 'Expression'. In the final column, 'Gloss', there is a kind of translation into adult language of what was meant.

Between 12 and 17 months Nigel extended and enriched his use of these functions, and also developed a new one: the Imaginative function, which involved using meanings for the purposes of playing. Halliday dubs it informally the 'Let's pretend' function.

Furthermore, the 'I wonder' personal mode developed into the Heuristic[11] function – that is, the function of organizing experience (the 'Tell me why' function). This involves asking questions (like 'What's that?') and making observations (like 'That's a . . .').[12]

Much later the child will progress to the notorious 'Why?' phase. The word 'notorious' is mine, not Halliday's, and I use it because many

139

Figure 8.1 Halliday: Nigel at 12 months
Courtesy of M. A. K. Halliday and Cambridge University Press

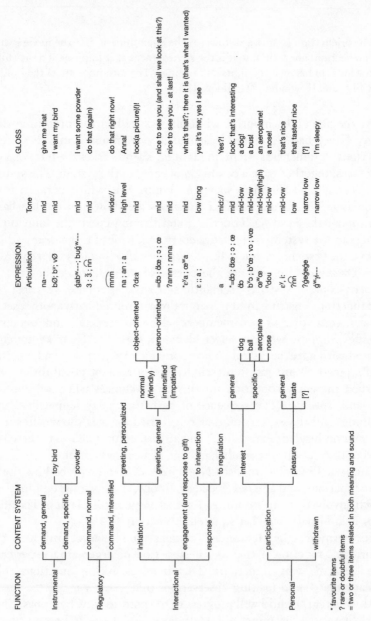

adults find this period a bit of a trial (if a relatively pleasant one). After they have given their best answer to the question, the child will simply come back again with 'Why?' and no matter how often the adult answers the question, a new prompt will appear immediately.

I suppose this is just the child's enjoyment of his/her new-found power in being able to ask that question and almost automatically get a response from the adult, so that for a while the question seems more important than the answer. However, asking 'Why is that?' is a very important use of language for the developing child, and, as Halliday says, 'The emergence of this "meaning for learning" function is perhaps the critical factor in the shift from protolanguage to language, the move into the mother tongue' (1979: 178).

Halliday (1975) lists a seventh function, the Informative function, informally called the 'I've got something to tell you' function. Although this plays a large part in adult language, it doesn't emerge until last in the child's language, and it arrives considerably after the others.

Near the end of Phase 1 (the protolanguage phase) there were about 50 meanings that Nigel could use. (It's very difficult to be exact about the number, because not all the meanings are used every day, or even every week. Some seem to drop out, and others emerge.)

In the description of the use of these functions, the emphasis is mainly on Nigel's active use of them to communicate messages to others, and the question arises whether he also 'used' the functions in the sense of understanding them. Halliday points out, in a private communication, that he thinks that children do 'use' the functions in this sense all the time, as when an adult says 'Be quiet!' (and the child responds by being quiet).[13] This has a regulatory function. But the fact that the main concentration is on the child's use of the functions in speech 'was simply my decision as observer/investigator to concentrate on what Nigel said rather than on what he heard and understood'.

8.4 The transition (Phase 2)

Nigel then entered Phase 2, the transition into the adult linguistic system. The transition is ushered in by a very marked increase in the number of meanings. In Nigel's case it went up quickly to about 150. This increase has been observed by linguists of all theoretical persuasions, and is often called 'the vocabulary explosion' (see p. 5–6).

For Halliday it isn't only a vocabulary explosion, but a meaning and grammar explosion as well, though of course the three things are intimately linked. The explosion in grammar and meaning may not be as obvious as the explosion in vocabulary, because the evidence for it is often in what children hear and understand, rather than what they say. On average the explosion in all three manifestations occurs at around 18 months.

Halliday observes that at the beginning of Phase 2, the child can use only one function at a time. (S)he can be an observer or an intruder, but not both at the same time. But by the end of Phase 2, the child has learnt to be both things at the same time. This is a distinguishing characteristic of adult language. In Nigel's case, Phase 2 continued until roughly the end of his second year (Halliday, 1975: 30).

At some time during Phase 2, the Personal and Heuristic functions join. You'll recall that the Personal function involves the use of language to 'express the child's uniqueness, in contradistinction to his environment' (Halliday, 1975: 20). It is the 'Here I come' function, and it sets the boundary between the child and the environment. The Heuristic function is the one that uses language to explore that environment – the 'Tell me why' function. The two merge into one, which Halliday calls the Mathetic (learning) function.

Thus the identification by the child of her/his 'self' becomes part of the same function that uses language to explore the rest of the universe. Both involve 'language as learning'. This function inevitably introduces new meanings, for which new vocabulary items are needed. Furthermore, new structural resources become necessary.

What are these structural items of which children feel the need at this stage? One example is *classes*: word-classes (such as noun and verb), as well as classes of phrases, clauses, etc. Furthermore, the classes are associated with structural functions like actor, process and goal. (Reminder: Halliday uses the word 'functions' in two senses: there are 'functions in structure' like the ones we are referring to here, and 'functions of language', like the ones referred to in the preceding paragraph.)

A second important change occurs at about the same time as the Personal and Heuristic language functions come together into the Mathetic function. The other language functions seem to coalesce, too, into what is called the Pragmatic function. It involves 'language as doing' – that is, language as it is used to interact with other people and to control objects and other people. These activities generate more meanings, and hence more lexical items and more structures (e.g. Request + Object of desire).

142

Thus it comes about that the transition from protolanguage to the mother tongue leads to the emergence of grammar.[13] Why should that be so important? Well, you may recall that I said earlier that proto-language contained only two levels: content and expression (meaning and sound or gestures), with no grammatical level in between. But adult language isn't like that. In between the semantic and the phonological components of adult language there's a 'bridge', which is the grammatical level.

Most important of all, the emergence of grammatical structure makes it possible to use the Pragmatic (doing) and the Mathetic (learning) functions together in the same utterance. Previously the groups of functions which became these two could be used separately by the child, but not at the same time.

Parallel with the development of vocabulary (at about 18 months) goes the development of dialogue. Halliday comments that dialogue could serve as well as vocabulary to mark the beginning of Nigel's Phase 2 (1975: 48).

In dialogue, people adopt various roles and assign roles to others: speaker, addressee, respondent, questioner, persuader, etc. Although these roles are specialized in that they apply only to linguistic acts, they also have a more general developmental significance in that 'they serve both as a channel and as a model for social interaction' (Halliday, 1975: 48). In any act of speaking, the role of speaker is assumed by the person engaged in the act; but in dialogue, more than that happens. The speaker's role means more than just 'I'm talking to you'. It may mean, for example,

'I am demanding information, and you are to respond by supplying it'. Dialogue involves purely linguistic forms of personal interaction; at the same time, it exemplifies the general principle whereby people adopt roles, assign them, and accept or reject those that are assigned to them. (Halliday, 1975: 49)

Nigel is said to have worked out the principles of dialogue in two weeks near the age of 18 months. At the end of this time he was able to respond to a Wh question 'provided the answer was already known to the questioner'; e.g. 'What are you eating?' – 'Banana'. He could also respond to a command by doing what was asked; respond to a statement with signals of attention and continuation of the conversation; respond to a response to something he had said; initiate a conversation and

143

respond to what the other person said. At that stage his only method of initiating a conversation was to ask 'What's that?'

The capacity to engage in dialogue gives the child a new power to use language with the Mathetic (learning) function. (S)he can now ask directly for information and for words. But equally important is the capacity of dialogue to lead to the beginning of Phase 3, the completion of the adult system:

> Through its embodiment of linguistic role-playing, dialogue opens the way to the options of mood (declarative, interrogative, etc.), and thus to the entire interpersonal component in the language system. This is the component whereby the speaker intrudes or, as it were, builds himself into the linguistic structure, expressing his relations with other participants, his attitudes and judgments, his commitments, desires and the like. (Halliday, 1975: 50)

The emergence of grammar and of dialogue, then, are the two main developments during Phase 2 that lead to progress into Phase 3 and hence to the adult linguistic system. But although the principles of grammar and dialogue have been absorbed by the beginning of Phase 3, the process of mastering them has only just begun.

Although the protolanguage is not the mother tongue – not the adult language – the fact that it exhibits semantic functions provides the source for the later development of the so-called metafunctions of adult language. The 'active' (Interpersonal) component of the adult semantic system and the 'reflective' (Ideational) component (see below) have been present, in a sense, right through, almost from birth. The semantic system at every stage is represented not by a set of rules, but by a system of choices, which are associated with conditions of entry.[14]

8.5 The adult language (Phase 3)

In Phase 1, the half-dozen or so functions can be equated with uses of language. In the adult language of Phase 3, there are only two main functions, the Ideational and the Interpersonal. How do the functions in Phase 3, then, relate to those in Phase 1? And in particular, why does Halliday use the terms Mathetic and Pragmatic when he's describing how the original half-dozen or so functions reduce to two during Phase 2, but a different set of terms, Ideational and Interpersonal, when he refers to adult language?

The answer is that Mathetic and Pragmatic refer to separate functions, which represent a choice. Every utterance represents either one or the other of these functions, but never both at the same time. The distinguishing mark of adult linguistic performance, however, is that both functions (Ideational and Interpersonal) can be used in the same utterance. Halliday adds, in a personal communication:

> It's important to note that 'ideational' and 'interpersonal' aren't in fact a new set of terms for 'mathetic' and 'pragmatic' – the semantic resources get totally realigned. What happens is that: (1) the *content* component of *both* mathetic *and* pragmatic evolves into the ideational; while (2) the *contrast between* the mathetic and the pragmatic evolves (vastly elaborated, of course) into the interpersonal. (In grammatical terms, the content of both becomes transitivity, while the contrast between them becomes mood.)

There is a third function in adult language, called the Textual function. Text is language that is being used, as opposed to language that is just being cited; so a list of words or sentences is not text.[15] The Textual function allows a speaker or writer to operate in discourse in a way that is relevant to the situation. Notice the phrase 'a speaker or writer'. We are used to thinking of text as written language, but Halliday means the word to cover spoken language too.

We've seen that the adult semantic system contains three functions: the Ideational, the Interpersonal and the Textual. They are all activated (simultaneously) by aspects of the context in which language is being used. For example, the Ideational function is activated by what kind of social process is going on in the conversation.[16] The Interpersonal function is activated by the social relations existing among the people involved in a conversation.[17] The Textual function is activated by 'what part the conversation is playing in the total unfolding scene' (Halliday, 1978: 75).[18]

Not only are the three functions motivated by different aspects of the social context; they are also manifested in different ways in the language used in the conversation. The Ideational function is realized in the structures consisting of verbs and their associated noun phrases,[19] in the names of things referred to in those noun phrases, and so on. The Interpersonal function is manifested in such matters as the grammatical 'mood' of the sentence (indicative (declarative/interrogative) or imperative, etc.), in modal verbs and adverbs, and in comments and expressions of attitude that occur in the conversation.

145

In these ways, Halliday sees a direct connection between what is being said, the context in which it is being said, and the nature of the language being used. Thus, 'much of the speech a child hears around him is, typically, relatable to its context of situation in recognisable and systematic ways' (1978: 74). The implication is that this helps the child's language development. Because of what the child can see, hear and feel during a conversation, (s)he is often made aware of the attitudes of the other participants, and how they feel towards each other.

In several places (e.g. Halliday, 1978: 93; 1979: 180–1) Halliday comments with admiration on the 'tracking' abilities of the mother or whoever else is closest to the child. By this he means the way the mother (or other) is able to respond to the sounds and gestures the child makes, even before the child can really speak the language:

> At any given moment, she knows what he knows; not only does she understand him, but she knows the limits of his understanding, and talks to him so that he gets the message – not of course the literal message that the adult gets from it, but a message that he can interpret in the light of his own functional resources for meaning. (1979: 181)

Halliday thinks that, under favourable conditions, tracking of this kind can assist in developing the child's language and also his/her ability to use that language to learn other things.

While we are considering mothers and other language-nurturers, it's as good a time as any to mention a matter that brings Halliday into direct confrontation with one of Chomsky's claims. We have already seen, in the chapter on motherese (Chapter 7), that Chomsky alleged (1968: 23; 1972: 27) that the native speaker acquires the language 'on the basis of very restricted and degenerate evidence'. He also said (1965: 4):

> A record of natural speech will show numerous false starts, deviations from rules, changes of plan in mid-course, and so on. The problem for the linguist, as well as for the child learning the language, is to determine from the data of performance the underlying system of rules that has been mastered by the speaker–hearer and that he puts to use in actual performance.

Halliday (1975: 45) has a different view:

146

Despite a commonly held belief to the contrary, the speech which the child hears around him is, in the typical instance, coherent, well-formed and contextually relevant. In interaction with adults he is not, in general, surrounded by intellectual discourse, with its backtracking, anacolutha,[20] high lexical density and hesitant planning; but by the fluent, smoothly grammatical and richly structured utterances of informal everyday conversation. He has abundant evidence with which to construct the grammatical system of his language. What he hears from other children, naturally, is different – but it is different in ways which serve him as a guide for his own efforts. (This is not, of course, an argument against the nativist hypothesis.[21] But it is an argument against the *necessity* of an interpretation in nativist terms.)

8.6 Conclusion

8.6.1 THE SCOPE OF HALLIDAY'S WORK

In this chapter, as in the preceding ones, I have concentrated on the development of the spoken language in young children, but it should be said that Halliday does not stop there. He is interested in pursuing children's language development into the school, and he and his followers have produced an extensive literature about language in education.

In Chapter 5 I reported that Chomsky said that virtually all children have the capacity to acquire language, and that that capacity is not correlated with intelligence. I remarked then that that didn't mean that intelligence had nothing to do with performance in language. As long as we're talking about the 'mere' ability to acquire language for the purposes of everyday communication, then Chomsky would claim that there is no correlation with intelligence, but he would readily admit that when it comes to people's ability to use language with finesse and artistic creativity, there is a correlation with intelligence and with individual skill.

Halliday has been concerned with the educational aim of developing skill in language to each child's maximum potential. This, of course, involves written as well as spoken language. People working within Halliday's model have written extensively on language and education. (For one example, see Christie, 1985.)

Halliday has also been interested in writing more generally about the linguistic analysis of language, and the model he has produced is known

147

as systemic-functional grammar (see Halliday, 1961, 1967–68, 1994, and many other works, some of which are listed in the bibliography of the 1994 volume.)[22]

Another area of interest, for both Halliday and his followers, is the study of units of language larger than the sentence (see, for example, Halliday and Hasan, 1976; Martin, 1992). Halliday's interests also include language in poetry, automated computer analysis of language – in fact almost any area that concerns language. If you would like to get a quick sampling of his earlier writings, try Kress (1976).

Halliday's work has been very usefully complemented by that of Clare Painter, who did her postgraduate work with him at the University of Sydney (Painter, 1984). While following closely the paradigm established by Halliday, she contributes some original perceptions of a persuasive kind in her accounts of how her son Hal 'learnt how to mean'.

8.6.2 SEPARATE PLANETS

Halliday's account of language development contains many important insights which cannot even be studied within a generative model. (Conversely, the important insights gained by generative linguistics cannot be accommodated within Halliday's model.) Halliday says they are complementary, not contradictory, and that seems a fair statement. Maybe the details of that complementarity will one day be spelt out, but at present it seems like a forlorn hope. To pass from one model to the other is to enter a different world, and it is difficult to see, at present, how the two sets of insights can be brought together.

Notes

1. Halliday has recently written (in a private communication): 'Now I wouldn't see it as a *product* of consciousness but rather as an essential *aspect* of it. (I wrote somewhere, in relation to Gerald Edelman's work on the evolution of the brain, that "higher-order consciousness [his term] is meaning".)'
2. For details of some experiments that seem to support this notion, though the authors are not followers of Halliday, see Mehler and Dupoux (1994).

3. These are average figures; as in everything else, there is individual variation.
4. An invaluable reference book for technical terms in Halliday's writing is de Joia and Stenton (1980).
5. Although, as Halliday has pointed out to me, this would be a fairly standard view in (what used to be called) symbolic anthropology.
6. I avoid the word 'acquired' here and throughout this chapter because in various places (e.g. 1978: 89) Halliday objects to it, saying that it implies that language is a commodity that the child has to get from 'out there'.
7. I apologize to the baby for desexing him/her, here and elsewhere, but I can't bring myself to write, 'If the baby cries because he/she has a safety pin sticking into him/her, that is a communicative act, sending a message that he/she is in pain.'
8. Of course, they could be built into a code as items that did have meaning.
9. See (Gruber, 1976). It would appear that Gruber arrived at these notions independently of Halliday, but Halliday's notion of functions goes back to the late 1950s. (See his comment to this effect in the foreword to de Joia and Stenton, 1980: x.)
10. Michael Halliday has explained to me that he uses the term *content systems* here, rather than *semantic systems*, because the latter 'is usually used in the context of adult language, where it is distinct from lexicogrammar (syntax). But ... there is no lexicogrammar in protolanguage; only a single, undifferentiated system of "content" (in Hjelmslev's sense, contrasting simply with "expression"); so the term "content systems" seems to capture that better.'
11. *Chambers Twentieth Century Dictionary* defines the adjective *heuristic* as follows: 'serving or leading to find out; encouraging desire to find out ...'.
12. This development is rather more complex. For a very interesting and more extensive account, see Halliday (1984).
13. 'Grammar means lexicogrammar; that is, it includes vocabulary' (Halliday, 1974: 86).
14. In answer to my question as to what he regards as the difference between a rule and a system of choices, Halliday gave the following quite extensive answer, which I think is worth presenting in full. (I do so with his permission.) 'I think that a system of choices is conceptually very different from a set of rules: it treats language as a resource (for making meaning) rather than an inventory (of structural devices). But to make this more explicit: a system of choices is a paradigmatic concept, in which describing something *consists in* relating it to everything else; whereas a set of rules is a syntagmatic concept, in which relating something to something else is added as an afterthought. (That's the basic difference, I think,

between "choice" and "rule".) Then, a system of choices is openended, whereas a set of rules is finite (that's the basic difference between "system" and "set" – there's nothing corresponding to the concept "the set of all possible sentences"). Thirdly, a system of choices is "semogenic" (meaning-creating), whereas a set of rules is meaning-expressing, and so the meaning must somehow exist outside it. Fourthly, perhaps, a system of choices has a history: it is constantly changing in interaction with its environment; whereas a set of rules is taken outside history – not that rules can't change, of course, but it requires extra energy to change them, since a rule is essentially a static concept.'

15. (Compare the traditional distinction between 'use' and 'mention'.)
16. Halliday uses the term 'field' to refer to this social process.
17. Halliday uses the term 'tenor' to refer to these relations.
18. Halliday refers to this as the 'mode'.
19. That is, what Halliday calls transitivity structures.
20. *Chambers Twentieth Century Dictionary* has this to say: *anacoluthia*: want of syntactical sequence, when the latter part of the sentence does not grammatically fit the earlier. *Anacoluthon*: an instance of anacoluthia; pl. *anacolutha*.
21. 'The nativist hypothesis' means the hypothesis that there are innate principles of some kind. It is sometimes referred to as 'the innateness hypothesis', though Chomsky in various places has objected to that phrase being attributed to him, on the grounds that virtually all linguists and psychologists, including behaviourists, accept that some things are innate, and the only question is where (and how) to draw the line. We have already seen that Halliday accepts that children have an innate disposition to pay more attention to human beings than to objects. He also believes there are innate *semiotic* principles: 'that the human infant is genetically predisposed to mean ... The issue, I think, is to what extent these are *linguistic* principles. If it means that the human brain is capable of construing a system having the properties of adult language, then of course it is – but it has to *develop* to this point ... It is not that way at birth ... So I do not believe there is any blueprint for a grammar etched into the neonate brain.' (Private communication.)
22. In his foreword to de Joia and Stenton (1980: viii), Halliday says 'I am not really a theoretician; I have been interested in theoretical matters only because I had to be, because it was necessary to construct some new theoretical framework in order to accommodate certain aspects of the interpretation I wanted to suggest.' Seems like a good qualification for being a theorist.

9. The two hemispheres of the brain – A

9.1 The physical brain

In Chapter 6 we saw that Chomsky's claims about how language operates were said to be true *in principle*, even though he could provide no physical description of where the operations were located in the brain. But obviously the physical brain *is* involved in the operations of language, and it's time we looked at what's known about the way it's involved.

The human brain has two 'hemispheres', as can be seen in Figure 9.1. In appearance, it seems perfectly symmetrical; we can't detect any obvious difference of shape between the two sides. But there's good reason to think that the two hemispheres have rather different functions. The left side seems to have more to do with language and mathematical calculation than the right side.

A warning is necessary, however. It's sometimes said that 'language is on the left side of the brain', but that's a great oversimplification. The matter is much more complex than that, as we shall see. That's why I made such a cautious statement: *The left side seems to have more to do with language and mathematical calculation than the right side.*

On the other hand, the right side of the brain seems to have more to do with spatial relationships, and with an appreciation of jokes, irony and other non-literal meanings. Again, it would be an oversimplification to say that spatial relationships and the machinery for understanding non-literal meanings are on the right side of the brain. There have been a number of books with titles like *Draw on the Right Side of Your Brain*, *Use Both Sides of Your Brain*, etc., but however good the books may be in themselves, such titles give a false notion of the way the brain functions.

151

We'll return to this matter later; for the moment I'm simply trying to give a broad impression of the two sides of the brain.

Figure 9.1 The two hemispheres of the human brain, viewed from above
Copyright Laura Maaske

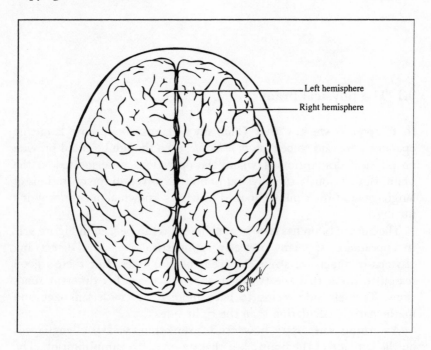

You probably know someone who's had a stroke. Were the speech and language of that person affected adversely? Perhaps you know a number of people who have had strokes. Did the strokes affect the speech and language of all of them? What's interesting is that certain stroke victims lose some or all of their ability to speak or use language, whereas others don't. Why should that be?

A stroke usually[1] involves a stoppage of the blood supply to some part of the brain, and that causes damage to the region in question. The blood's supplied separately to the two hemispheres, so if the supply's blocked to only one hemisphere, as is nearly always the case, that's where the damage will be.

152

If the damage is in the left hemisphere, there's highly likely to be some effect on speech and language, though how bad it is will depend on where and how extensive the injury is. Loss or partial loss of speech and language is called aphasia, and treating it takes up a good deal of the work of speech pathologists (or therapists – the choice of terms is different in different countries).

If the damage is to the right hemisphere, there may still be some interference with language abilities, but it's likely to be less immediately noticeable, and to be rather different in kind. People who have suffered damage to the right hemisphere often appear not to have much wrong with their speech. But after a while it may emerge that they do have certain difficulties. Their problems arise when they have to deal with complex uses of language; for example, presenting or following a logical argument, a story or a joke, or understanding the use of irony, and so on.

An appreciation of the role of the right brain in language has been steadily growing for thirty years or so. Right-hemisphere participation has been demonstrated for a large range of language processes (Beeman and Chiarello, 1997; Chiarello *et al.*, 1990). Whichever side the stroke is on, some improvement towards recovery can often be made with the help of a speech and language pathologist, but if the damage is severe, progress in that direction will be very slow or non-existent.

In the past few decades there has been a lot of research that suggests that the right hemisphere makes an important contribution to processing the semantic ingredient of individual words and semantic relationships between words. But the left hemisphere makes an even stronger contribution to these matters. Some have suggested that the right is more able to cope with words that are short, concrete, frequent, and able to be thought of in images.

Some patients who have right-hemisphere damage show what is called 'left neglect'. They tend to ignore the left side of objects and of scenes in the outside world. Also, very importantly for their language performance, they ignore the left-hand side of written or printed sentences, of pages of books, and of drawings. They tend to bump into things that are on their left, to bisect a line too far to the right (because they have ignored the leftmost part of the line), and so on. This is not the result of any inability to see, because such patients tend to neglect the left side of even their own mental images.

This was demonstrated by Bisiach and his colleagues with some Italian patients who exhibited left-neglect (Bisiach *et al.*, 1981; Bisiach

153

and Luzzatti, 1978; Hellige, 1993). The subjects, who knew Milan well, were asked to imagine they were in the square that's in front of the cathedral and were standing on the opposite side of the square, looking towards the cathedral. They were then asked to describe what they could see in the square, in their imagination. They described all the buildings very well, except that they completely omitted any reference to the left side of the square.

Next, they were asked to imagine that they were standing on the steps of the cathedral with their backs to it (i.e. now facing the other way). They then had to describe what they could see from that viewpoint, in their imagination. They gave very good descriptions of all the buildings that would be on their right, but ignored all the ones that would be on their left. Of course, the interesting point is that what was now on their left had been on their right in the previous task, and what was now on their right had been on their left. So it wasn't that they didn't know what was on both sides, or couldn't imagine it vividly; it was just that they neglected whatever side was on their left at the moment.

If asked to draw a clock face, a person with left hemi-neglect will often show all the figures from 1 to 12 crowded onto the right-hand side of the clock, with nothing on the left-hand side at all.

Occasionally, patients who have damage to the left hemisphere show right-neglect, but it is much rarer and less severe.

Let's return now to the main theme of strokes. They mostly attack elderly people, but sometimes the victims are young people – even children. The younger the person is, the more likely they are to make a significant recovery.

Another effect of stroke is that the victim will often be partly paralysed on one side of the body or the other. The functioning of one side of the body is largely controlled by the opposite hemisphere; that is, the left side of the body is controlled by the right side of the brain, and the right by the left. So if the damage from the stroke is on the right side of the brain, the left side of the body is likely to be affected, while if it is on the left side of the brain, the right side of the body is likely to be affected.

The effect of strokes is one piece of evidence that the left and right hemispheres are different in their functioning, and that the left hemisphere has more to do with language than the right.

It isn't always a stroke, of course, that causes brain damage and language impairment. Very similar consequences may be the result of a car accident, war wounds, or some other disaster.

154

Figure 9.2 The left side of the human brain, showng Broca's and Wernicke's areas
Copyright Laura Maaske

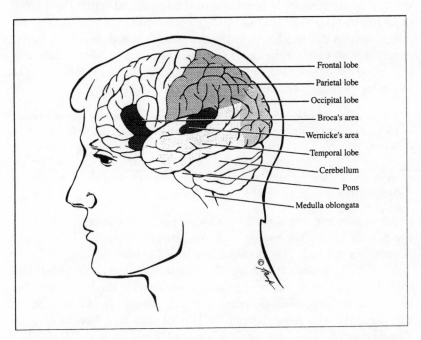

So far I've talked vaguely about 'the left side of the brain' in relation to speech, but it's possible to be more precise than that. There are two areas in the left hemisphere that are crucially related to speech and language, and if they're damaged by a stroke, there will almost certainly be speech and language problems as a result. They're known as 'Broca's area' and 'Wernicke's area', and Figure 9.2 shows where they are.

Damage in Broca's area tends to be associated with difficulties in speaking. The patients' utterances, if they make any, are likely to be understandable but brief. They often leave out grammatical morphemes such as the -*ed* endings on verbs to indicate past tense, or the -*s* endings on nouns to indicate plurality. They're also inclined to leave out 'little words' or 'function words': determiners like *the* and *a*, prepositions like *in* and *for*, auxiliary verbs like *could* and *have*, and so on. But the aphasic person with a lesion in Broca's area can usually understand a good deal of what other people say.

155

On the other hand, people with damage in Wernicke'e area tend to have difficulty understanding what others say. Their own utterances are frequently fluent but virtually meaningless to the listener. They insert words that are seemingly unrelated to the topic, and speak a good deal of jargon (use a good many unintelligible words).

If aphasia is due to a lesion in Broca's area it's called 'Broca's aphasia', or sometimes 'motor aphasia'. If it's due to a lesion in Wernicke's area, it's called 'Wernicke's aphasia', or sometimes 'sensory aphasia'. The following pertinent comment is by Gregory (1987: 809):

> the form of aphasia described by Wernicke was marked by a severe defect in the understanding of speech, and correspondingly became known as *sensory aphasia*. This term, however, is by no means totally appropriate as expressive disorders undoubtedly occur in Wernicke's aphasia, but they are disorders in word usage and word choice rather than disorders in the articulation or expression of speech.

Sometimes the damage covers a larger part of the language area and the patient shows the two sets of symptoms relevant to Broca's and Wernicke's aphasia. This is called 'global aphasia'.

Until fairly recent times it was thought that aphasia could be labelled entirely according to where the damage occurred in the brain, but that is no longer regarded as true. For one thing, it often happens that patients who have damage in Broca's area will have somewhat different symptoms from each other (and likewise with Wernicke's area). For another thing, modern technology has shown that the picture of language activity in the brain is much more complicated than my account suggests. You'll see some of the details in the next chapter.

Very occasionally, the left side of the brain can be badly damaged without any apparent effect on speech and language. Antonio Damasio (1994) recounts the fascinating story of a man named Phineas Gage. In 1848, at the age of 25, Gage had an extraordinary accident. He was a railway worker, head of a large gang of workmen laying track across Vermont. Their job involved blasting rocks out so as to make way for the track. One day an explosion occurred prematurely. An iron bar which Gage was using became a projectile which entered his left cheek, travelled through the base of his skull, through his brain and out through the top of his head. The bar, 'covered with blood and brains' (Damasio, 1994: 4), continued on and landed 100 feet (30 m) away. The bar was 3 feet 7 inches (1 m) long and $1\frac{1}{4}$ inches (3 cm) in diameter. It weighed $13\frac{1}{4}$ pounds (6 kg).

Gage miraculously escaped death, but, even more miraculously, this man who had had an iron bar driven with great force through his left hemisphere was able to speak a few minutes later, and continue to speak as though he had no problem with it. Seeing that this was so, the doctor who was brought to the scene addressed his questions to the patient, who gave a clear account of what had happened.

Phineas Gage seemed to have come through his dreadful accident with minimal damage, and he made a complete physical recovery, apart from losing vision in his left eye. His limbs were not paralysed, and his speech was not affected. His senses were still functioning.

Unfortunately, though, it soon emerged that he'd undergone a personality change. Previously he'd been a pleasant and popular man, regarded by his employers as outstandingly efficient. Now he treated people irreverently, was impatient of being blocked in what he wanted to do, and was given to profanity (which had not been so previously). He became so changed that his friends weren't able to recognize him as the same person, and his former employers wouldn't re-employ him. After that, Gage drifted from one job to another and eventually started to have epileptic seizures. In 1861, at the age of only 38, he died from a very severe seizure.

We can be interested in the story of Phineas Gage for two reasons. First, because it's hard to beat as a story of a human being coming to a tragic decline through no fault of his own, and second, because the fact that a person can have a large bar driven through the left hemisphere of his brain and emerge with his speech and language intact is of great scientific interest and helps to throw more light on what this chapter is about: the relationship between language and the brain.

9.2 The origins of knowledge about aphasia

Although aphasia has been reported ever since the time of the ancient Greeks, it was only in the nineteenth century that knowledge as to its true nature started to be discovered. Three people were most responsible for this: Marc Dax, Paul Broca and Karl Wernicke, though many others played important supporting roles.

9.2.1 MARC DAX

Knowledge about the different functions of the two hemispheres of the brain began to appear in the middle of the nineteenth century, but grew rather slowly from then on.

In 1800 a French doctor named Marc Dax set up a quiet practice in the country, near the village of Sommières, which lay between Nîmes and Montpellier, not far from the Mediterranean. Because some of his patients were soldiers and had war wounds, Dax began to practise as a military surgeon. (But not exclusively: he also had civilian patients.)

Some of his patients had brain damage, and some of those suffered word memory loss. One, whose name was Broussonnet, was quite a famous naturalist. His sudden loss of word memory was followed by an attack of apoplexy – that is, a sudden loss of sensation and motion. Such an attack is generally the result of haemorrhage or thrombosis (a clot). Dax assumed that the brain damage was causally connected to the loss of word memory. He had no way of finding out which side of the brain had been damaged, but at the man's funeral he learnt that an autopsy had revealed that there was a large ulcer in the left side of the brain.

Up until 1811 Dax had had three patients who had suffered sudden loss of word memory, and he remembered that all three had had a lesion (an area of damaged tissue) in the left hemisphere. Over the next few years he had more such patients, and he carefully observed which side of the brain was affected. In 1836 he went to a medical conference in Montpellier and read a short paper called 'Lesions of the left half of the brain, [which] coincided with the forgetting of the signs of thought'.[2] He had never presented a paper at a conference before, and he never presented one afterwards.

The ancient Greeks had observed that loss of speech sometimes followed brain damage. But Dax's observation that there was a correlation between the loss of speech and the fact that it was the left side of the brain that was damaged was one of the most important discoveries of modern times. After presenting his evidence in his paper, he remarked:[3]

> From all that precedes, I believe I am able to conclude, not that all diseases of the left hemisphere necessarily interfere with verbal memory, but that, when this type of memory is altered by a brain disease, we must look for the cause of the disorder in the left hemisphere, and still look for it there even if the two hemispheres are both diseased.

A little later in the paper, Dax comments,[4] 'There now remained a very interesting problem to resolve: why does it happen that damage to the left cerebral hemisphere is followed by loss of memory for words, but not damage to the right hemisphere?' A very interesting problem indeed. He said he hoped that while they were waiting for a satisfying solution to that problem, his work would be of some use in the diagnosis and therapy directed at diseases of that kind.

This paper, which was so significant in the light of later history, fell like a stone into the conference pond. It aroused almost no interest, and was soon forgotten. Poor Marc Dax! He died the next year without knowing that he had presented a paper that should have been a sensation, and which would still be recognized over a century and a half later.[5]

9.2.2 Paul Broca

Some years later, in 1861, a Parisian neurologist and surgeon named Paul Broca came into contact with an old man who was in hospital because he had a serious leg infection. But Broca became interested in something else about this patient: he had been paralysed on one side of his body for many years, and he had also lost his ability to speak, except for a few words. One of those 'words' was *tan*, and it came to be applied to him like a name. (His actual name was M. Leborgne.)

A few days after Broca met him, 'tan' died, and Broca then did a post-mortem examination. He found there was a lesion in part of the left frontal lobe. At the next meeting of the Anthropological Society in Paris, Broca reported his observations and exhibited the brain to the audience. It aroused little interest.

A few months later, Broca was able to report to the Anthropological Society about a second patient who was a similar case, and had a similar lesion. This time, for some reason, Broca's report drew a very enthusiastic response.

A vigorous debate broke out following that meeting. Broca was reluctant to become a protagonist in the debate, but in spite of that he became recognized as the main proponent of the theory that functions in the brain were associated with particular regions within it.

Ornstein (1997: 50) and Springer and Deutsch (1989: 11) both say that Broca was at first unaware of the link between the left hemisphere and the speech loss in his two patients; and that's possible. But it's also possible, and perhaps more likely, that he was reluctant to speak about it until he had more evidence. That would be consonant with the scrupulous scientific caution he showed throughout his research about drawing conclusions before he had enough evidence.

In any case, he said nothing about it for two years. By then he had eight cases, all with lesions on the left side, but he simply drew attention to it, saying, 'I do not attempt to draw a conclusion and I await new findings' (quoted in Joynt, 1964). To us, with the benefit of hindsight, that may seem overly cautious, but Broca obviously had a great deal of scientific integrity and wasn't rushing to conclusions. He seems not to have heard of Marc Dax or his paper (but hardly anyone had).

Finally, in June 1865, at another meeting of the Anthropological Society of Paris, Broca made his claim: 'Just as we guide the movements of writing, drawing, embroidery, etc. with the left hemisphere, so we speak with the left hemisphere.'[6]

Figure 9.2 shows the area that has come to be called 'Broca's area'. Technically, Broca's area is described as being in the posterior part of the third frontal convolution on the left side of the brain, which is just in front of the motor cortex. The cortex is a thin layer of 'grey matter' which covers the surface of both hemispheres, and the motor cortex is that part of it which is responsible for voluntary muscular activity, including that involved in speech.

Broca also claimed that the hemisphere controlling speech is on the same side as the preferred hand. This later turned out to be over-simplified, but he was thinking in the right direction. We will take up the question of the correct version of handedness later in the chapter, in Section 9.2.4.

Broca noted that damage to the left hemisphere interfered not just with speech, but with language more generally. Thus, damage to the left hemisphere sometimes caused difficulties in reading and writing. These observations were soon confirmed by a number of researchers.

The next episode should be called Son of Dax. Gustav, son of Marc Dax, who was also a doctor, wrote a letter to the medical press claiming that Broca had deliberately ignored his father's earlier paper. Broca's answer was that he had never heard of Dax or his paper and that he could find no record of the paper having been delivered in 1836. Gustav Dax then not only located the paper, but published the text of it.

A row broke out about this claim, and some even suggested that the younger Dax had written the paper himself. Broca then personally went

160

to Montpellier and examined all the records of medical meetings, but he couldn't find any evidence of such a paper, nor even any evidence of a programme for a meeting with such a title on it (Joynt, 1964: 211). There has been controversy ever since about who was right in this argument, and who deserved the credit for first linking damage to the left hemisphere and loss of language. In 1877, after Broca had presented a paper, he was asked to comment on the debate. According to Joynt (*ibid.*), Broca stated that he had personally examined the papers of Marc and Gustav Dax in regard to their style and their mode of expression and convinced himself that they were different. He admitted that Marc Dax had undoubtedly prepared the paper in 1836, but said he (Dax) had not read or published the report – perhaps, as Broca states, because there was no good pathological verification of these data.

In any case, it is certainly true that the evidence that Broca put forward was more impressive than what Dax had written in his paper. He gave a more accurate description of the area of the lesions, and gave full case-histories of his patients.

9.2.3 KARL WERNICKE

The next important progress was made in 1874 by a 26-year-old German neurologist named Karl Wernicke. He presented a paper (Wernicke, 1874) in which he described nine patients with different kinds of aphasia. He used the first two of them to argue that there is a second speech area in the brain, in addition to Broca's area.

The area that Wernicke was referring to is in the posterior third of the first convolution (or gyrus) in the temporal lobe (see Figure 9.2). It extends into a deep fissure called the Sylvian fissure. Wernicke's area, as it is known, lies behind the area of the cortex that is specialized for hearing. Remember that Broca's area lies near the area of the cortex that is specialized for speech movements. So Broca's and Wernicke's areas lie adjacent to the parts of the cortex that control speaking and hearing respectively.

Both of the patients who were used by Wernicke to argue for a second language area were fluent in their speech and used normal intonation patterns, but what they said didn't make sense (Caplan, 1987: 50). Wernicke (1874: 66–7) described the first of these two patients as follows:

> Susanne Adam, ... 59 years old, fell ill suddenly, with no known cause, on 1 March 1874. ... Although she spoke in a confused manner she still expressed many things correctly, but answered questions in a completely confused way ... she mixed the meaningless word 'begräben' into everything she said ... her condition was considered to be simply a confusional state and, since no physical illness could be found, she was transferred to the psychiatric ward ... the patient can under certain conditions say everything correctly, but she understands absolutely nothing.

Wernicke described her as making good progress subsequently. On 20 April 1874 he judged her to be continuing to make progress; however, if she was asked to write about something of her own choice, she couldn't achieve more than a few words; likewise she couldn't write down words from dictation. Perhaps surprisingly, though, she was able to copy words accurately if they were written down for her. Wernicke comments, 'Agraphia is thus her most striking language disturbance at this time' (p. 70).

He described the second patient like this (pp. 70–1):

> Susanne Rother, 75 years old ... was admitted to the Allerheiligen Hospital on 7 October 1873. She showed all the signs of extreme senescence. ... Her mental condition was regarded at the time as a confusional state associated with aphasia. She answered all questions directed at her in a completely confused way, and carried out commands either not at all or in a completely confused manner, which at the time gave the impression of apraxia[7] ... she ... showed little urge to communicate. Her (spontaneously used) vocabulary thus seemed small in contrast to that of the case described above but was nevertheless large enough that motor aphasia[8] ... could not be considered. The presence of aphasia could be recognized by her substitutions and distortions of words.

This patient died in December of that year, and a post-mortem was carried out on her. It showed that she had had a stroke which had caused softening in the first convolution in the temporal lobe, on the left side of the brain. And in the case of the other patient (Adam), Wernicke says, 'we are also justified in assuming a focal lesion in the left first temporal convolution' (p. 73). By careful description and cautious argumentation, Wernicke managed to show that these two cases were certainly not cases of Broca's aphasia, and to make a convincing case for the existence of a second language area.

But he proceeded to do more than that. He gave a detailed description of the types of aphasia that were associated with this area, accounting for each one by the location of the lesion. He went on from there to outline a general theory of language and language disorders. His work has had a continuing influence on subsequent theory (Geschwind, 1969).

Wernicke's life seemed to be blighted in various ways, in spite of his success with aphasia. He had been trained as a psychiatrist, and wanted to make his mark primarily in psychiatry. He wrote a book on the subject, but it didn't have the effect he had hoped for. Then, because of a fierce row that he had (quite early in his career) with the administrators of the hospital where he worked, his career was blocked in various ways.

On 13 June 1905 Wernicke went for a bike ride with a colleague. As they rode past a timber-wagon loaded with logs, Wernicke fell and the wagon ran over his breast-bone. He lived just four more days, until 17 June. He was 57 (Geschwind, 1969: 10).

9.2.4 HANDEDNESS

You'll remember that Broca said that language was on the side of the preferred hand, and I remarked that this conclusion was oversimplified, though it was in the right direction. What is the truth, then, about the relationship between speech/language and handedness?

Estimates of how many human beings are right-handed frequently say about 90 per cent, but it isn't as certain as that. Holder (1997) says the figure is between 70 and 95 per cent. Why such a wide disparity? Because scientists haven't agreed on what the criteria should be. How do you assess someone who writes with the right hand but plays tennis with the left hand? It may mean that the person is basically left-handed but has been forced or encouraged to write right-handed at school; however, that doesn't have to be the explanation.

In any case, it's clear that the vast majority of people are right-handed, and that appears to be true in all cultures. Furthermore, cave-drawings, tools and weapons from prehistoric times have been used as evidence that the majority of people were right-handed even in those days.

Nicholas Toth (1987) studied artefacts in northern Kenya going back various lengths of time, from roughly $1\frac{1}{2}$ million to roughly 2 million years. Among them were a great many stone tools and pieces that had been rejected during their manufacture.

Toth went to the trouble of making such stone tools himself out of similar stone from the area (mainly 'a medium-grained lava') so that he could find out which of several known techniques of ancient toolmaking had been used there. He found that the only technique used there had been the one known as 'hard-hammer percussion', in which a core was struck glancing blows with a stone hammer, so as to remove a number of flakes.

There were two ways of doing this: the toolmaker could either strike alternately on both sides of the core so as to produce flakes with two faces, or strike only on one side so as to produce flakes with only one face. It was the second of these that interested Toth, because it made different markings on the stone depending on whether the toolmaker was left-handed or right-handed. The technique is to hold the core in one hand and strike with the other.

Toth concluded that the preference for the right hand had already developed among human beings by between 1.9 and 1.4 million years ago (1987: 110).

Land mammals are not the same as humans in handedness – or 'pawedness'. About 50 per cent of land mammals favour the left paw and about 50 per cent the right one. It isn't altogether clear why there should be this difference between humans and animals, but the fact that animals don't have language means that they have a somewhat different brain organization from that of humans.

Perhaps handedness is hereditary in humans. (But then, why not in animals?) Statistics show there's a strong correlation between the handedness of parents and that of their children. But, as Springer and Deutsch (1989: 147) remark:

> Two left-handed parents could provide a child with different experiences relevant to the determination of handedness, just as they might provide specific genes. Nature (genes) and nurture (experience) are confounded in these figures, making it impossible to sort out the contribution of each.

That's the usual state of affairs, of course, with nature and nurture (see Medawar, 1961: 122–4).

How does the matter of handedness tie in with the organization of language in the brain? In a famous study at the Montreal Neurological Institute, investigators anaesthetized one hemisphere or the other in turn, using sodium amobarbital. They then carried out language tests which showed that the vast majority of right-handers (over 95 per cent of them) had speech and language predominantly in the left hemi-sphere, and that 70 per cent of left-handers did too. Fifteen per cent of the left-handers had speech and language in the right hemisphere, and 15 per cent had speech and language represented on both sides of the brain. The validity of these results depends to some extent on whether there were any cases of mixed handedness among the subjects.

Some studies have shown that left-handers have a better chance of recovery from strokes than right-handers. It isn't obvious why.

9.2.5 DIFFERENCES BETWEEN THE SEXES

Psychologists have used a number of tests to see if there is any difference in the performance of males and females in various cognitive tasks, including language tasks (see, for example, McGlone, 1978, 1980; Springer and Deutsch, 1989; Joanette *et al.*, 1990; Hellige, 1993; Kimura, 1993).

The general conclusion has been that females perform better than males across a number of language skills, do better on arithmetical calculations and give faster (correct) responses in certain tasks of visual perception. An example of the latter would be the task of picking which two pictures match exactly in a set of very similar ones. One of the language tasks on which females outperform males is that of listing words that all begin with the same letter, or which are all related semantically. ('List as many words as you can think of having to do with school.')

Males, on the other hand, perform better than females in certain tasks of visual perception (such as finding a shape which forms part of a larger pattern of shapes). They also perform better than females on some spatial tasks, such as mentally rotating an object or figure, as well as on problems where mathematical reasoning is required.

These are, of course, statistical differences: they don't mean that every female will be better at language tasks than every male, or every male better at tasks of visual perception and spatial ability than every female. As Hellige (1993: 233) puts it:

> Of course, there is substantial overlap in the performance of the two sexes for all of these tasks, and the differences in the means are typically small relative to the variance. The determination of these sex differences in cognitive ability is likely to involve complex interplay between biological and environmental factors.

One possible kind of explanation for these differences between the sexes is that there are differences of anatomy or function or both in the brain. Various differences of these kinds have been claimed.

A number of research studies have purported to show that males are more strongly lateralized than females, both for language and for spatial relationships. That is, those skills are more spread out over both hemispheres in females. If so, this might explain why males are more likely than females to suffer aphasia after a left-side stroke. The idea is that in females the relevant processes can be more readily carried out on the right side of the brain if a stroke occurs on the left side. A related claim is that a part of the corpus callosum called the splenum is larger in females than males. So where is the corpus callosum? The two hemispheres are divided by a deep fissure called the median longitudinal fissure. But that doesn't go all the way down through the cerebrum; beneath it there's a thick bundle of nerve fibres, the corpus callosum, which joins the two hemispheres. Concerning the claim that the splenum is larger in females than in males, Kimura comments drily, 'This finding has subsequently been both refuted and confirmed' (1993: 84).

If women suffer lesions in the front part of the brain, they are more likely than men who are similarly affected to suffer aphasia. Kimura (1993: 87) says:

> Because restricted damage within a hemisphere more frequently affects the posterior than the anterior area in both men and women, this differential dependence may explain why women incur aphasia less often than do men. Speech functions are thus less likely to be affected in women not because speech is more bilaterally organised in women but because the critical area is less often affected.

I have given you an (admittedly sketchy) outline of what is known about the brain in relation to language. But suppose we had enough time and space to fill out this sketch until I had described in much greater detail what is known of the matter at present. It still wouldn't say very much about some of the deeper questions about the relationship between language and the brain.

Linguists can make a fairly sophisticated attempt to give a systematic description of how language is constructed and the principles by which it is organized. And neurologists can make an increasingly sophisticated attempt to describe where language is located physically in the brain (though much is still not known). The problem is how to get the two descriptions to come together. I began this chapter by pointing out that linguists like Chomsky attempt to explain the linguistic principles that drive language, but that they make no attempt to describe how the principles are manifested physically in the brain. There is simply no known way to do it.

It may not just be that no one is clever enough to think of a way of doing it; there may be no possible way of doing it. There are scientists who believe that all scientific claims can be reduced to physics. They are known as 'reductionists'. But there are others who don't believe that that is either possible or desirable.

It's usually assumed that the abstract principles of linguistics must be shown to relate to the actions of neurons in the brain, but Chomsky, for one, challenges this assumption, and even suggests that the boot may be on the other foot: that it's the linguistic facts that seem secure, and the physiologists and physicists who may have to develop new theory to cope with these linguistic facts. If any readers would like to pursue the arguments Chomsky advances, and feel equipped to do so, they should read Chapter 2 of Chomsky (1996a).

Notes

1. It can also sometimes be caused by bleeding.
2. Lésions de la moitié gauche de l'encéphale coincidait [*sic*] avec l'oubli des signes de la Pensée. – Lu au Congrès méridional tenu à Montpellier en 1836, par le docteur Marc Dax. (Dax, 1865)
3. 'De tout ce qui précède, je crois pouvoir conclure, non que toutes les maladies de l'hémisphère gauche doivent altérer la mémoire verbale, mais que, lorsque cette mémoire est altérée par une maladie du cerveau, il faut chercher la cause du désordre dans l'hémisphère gauche et l'y chercher encore si les deux hémisphères sont malades ensembles.' Here and in what follows, the translations are by Ray Cattell.
4. 'Il restait maintenant un problème fort intéressant à résoudre: d'où vient que les altérations de l'hémisphère cérébral gauche sont suivies de l'oubli des mots, à l'exclusion de celles de l'hémisphère droit?'
5. For further details, see Ornstein (1997) and Springer and Deutsch (1989).

6. 'De même que nous dirigeons les mouvements de l'écriture, du dessin, de la broderie, etc., avec l'hémisphère gauche, de même nous parlons avec l'hémisphère gauche.'
7. 'An inability, not due to paralysis, to perform voluntary, purposeful movements of parts of the body, caused by brain lesion' (*Chambers Twentieth Century Dictionary*).
8. That is, Broca's aphasia.

10 The two hemispheres of the brain – B

10.1 Twentieth-century technology

As we've seen, the fact that language and speech are most closely associated with the left hemisphere in most people was demonstrated in the nineteenth century through post-mortems carried out on brains that had had some injury.

During the twentieth century, new technology and new techniques have confirmed many times over the basic insights of Dax, Broca and Wernicke, while at the same time extending and complicating the picture of how the hemispheres work in relation to language. In this section we look at some of the techniques that have been used.

10.1.1 'SPLIT-BRAIN' OPERATIONS

Perhaps the most dramatic growth in knowledge about the differences between the left and right hemispheres came about because of so-called 'split-brain surgery'. It was carried out on patients with very severe epilepsy, and involved severing the two hemispheres from each other, so that, at least in theory, there could be no communication between them. That might seem like a monstrous thing to do to any human being, but the members of the medical team who carried out the operations assure us that the patients in question had no hope of a normal life without the operation, since they were subject to repeated and violent epileptic seizures.

If you look down at a human brain from the top (or, if there isn't one to hand, a picture of a human brain looked at from the top, such as

Figure 9.1 on p. 152, will do), you will see that the two hemispheres are divided by a deep fissure called the median longitudinal fissure. Beneath it there's the thick bundle of nerve fibres, called the corpus callosum, which joins the two hemispheres. The idea of the split-brain operations was to sever the corpus callosum so that there could be no communication between the hemispheres thereafter. This was to stop the cycle of epileptic seizures from being passed from one hemisphere to the other.

About 30 such operations were carried out in the United States in the 1940s, and the results were studied intensively. The leader of the medical team, Roger Sperry, was given a Nobel Prize in 1981 for his work.

Before the operations were carried out, it was expected that they would produce various changes in behaviour in the patients, as had happened in other cases in which patients had had lesions in the corpus callosum. Sperry and his co-workers were surprised, then, to find that the everyday behaviour of the split-brain patients after the operation didn't seem to be changed very much. Sperry commented (1974: 6) that speech, verbal intelligence, calculation, established motor co-ordination, verbal reasoning and recall, personality and temperament were all preserved 'to a surprising degree'.

But despite this apparently good outcome, they were able to demonstrate that there were a number of impairments. Sperry summarizes as follows:

> The left and right hemispheres, following their disconnection, function independently in most conscious mental activities. Each hemisphere, that is, has its own private sensations, perceptions, thoughts and ideas, all of which are cut off from the corresponding experiences in the opposite hemisphere. Each left and right hemisphere has its own private chain of memories and learning experiences that are inaccessible to recall by the other hemisphere. In many respects, each disconnected hemisphere appears to have a separate 'mind of its own'. (Sperry, 1974: 7)

They demonstrated that if a split-brain patient were blindfolded and asked to feel an object with one hand, it made a dramatic difference whether it was the left or the right hand that carried out this task.

As we have seen, in most normal individuals the limbs on the right side of the body are most directly connected to the left side of the brain.

If the split-brain patient felt the object with the right hand, therefore, there was no difficulty in naming the object, since speech is mainly on the left side of the brain, too.

On the other hand, the left side of the body in most normal people is most directly connected to the right side of the brain. Such a normal person would have no difficulty in naming something held in the left hand, because when the message arrived in the right side of the brain, it would be redirected to the left side and processed in the speech centre. But a split-brain patient can't make that transfer. Since the two sides of the brain are cut off from each other, no message can cross the corpus callosum. For that reason, the split-brain patient who feels an object with the left hand can't name it. Nevertheless, the patient will be able to retrieve the object if it's placed among a number of other objects which are all hidden from sight.

For similar reasons, such patients are also unable to name objects seen in the left field of vision or felt with the left foot, or smells experienced through the right nostril. (Smell contrasts with the senses of sight and touch in being ipsilateral – that is, the right nostril sends information to the right side of the brain, and the left to the left.)

Sperry (1974), Joanette *et al.* (1990) and others warn against the dangers of generalizing too freely from the split-brain cases to normal brains. Joanette *et al.* point out that the split-brain subjects had all suffered from severe epilepsy and in consequence had suffered injury to the brain early in life. Furthermore, their medical histories were all different and they can't be regarded as a unified group.

10.1.2 OPERATIONS WHICH REMOVE ONE SIDE OF THE BRAIN

Brain science owes quite a lot to sufferers of epilepsy (that is, very severely affected ones), in that they have been the guinea-pigs not only for split-brain operations but also for operations to remove one hemisphere or the other (hemispherectomies). Again, it seems like a horrific thing to do to another human being (and no doubt is), but again we are assured by the surgeons that the people who have this kind of operation would have continued to suffer a great deal in their lives if they had not had it. By comparison, their lives after the operation seem to have been better.

In the light of the fact that there has always been a certain amount of unjustified community avoidance and fear of people with epilepsy, it's important to say that there are many epilepsy sufferers who live normal lives and who aren't noticeably different from other people. The cricketer Tony Greig, who has been very successful in business as well as in cricket, is an epileptic, for example.

Some of the operations to remove a hemisphere have been carried out on children whose brains had undergone calcification and degeneration of one hemisphere as a result of severe epilepsy. Actually, the operation isn't always a matter of removing the hemisphere entirely. 'The term "hemispherectomy" is applied to surgeries in which all or large amounts of cortical tissue, including the motor and sensory strip, are removed. The term also includes hemidecortication'[1] (Carson *et al.*, 1996).

Three children who were studied by Dennis and Whitaker (1976) had (the cortex of) one hemisphere removed when they were only 5 months old, in order to prevent years of epileptic activity before inevitable removal. Damage to one side of the brain was threatening to cause damage to the other side as well. When Dennis and Whitaker studied these children, they were 9 to 10 years of age.

One of the children had had the (cortex of the) right hemisphere removed. He had no difficulty in making correct judgements about the following sentences:

a   *I paid the money by the man.
b   *I was paid the money to the lady.
c   I was paid the money by the boy.

That is, he said that (a) and (b) were ungrammatical and that (c) was acceptable. The other two children had had the (cortex of the) left hemisphere removed and they were unable to make these judgements. Dennis and Whitaker drew the conclusion that these two children were unable to understand the meaning of passive sentences correctly. They had similar difficulty with other sentences which departed from the normal order of an active sentence.

People who have suffered a stroke in the left hemisphere often have difficulty with such judgements, too. In a sentence like *The policeman was killed by the gangster*, they would be unable to say which person died. It's as if they can't interpret the signals *was*, *-ed* and *by*, which most people use (unconsciously) as clues to the syntax and the related semantics.

Dennis and Whitaker also studied a 16-year-old girl who had suffered brain damage at the age of between 5 and 7 weeks, which caused profound epilepsy in the left hemisphere. All treatments were unsuccessful over the years, and at the age of 16 the whole of her left hemisphere was surgically removed. The temporal lobe was then seen to be about a quarter of its normal size, and there were other abnormalities.

She was given linguistic tests, and it emerged that she had great difficulty with passive sentences. She interpreted them as though they were active sentences – that is, she interpreted a sentence like *I was paid the money by the boy* as though it meant *I paid the money to the boy*. Again the structural signals were ignored, as if the girl had just heard *I – paid – the money – the boy*.

Dennis and Whitaker say that her error rate was greater than she could have achieved by chance. Remember, she was working with only a right hemisphere. Such cases provide further evidence that the left hemisphere is crucial to the successful processing of syntax.

Dennis and Whitaker draw attention to the fact that when very young children suffer damage to the left hemisphere, they recover better than adults who suffer similar damage. It has been known for over a century that if children under about 3 suffer damage to the brain's language areas in the left hemisphere, their language learning is considerably impeded; but they usually recover to a large extent, and do learn language. Similar damage in adults is far less likely to lead to such a good recovery. Over 90 per cent of adults who suffer a lesion in the left hemisphere (usually through a stroke) will suffer significant interference with language processing, which will probably be permanent.

As far as children are concerned, there's some evidence to suggest that the left side of the brain doesn't become the dominant side for language until sometime during childhood. That process is called 'lateralization'. According to Lenneberg (1967), lateralization takes place some time between 2 years of age and puberty, and those are the bounds that he set for normal language acquisition 'by exposure'.

But a different view was put forward by Stephen Krashen (1973). He claimed that lateralization is a matter not of age, but of exposure to the language. At whatever age a child is exposed to language experience, lateralization will occur. He believed the process was normally complete by 5 (since most children have virtually learned their language by then), but that there should be nothing to stop someone from learning language after that, whenever (s)he was exposed to it.

To return now to Dennis and Whitaker, they say there are two competing explanations for the child's effective recovery from strokes:

1. When there is damage to either hemisphere, the other side can take over the functions which normally would have been carried out by the damaged one. This suggests that lateralization (say of language to the left side) must be something that develops after birth, and that it has not yet developed by early infancy.

2. The other possibility is that the differences between the two hemispheres are already present in early infancy, but that the young brain has a very great ability to reorganize itself if it needs to do so because of damage to particular areas. This property is called 'plasticity'.

Some of the children studied by Dennis and Whitaker had sustained brain damage at the age of only a few weeks. The fact that in later years they were unable to correctly interpret passives and certain other syntactic structures led the investigators to the conclusion that there are limits to plasticity and that the asymmetry in the brain is already present early in life.[2] So choice 2 is preferred.

Michael Gazzaniga (1988) makes a claim which is difficult to reconcile with the results of Dennis and Whitaker. Gazzaniga first tells his readers that the normal pattern in adults is that injury to certain regions of the left hemisphere has serious effects on language and thought processes, while injury to corresponding parts of the right hemisphere causes problems with spatial orientation. He goes on:

> Injury to the young child's brain produces a wholly different picture. Damage to the right hemisphere during the first year of life produces grave consequences for both verbal and spatial functions later on. Remarkably, damage to the left affects spatial processes only, with verbal processes being almost completely spared. In other words, the specific brain functions active during the development of language and thought mechanisms are located in brain areas distant from their final location. (Gazzaniga, 1988: 62–3)

This fascinating claim seems to conflict with the report of Dennis and Whitaker that children who had had their left hemisphere removed at the age of 5 weeks showed typical left-side language deficits at a later age. There is a certain amount of latitude provided by the difference between '5 weeks old' and 'during the first year of life', and there may well be considerable individual differences. As with many questions to do with brain and language, the truth is not yet clear.

174

10.1.3 BRAIN SCANS

Great progress has been made in studying the relationship between language and the brain in recent years by using modern brain-scanning techniques (Posner and Raichle, 1994; Raichle, 1994).

Computerized axial tomography (CAT)

A CAT scan is a computerized X-ray which gives pictures of cross-sectional slices of the brain. CAT stands for 'computerized axial tomography', though it is now usually called just CT, for 'computerized tomography'. This process gives fuller and better information than ordinary X-rays. Its primary use is in medical investigations, such as searching for a suspected tumour on the brain, or searching for the site of lesions suffered by stroke victims. It doesn't always find what it's looking for, especially if it's made too soon after the cerebral damage or if the lesion is very small, but CT scans are nevertheless a very effective diagnostic tool. It is a tool that is of some, but limited, relevance to research in language.

Positron emission tomography (PET)

A positron is an elementary particle which is like an electron except that it has a positive charge, whereas the electron has a negative one.

A CT scan can show the brain's shape and structure, but not how it's functioning. One of the restrictions traditionally suffered by researchers studying language and the brain was that they couldn't cut a hole in the top of the head and look in,[3] and they wouldn't have seen much that was relevant if they had. Well, that restriction still holds, of course, but PET scans allow researchers to see the brain in action while it is processing language – a truly remarkable development.

A PET scan can show the details of the blood-flow in the brain, and so demonstrate which parts of the brain are active while a subject is doing particular mental operations. It can also show details of glucose or oxygen metabolism (chemical changes) in the living brain.

In PET, radioactive water is injected into the bloodstream. This is said not to be harmful to the subject:[4] it reaches the brain in 1 minute and after about 10 minutes it has decayed to the extent that it

175

is no longer appreciably radioactive. Meanwhile, its radioactivity makes it easier to localize exactly the distribution of particles in the brain.

In recent years, investigators have used the technique to study differences in the hemispheres during particular cognitive tasks; and that, of course, is of great interest to language researchers. In one study,[5] seven subjects were given repeated PET scans while they carried out tasks in four stages (Raichle, 1994: 39):

1. Fixate the vision on a '+' symbol on a video monitor. That's all: just look at the '+'.
2. Observe single nouns (e.g. *plate*, *scissors*, *child*, etc.), flashed on the screen, while maintaining the fixation on the '+' symbol. That's all that was required in this phase: merely looking at them. The nouns either appeared just under the '+' sign or were spoken through earphones.
3. Look at cue words on the screen and repeat them aloud. (This adds motor output.)
4. Respond to a noun that names an object (flashed on the screen) by giving a verb that describes some use of the object; (for example, *wood – chop*; *meat – cook*. (This adds semantic processing.)

At each of these stages a PET scan was carried out to show the details of blood flow in the brain. The investigators were able to show changes in the pattern of blood-flow as the tasks changed. Even the task which required 'just looking at words' caused some activity in the right hemisphere (because of the graphic shapes of the letters, which were lateralized to the left hemisphere).

The researchers suggested that the subjects were responding to the sight of the words with a reflex action of performing some linguistic analysis, even though they were not asked to do so.

Interestingly, the level of activity in these areas of the left hemisphere did not change when they were asked to read or vocalize or carry out the semantic task, suggesting that they had already done some form of linguistic analysis during passive presentation of the cue words.

This kind of research is expected to produce very interesting results in the future. A crucially important finding from such research has been that many areas of the brain are involved in even the simplest task, so any simple formulation of hemispheric specialization, such as saying that 'language is on the left side of the brain', is wrong.

Then what about the discoveries of Dax, Broca and Wernicke, which seemed to say that there are language centres in fixed local areas of the brain? It's certainly true that damage in Broca's or Wernicke's area can cause breakdowns in language performance, as happens with many stroke victims; but while it's a *necessary* condition for successful language performance to have such areas intact, it isn't a *sufficient* condition, as we can deduce from the fact that the research with PET scans shows that many areas of the brain are involved in even the simplest tasks. And, as reported earlier, two stroke victims can have lesions in, say, Broca's area, apparently in the same place, but have somewhat different symptoms as far as their language is concerned. That's just to make life interesting for speech pathologists.

Magnetic resonance imaging (MRI)

Magnetic resonance imaging also has relevance to language research, as well as to medical probes. Its advantage is that it isn't invasive, as CT scans are. CT scans carry the same dangers as X-rays, in that they expose the body to radiation, but MRI scans don't: they depend on ultrasonics rather than radiation. Like CT scans, though, MRI scans produce high-quality images of cross-sections of the brain. (See Greenfield, 1997; Posner and Raichle, 1994; Raichle, 1994.)

The equipment generates a strong magnetic field, which, together with radio waves, causes hydrogen atoms in the body to give off small electric signals. That makes it possible to detect where the hydrogen molecules are, in living tissue. Since hydrogen molecules occur in water (H_2O), there are a lot of them in the human body. By using these small electric signals, the machine can generate an image showing tissue and bone marrow. MRI is used in the detection of cancer, and is able to detect some brain tumours that are too small to show up on an X-ray or a CT scan. It is considered to be the most promising of the body-imaging diagnostic tools now available.

The technique is safe enough to allow studies of the brain to be carried out on many more subjects in the future than has been possible in the past. One field to which the technique can be applied is differences of function between the hemispheres.

A development called 'functional MRI' (fMRI) adds to the picture provided by MRI by showing also the areas where the greatest activity is taking place in the brain. The blood contains glucose and oxygen,

177

which are attracted towards any neurons that fire. They add fuel to the firing, and show up the areas where there is most oxygen. The technique gives a very good means of tracking the ebb and flow of brain activity occurring in response to stimuli (Carter, 1998: 26). According to Raichle (1994: 41), the advantages of fMRI over other forms of scanning are as follows:

1. Nothing, radioactive or otherwise, has to be injected to obtain a signal. The signal comes directly from the change in the concentration of oxygen in the veins in the brain tissue.
2. MRI permits the investigator to identify the anatomical structure where the active regions are, as well as the material which is stimulating them.
3. The spatial resolution is quite good (better than PET's resolution).
4. When it is properly equipped, MRI can monitor, in real time, the rate of change in the oxygen signal that is induced by the blood-flow.

MRI is also said to carry little, if any, biological risk.

10.1.4 OTHER TECHNIQUES

Less spectacular than split-brain operations, but very useful nevertheless, are various techniques that have been developed in the twentieth century with the aim of finding out more about the differences between the two hemispheres.

Dichotic listening tests

Dichotic listening tests involve a procedure in which different programmes of sounds (words, including digits, tunes, etc.) are played simultaneously in the two ears of a subject through stereophonic earphones, hooked up to a dual-channel tape recorder. For instance, the stimulus in the left ear might be 'three', while the simultaneous stimulus in the right ear is 'six'. The first use of the technique was made by the psychologist Donald Broadbent in 1954, in order to study memory and attention.

The first use of it to study differences between the ears in hearing acuity was made by Doreen Kimura, working at the Montreal Neurological Institute, in the early 1960s. She played three pairs of competing digits, for example 'three' in the left ear and 'six' in the right ear, with intervals of half a second between each pair and the next. The onset of the sound in each case was synchronized so that each word in a pair began at exactly the same time as the other. The subjects were asked to report all the ones they could remember, out of the six. The order of recall didn't matter. Most normal right-handed people reported more items correctly for the right ear than the left ear.

Kimura then proposed two hypotheses:

- that the left temporal lobe was specialized for speech; and
- that the path connecting the right ear to the left side of the brain was more effective than the path connecting the left ear to the right side of the brain.

This conclusion was strengthened by investigations that showed that patients who were known to be right-hemisphere dominant for speech showed superiority in the left ear.

Kimura's discovery (1961) provided the first clear demonstration that in the normal brain, the functioning of the two hemispheres is different. (Remember, Dax's and Broca's patients were brain-damaged.)

Kimura then tested to see if the right side of the brain was also specialized. The effects that right-brain surgery had had on patients had already suggested that the right side was specialized for musical tone. Kimura administered dichotic listening tests again, this time using two different snatches of music (excerpts from concerti grossi of Handel). The two ears heard different snatches simultaneously, then four such excerpts played one after another. The subject had to identify which two (s)he had just heard.

The same normal subjects who had favoured the right ear when listening to digits (that is, words) showed a left-ear superiority when listening to music (Kimura, 1964).

The difference in performance of the two ears with normal patients is very small, though it is said to be statistically reliable.

Sodium amytal

In 1949 Juhn Wada presented a technique which allowed one hemisphere at a time to be anaesthetized, thus effectively isolating it from the other one without the need for surgery (Joanette *et al.*, 1990: 37–8; Springer and Deutsch, 1989: 22). The effect was only temporary, but was very useful for displaying the different performances of the two hemispheres.

With the aid of the Wada test, it is possible to determine which hemisphere is specialized for language. This is especially useful before operations which might interfere with the speech centre accidentally without the benefit of this knowledge.

The two main arteries of the neck are the carotid arteries, located on each side of it.[6] Wada injected sodium amytal (sodium amobarbital) into the carotid artery on one side of the neck at a time. If the injection is on the side where language is dominant (in most people, the left), it renders the patient unable to answer questions, but if the injection is on the other side, this doesn't happen. Thus it provides a means of checking which is the dominant side for language.

Joanette *et al.* (1990: 37, fn. 5) explain why the test is not used very often: 'Given that this technique is relatively invasive and not without a certain amount of risk, its application to aphasic populations would probably not be authorised by contemporary ethical committees.'

Electrical activity in the brain

Electrical activity takes place in the brain, and the frequencies can be graphed by an electroencephalogram (EEG). It can be shown that when verbal tasks are being carried out by the brain, there is more electrical activity in the left hemisphere than the right one. This provides yet another way in which left-side dominance for language can be demonstrated.

An electroencephalogram is simply a graph recording electrical activity in the brain. A part of the graph is called an evoked potential. It shows a series of deviations from the baseline, in either a positive or a negative direction. It graphs about 500 milliseconds of activity after the stimulus ends. A person using this device for research can measure the amplitude (height) of the deviations and also the latency –

that is, the period from the time the stimulus begins to the time the electrical activity begins.

A central research question is whether there is a difference in the pattern of electrical activity between the left hemisphere and the right, when the brain is carrying out verbal tasks. There is a large literature on the research that this has provoked, and we will not go into the details here. For our purposes, it is sufficient to say that the results do provide further evidence that speech is mainly processed in the left hemisphere.

10.2 Conclusion

The research findings that have been outlined in this chapter have taken neurological studies a long way in the twentieth century. There is reason to hope that even more exciting developments might take place in the twenty-first century.

Yet in spite of this increase in knowledge, the clinical problems posed by aphasia are still difficult. The real hurdle is that, at present, if a brain is damaged, it cannot be put back the way that it was. Most treatment is aimed at achieving as much improvement in the patient's condition as is possible, and then re-educating the person to live with his/her disability as successfully as possible.

But as valuable as knowledge about the hemispheres is for helping aphasic patients, that is not its only value. Knowledge about the hemispheres also touches virtually every question about normal use of language.

Notes

1. That is, removal of half the cortex.
2. However, as Springer and Deutsch (1989) note, their conclusions have been criticized for being premature, given that they didn't use control groups for comparison with these subjects and that there were problems with their statistical analysis. The questions remain open, then.
3. Though that is sometimes done for other reasons.
4. I am grateful to Neil Smith for drawing my attention to the fact that the use of PET is excluded for women of child-bearing age in the UK, which suggests that at least some experts believe it is potentially harmful for such people.

5. By Marcus E. Raichle, Steven E. Petersen, Michael I. Posner, Peter T. Fox and Mark A. Mintun, carried out at the Washington University Medical Center in 1988.
6. If you take very active physical exercise and need to know what your pulse rate is, you can work it out from feeling the pulse in the carotid arteries with your fingers.

11. The bounds of language acquisition

11.1 Introduction

This chapter will discuss three cases in which there's a question as to whether language acquisition is involved. They are all in some way 'out of the ordinary'. The aim will be to define what does and doesn't fall within the bounds of 'language acquisition'.

I'll begin by considering deaf children who learn to use sign language, and ask whether what they achieve represents language acquisition. Clearly they're atypical in one sense – that they use a channel of communication that isn't the usual one: they communicate principally with their hands, faces and bodies instead of with sound. But do they still fall within the bounds of language acquisition in the true sense?

Language acquisition requires not only a child to acquire it, but also parents, other adults and the children's peers to provide language input. So as the second case we'll briefly examine what happens with children whose parents are profoundly deaf and whose speech as a consequence is atypical.

Finally, I'll discuss the case of a girl called Genie (though that is not her real name) who suffered extreme physical, mental, emotional and social deprivation during her childhood. When she was discovered at the age of $13\frac{1}{2}$ she had virtually no language. An attempt was made to teach her English, but since she was not an infant when she began, the question arises whether her achievements represent something resembling ordinary language acquisition.

Our conclusions will be somewhat different in each of the three cases.

11.2 Deaf children

11.2.1 INTRODUCTION

Deaf children come to language in different ways. Those who have speaking, non-deaf parents (the majority) are obviously going to have a different exposure to language from those whose parents are deaf and use sign language (between 5 and 10 per cent, according to Gallaway and Woll, 1994).

We might expect that deaf children in the first group would be more likely to make use of lip-reading, and ones in the second group would be likely to pick up signing from their parents in the natural course of events, in much the same way as a hearing child picks up a spoken language. However, while that's broadly true, matters aren't quite so straightforward, as Mogford (1993: 114) points out:

> Deaf children can be born to deaf or hearing parents, each of whom will have a preference for spoken or sign language depending on their own first language, social contacts, experience in education and beliefs. Parental preference means that some deaf children learn sign language as a first language and others spoken language.

Mogford goes on to say that if sign language is the first language, it's likely that the child will later also learn spoken language, and if the first language is spoken, children will probably acquire some signing later on. 'Thus there are no clear divisions between signers and speakers, nor is the first language mode entirely predictable from the parents' hearing status.'

The choice between signing and lip-reading (where there is a choice) is a difficult one. There are many areas of life to which signers who don't lip-read are denied access. Pharmacists, bank tellers and people who serve in fruit shops are usually not able to sign. However, some banks and other institutions are now introducing access programmes to overcome this problem. As we'll see shortly, though, signing is a true language, as much so as any spoken language, with all the richness that that implies, whereas lip-reading is only partially adequate as a means of accessing a spoken language.

Courses in lip-reading are given by some educational institutions, but it can take quite a long time to master the art. (There's great variation among people in this, as in every other endeavour in life.)

184

Lip-reading may be better than signing in that it allows access to more activities and allows the deaf person to understand more people; but signing is more efficient for fluent users. Signers are not restricted to communicating only with certain racial or national groups, as non-signing speakers of other languages are. On the other hand, they are restricted to communicating only with other signers.

Since many people have misconceptions about sign languages, it will be worth looking at one of them in some detail – just enough detail to show how it works. We'll tackle this task below. As Poizner *et al.* (1987) make clear, American Sign Language is a language in the full sense. Its structure is highly complex, in the way that the structures of spoken languages are. The main difference is in the modality it uses – that is, signs made with the hands, face and body, instead of signs produced with speech. The signs that make up a sign language are often thought of as being made simply with the hands, but the face and other parts of the body enter into the communicative act in important ways.

Deaf children with speech frequently have phonetic distortions in their speech. It's very difficult to reproduce sounds that you've never heard, or never heard clearly. A skilled teacher can help, but some of the distortion is likely to remain.

There's also a certain social isolation because of the communication problem. This can be severe, and is one of the factors that has to be dealt with in helping the child to acquire language, or acquire more language.

11.2.2 THE SCIENTIFIC INTEREST OF SIGNING

Signing has a unique interest to language scientists. Some fascinating facts about sign language have been revealed in recent years, especially by Ursula Bellugi and her colleagues at the Salk Institute for Biological Studies in San Diego, California. Those discoveries have shed considerable light on the nature of language in general.

There are numerous sign languages in the world, but the one that has been most studied is American Sign Language (ASL). That's the one on which Bellugi and her colleagues have concentrated their attention (Poizner *et al.*, 1987).

In ASL the signs stand directly for meanings, just as whole words do in spoken languages. Furthermore, the sign sequences have syntactic structure, just as sequences in spoken languages do. Some of the signs are iconic – that is, the physical nature of the sign suggests the meaning. For example, crying is indicated by a finger being drawn down each cheek, like tears flowing. Bellugi *et al.* (1993) say that symbols that suggest their meaning are probably more common in ASL than in spoken languages. Interestingly, however, they also have this to say (p. 148):

> Because of the transparency of ASL forms, one might expect that these would be systems profoundly influenced by iconicity. What we found, instead, was that their transparency at all levels appears to have little or no effect on acquisition.

In any case, historically (over the past hundred years) signs have tended to become less iconic and more arbitrary. There is similarly an arbitrary relationship between most words and their meanings in spoken languages.

Many people think of a sign language as being based on a spoken language like English, and in fact being a kind of coding from a spoken language into signs. But that isn't true, other than in finger-spelling. ASL is symbol-based, and is a language in its own right, not formed from any other language, as we'll see in more detail below.

In a spoken language like English, there are various levels of structure, but two extremely important ones are the phonological level (see Chapter 2) and the syntactic level (see Chapter 6). Likewise, in ASL there are two levels: (a) one that is internal to the structure of the sign, just as a large part of phonology is internal to the word; and (b) a syntactic level, showing the grammatical relationship between the signs.

Structure that is internal to the sign

Structure that is internal to the sign consists of the hand configuration, place of articulation (i.e. where the signs are made in relation to the body) and movement. Each of these has a limited set of alternatives, though there's a much larger set of theoretical possibilities, just as the set of phonemes in a spoken language is a limited set of the theoretically possible ones.

In ASL, the structure that's internal to the sign differentiates words from each other. As indicated by Poizner *et al.* (1987), the signs for *candy*, *apple* and *jealous* differ only in hand configuration (Figure 11.1),

186

Figure 11.1 American Sign Language: minimal contrasts involving (a) hand configuration, (b) place of articulation, and (c) movement
After H. Poizner, E. S. Klima and U. Bellugi, *What the Hands Reveal about the Brain.* Copyright MIT Press, Cambridge, MA, 1987

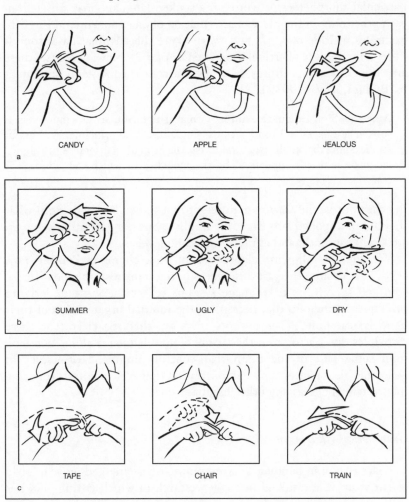

while the signs for *summer, ugly* and *dry* differ only in place of articulation (the forehead, nose and chin, respectively), and the signs for *tape, chair* and *train* differ only in movement. There are constraints (restrictions) on the ways in which sublexical components can be

187

combined – that is, the way components can be combined within symbols.

Just as certain signs may differ from each other only in place of articulation, as in the difference between *summer, ugly* and *dry*, so particular morphemes or words in a spoken language may differ from each other only in the place of articulation of one phoneme; in English, examples include *rum, run* and *rung*, where the terminal nasal sounds differ only in place of articulation (see Chapter 2). Now, of course, these are different kinds of things, but they illustrate the following statement by Bellugi, *et al.* (1993: 132):

> American Sign Language exhibits formal structuring at the same levels as spoken languages and similar kinds of organizational principles . . . Yet our studies show that at all structural levels, the form of an utterance in a signed language is deeply influenced by the modality in which the language is cast.

In other words, the *details* are different in a signed language from what they are in a spoken language like English, but the governing *principles* are similar in both, and apply at the same levels.

We find the following elaboration of these claims in Poizner *et al.* (1987: 5): 'despite the vast differences in the transmission modalities of sign and speech, both language systems reflect the same underlying principles, principles that determine the internal organization of their basic lexical units'. The authors then say that it's clear that these principles don't arise from the nature of sign language alone, but arise from some part of the brain that controls linguistic principles in general. This is part of their demonstration that ASL manifests the same inborn tendencies as any other language does.

Grammatical relations in ASL

The fact that sign languages have grammar has emerged only in fairly recent years, as a result of intensive research in which Bellugi and her colleagues have played a huge role. In a spoken language like English, some types of grammatical information are signalled by inflectional morphemes – that is, morphemes (parts of words) that signal grammatical information (tense, number, etc.). The inflectional morphemes occur on the ends of words, after the stem. In ASL they are often signalled by features of movement.

Grammatical relations in ASL are shown in several ways. One way is the order in which the signs are made. The order is frequently subject–verb–object, as in a spoken language like English, though with some verbs, like *welcome*, the order of the roles is reversed.

The noun phrases that are associated with a particular verb are assigned to a particular point on a horizontal plane in front of the signer and they can then be referred to again by pointing to the same place. This is parallel to what happens in a spoken language through pronouns; for example *I greeted Mary and kissed her*. This backward reference can occur in ASL even if many other signs have intervened, simply by pointing to the place where the antecedent sign was made.

11.2.3 ACQUISITION OF A SIGN LANGUAGE

In spoken languages, certain words such as the pronouns *I* and *you* are 'deictic' (pronounced dike-tic). This means that who or what they refer to changes according to who's speaking and who's being spoken to. So if John says *I am sick*, the reference is different from what it would be if Mary said *I am sick*. In ASL, deixis (the noun related to the adjective 'deictic'; pronounced dike-sis) is indicated by pointing, which is appropriate, since the literal meaning of the word (from Greek) is 'pointing'.

As Poizner *et al.* comment, you would therefore expect that the pronouns *I* and *you* would be easy to acquire in ASL, that they would be learnt very early, and that children wouldn't make mistakes with them. But that isn't so:

> Despite the identity of ASL pronouns with nonlinguistic gestures, the course of their acquisition is startlingly similar to that in spoken languages. Deaf infants between 9 and 11 months of age point freely for investigating and indicating and for drawing attention to themselves and others, as do hearing children. During the second year, however ... they seem to avoid such pointing ... The next period sees the re-emergence of pointing to self and addressee, but now as part of a linguistic system. At this stage, surprising errors of reversal appear in the children's pronominal signing. They sign (YOU) when intending self, patently ignoring the transparency of the pointing gesture. These pronoun reversals are also found in hearing children of the same age.[1] By around the age of $2\frac{1}{2}$ years, such reversal errors are completely resolved, just as they are in hearing children of the same age. (Poizner *et al.*, 1987: 22)

In spoken language, endings on verbs (or lack of them) signal various pieces of grammatical information; for example, agreement with the subject in number: *the cat plays with the wool*; *the cats play with the wool*. Agreements of this kind occur in ASL, too, but they're indicated by connections between spatial points.

There are many more complexities to ASL than have been described here. Anyone who wants to find out more should refer to Bellugi *et al.* (1993: 18), Poizner *et al.* (1987: 7) and Tarrter (1998: 151–203). My aim here is not, of course, to teach you sign language, but to outline some of its characteristics and give you some idea of why it is now regarded by linguists as a language in its own right, with many of the characteristics of spoken language.

As we saw in Chapter 9, the left hemisphere of the brain is dominant in language processing while the right is dominant in visuo-spatial relationships, among other things. Since sign language involves both language and visuo-spatial relationships, the question arises as to whether sign language is processed on the left or the right, or both.

Poizner *et al.* (1987) did extensive tests to determine what was happening in the case of six signers, of whom three had damage in the left hemisphere, and three in the right. From their study of the deaf people with left-side damage, they concluded that some areas of the left hemisphere are crucial for the correct functioning of language in people whose main means of communication is sign language.

By contrast, they found that those with damage to the right brain were not aphasic – that is, they didn't show language deficits. One subject had massive damage on the right side, in an area which would have caused her to be aphasic if it had been in the left hemisphere, yet 'astonishingly' she had no sign language aphasia (p. 159). In other words, although the damage was in an area which should have controlled her visuo-spatial abilities, she was able to sign perfectly. So it seems that left-brain dominance for language, which is manifested in people whose main means of communication is a spoken language, is also manifested in deaf signers.

It's worth noting that the work of Poizner *et al.* (1987) was reviewed rather unfavourably by Doreen Kimura (1988), who is herself a highly respected researcher in this field. While saying she has great respect for this group's earlier work (Klima and Bellugi, 1979) in adding to the available knowledge about the details of sign language, Kimura nevertheless is not happy with the evidence they provide for their most important conclusions. As the authors realized, it was important for them to demonstrate that the defects in the signing of those who had left-brain damage were actually due to a language deficit, and not to some other kind of deficit. *Apraxia* is a term used to refer to non-language programming defects. The authors argued that the defects in the performance of these signers could not be due to apraxia, so must be due to language deficits; but Kimura believes they have not been thorough enough in providing the evidence for this. (In fact, she points to the fact that they were relatively newcomers to the field, and challenges the extent of their knowledge.)

Kimura sums up her feelings like this:

> Two main themes run throughout the book: That the lateralization of visuo-spatial function in the brains of deaf signers is surprisingly similar to that of hearing subjects; and that the specialized function of the left hemisphere is explicitly tied to language. This reviewer was fairly convinced of the former before reading the book, and remains unconvinced of the latter after reading it. (Kimura, 1988: 375)

Discussion of these claims seems likely to go on for quite some time yet, but at least Poizner *et al.* (1987) have placed such interesting questions firmly on the agenda.

At the beginning of this chapter, the question was raised whether deaf children who became signers could be said to have acquired language normally. We can now answer that question with a confident 'yes'. If their parents are signers, they can pick it up from them just as speaking children pick up spoken language from their parents. The only difference is in the modality they use to communicate (hands, face and body instead of voice), but this is not a difference of language kind, only a difference of channel.

Bellugi *et al.* (1993: 149) sum up the situation well:

> The evidence demonstrates that, just as the structure of ASL exhibits the same formal patterning as spoken languages, the course of acquisition of grammatical processes in ASL is remarkably like that for spoken languages. These findings thus dramatically underscore that the biological substrate for the human capacity for creating and acquiring linguistic system is modality independent.

11.3 Hearing children of deaf parents

The hearing children of profoundly deaf parents may be faced with a special problem. Schiff-Myers (1987) presents a survey of studies on such children. At the end of it comes the following summary (p. 58):

> The research reported above indicates that some normal hearing children born to deaf parents have speech and language problems while others do not. Although the prevalence of problems in this population seems to be higher than in the population at large, factors other than the deafness of the parents have been identified as contributing to that difference ... the literature clearly shows that some hearing children develop speech and language normally, and that there are some aspects of speech and language that are rarely affected by the parents' deafness, even in children where problems have been observed.

I'm fortunate to have contact with a lady (call her Evelyn)[2] whose daughter is profoundly deaf, and married to a man who is also profoundly deaf. They have two sons (let's call them Jason and Ryan), who are not deaf. Jason is 8, and Ryan just 3. When Jason was about 6 months old, his mother went back to work, and Jason then attended family day care, run from the university in the city where they live. There, of course, he had speech input from the carers and the other children. Since he's now in primary school, he no longer goes to family day care, although Ryan does, for a couple of days a week.

Meanwhile, the boys' parents took the sensible step of moving into a house near the boys' grandmother and grandfather, Evelyn and Richard, so that they have regular speech input from them. Evelyn is a schoolteacher with a university education which includes psychology, and has a good understanding of what's needed.

I haven't been able to meet the boys face to face, since the city they live in is about 800 km from where I live, but Evelyn has very kindly recorded them for me in an everyday family setting, so that I could listen to their speech. At this stage Jason speaks normally. Ryan, being only 3, doesn't speak as well, and has characteristics in his speech that reflect the special context in which he has acquired language. But it's difficult to tell whether any imperfections are due to his early language environment or the fact that he has only just turned 3 – more likely both. Evelyn says that up until about 6 months ago he wasn't saying much at all, but he's certainly using language to communicate now. My judgement is that Ryan will come to speak just as well as Jason, given a bit more time. Their parents use sign language, and Ryan signs like a deaf child to his parents, but not to Jason. Presumably that's because he doesn't need to sign to Jason.

If we ask whether Jason has acquired language normally, the answer must be 'yes', even though the circumstances were unusual. And the same will be true of Ryan, if he comes to speak as well as Jason.

11.4 Severe deprivation: Genie[3]

11.4.1 ABOUT GENIE

> She could not stand erect, could not straighten her arms or legs, could not run, hop, jump or climb; in fact, she could only walk with difficulty. . . . She was incontinent of feces and urine. Her hair was sparse and stringy. She salivated copiously, spitting onto anything at hand. Genie was unsocialized, primitive, hardly human. (Curtiss, 1977: 9)

This is the description by Susan Curtiss of a $13\frac{1}{2}$-year-old girl called Genie, as she was in 1970. But how could she have got into such a condition? It's a horrifying story, but well worth learning about.

Genie was born in April 1957 into a household which was about as adverse as it could be from the point of view of a little child about to go through the period when language is normally acquired. Her father disliked children and declared he wouldn't have any; but in fact his wife bore four children, of whom Genie was the fourth. The first two had died, seemingly because of the adverse treatment they received, and the third one had developmental problems. There had also been domestic violence in the form of a vicious beating administered by the father to the mother just before she had the first child.

Genie was born with an RH blood incompatibility, like two of her siblings, only one of whom was still alive. In the second half of her first year, apparently her weight fell rapidly, after having been normal at first.

When Genie was 20 months old, an event occurred which was to prove cataclysmic for her. Her grandmother on her father's side was run over in the street by a truck, and was killed. When the truck-driver was acquitted of all charges, Genie's father acted very strangely. He moved the family into the house his mother had occupied and sealed them off from contact with the outside world.

Genie was a virtual prisoner. She spent most of every day harnessed to a child's 'potty' chair. At night she was put into a sleeping-bag which restrained her movements and then placed into a crib with wire mesh sides and top. She was badly nourished, and was given mainly baby foods to eat. Her mother, who was going blind, was unable to give her much attention.

Genie was exposed to hardly any language. There was no radio or TV in the house. If she made any vocal noise herself, her father beat her. Her father and brother both barked at her like dogs, and that appears to have been almost the only vocal input she got.

A dramatic change occurred in Genie's life when she was $13\frac{1}{2}$. Her father and mother had a terrible row, and the result was that her mother managed to leave home, taking Genie with her. They went to stay with Genie's maternal grandmother.

While they were there, Genie's mother learnt that she could apply for assistance because she was blind, and took Genie with her when she went to visit what she thought was the appropriate government department.

In fact it wasn't, but while she was there (at the Family Aids Department), one of the employees noticed how undernourished and poorly developed Genie was. With admirable alertness, (s)he not only noticed it, but drew the supervisor's attention to it, with the result that the mother was asked some pertinent questions and then the police were called in. The upshot was that charges were laid against Genie's parents.

On the day they were to appear in court, Genie's father killed himself. He left a note saying 'The world will never understand' – a prediction which is surely correct.

Because she was so severely malnourished, Genie was sent to the Children's Hospital of Los Angeles. Although she was chronologically 13 years 7 months old at this stage,[4] she is said to have had the physical development of a 6- or 7-year-old. Her height was only 54 inches (137 cm) and her weight only 59 pounds (27 kg).

The year was 1970, and a new era now began for Genie. In July 1971 she left hospital and went to live with a foster family. Various linguists, psychologists and psychiatrists began to study her and try to help her to take the long road of development that was necessary for her welfare. These carers seem to have been genuinely concerned to help Genie, and since they were distinguished experts in their fields, they represented a wonderful opportunity for her. But human motivations are never simple, and it was also true that Genie was a heaven-sent opportunity for them to make their mark by doing research on this most unusual case.

Let me sketch why Genie was such a gem as an object of research. Studies with non-human animals had shown that there is an optimum period for the development of certain characteristics, and this came to be known as the critical period. Critical periods had also been proposed for some human characteristics, and Lenneberg (1967) had claimed that there was a critical period for language development, which he estimated lasted from the age of about 2 to the age of puberty. A human being only had to be exposed sufficiently to language during the critical period in order to develop language normally.

When Genie was discovered, she didn't have language. Two important facts about her were relevant to Lenneberg's claim. In the first place, Curtiss reported that in 1970, breast development indicated that puberty had started for Genie. It was dubious, then, whether she was still in the critical period defined by Lenneberg. In the second place, it was not known for certain how much exposure to language she had had. All the evidence suggested it wasn't much. Genie's mother said Genie had begun to speak a few words before she was kept in confinement, and that she stopped shortly after she was confined.

Her lack of language when she was discovered, then, may have been due to the fact that she had had insufficient exposure to language, or to brain damage, or to emotional factors brought on by her horrific experience.

Lenneberg set forth two versions of his hypothesis: (a) a strong version, to the effect that a human being can't acquire a language naturally (by mere exposure) after puberty; and (b) a weak version, to the effect that *normal* language acquisition can't occur naturally after the critical period. The difference is that the weak version allows for the possibility that language might develop after the critical period, but that it wouldn't be normal.

As we saw in more detail in Chapter 9, in adults the left side of the brain is more specialized for language than the right side. But there is some evidence to suggest that the left side doesn't become the dominant side for language until sometime during childhood. That process is called 'lateralization'. According to Lenneberg, lateralization takes place sometime between 2 years of age and puberty, and those are the bounds that he set for normal language acquisition 'by exposure'.

195

But a different view was put forward by Stephen Krashen (1973). He claimed that lateralization is a matter not of age, but of exposure to the language. At whatever age a child is exposed to language experience, lateralization will occur. He believed the process was normally complete by the age of 5 (since most children have virtually learnt their language by then), but that there should be nothing to stop Genie learning language after that, whenever she was exposed to it.

Genie provided the opportunity for a playoff between these two competing theories. If Krashen was right, she should learn language normally; if Lenneberg was right, she would not learn it as well as normal children do, though she might learn it to some extent.

11.4.2 THE RESEARCH

Genie was taught, recorded, filmed and tested a great deal during the time she was being studied. A team of linguists, psychologists, psychiatrists and other scientists were given large grants of money to carry out scientific research on her. As one of them commented in a documentary film for television about Genie (Garmon, 1994), this put them in an invidious position. If they used these grants conscientiously, they were obliged to carry out the tests and the research; but this exposed them to the possible criticism that they cared about their research more than they did about Genie's welfare. On the other hand, if they concerned themselves entirely with Genie's welfare, they risked being found guilty of not using the research money to the best scientific advantage. Of course, they tried to do a bit of each, and fell between the two stools.

The time during which the research was carried out was marked by jealous rivalry about 'possession' of Genie and access to her, by suspicion and infighting, and a good deal of anger. Furthermore, the body that gave the research grants felt that not enough solid scientific data were being assembled for the amount of money spent. Eventually they declined to renew the grants and the study of Genie came to a halt.

In 1975 Genie returned to living with her mother in the house she had been brought up in. The mother had been acquitted of child abuse charges and wanted to look after Genie, but found she couldn't cope. A very dark period followed for Genie. She was assigned to a series of foster homes and was treated abominably: she was physically punished and abused. It seems unpardonable that this was allowed to happen.

Genie's mother brought lawsuits against most of the principal

196

researchers and the children's hospital, claiming that the researchers had carried out too many tests, at the expense of Genie's welfare. Eventually a settlement was reached, but it must have been a period of great pressure for all concerned, including Genie.

At the end of the film about her, it was said that she then lived in an adult-care foster home in southern California and that this was the sixth home she had lived in since the research ended. We would surely wish for a kinder, less isolated fate for Genie.

11.4.3 GENIE'S ACHIEVEMENTS

Let's now examine how far the attempts to teach Genie the English language succeeded. In more than four years of receiving highly expert tuition, only about 2,500 spontaneous utterances of two or more words were recorded. That means she rarely volunteered utterances. She spoke mainly in response to other people's questions, or to express her immediate needs. She often repeated any sequence she spoke.

The strongest part of Genie's language acquisition seems to have been vocabulary. Curtiss (1977) comments that Genie's early words were different from those of children who acquire their language at a normal age. Most of the words the latter use at first are nouns, whereas Genie used almost as many adjectives and verbs as nouns. Her early words included *walk*, *go*, *stopit*, *Genie*, *Mother*, *door*, *blue*, *red*, *no* and *don't*. Again, most children begin to construct two-word sentences when they have a vocabulary of between 30 and 50 words, whereas Genie waited until she had 100 to 200 or more before she embarked on her first two-word utterances.

Negation was an area of grammar where Genie's acquisition proved to be limited. The best study of the acquisition of negation at that stage is a paper, still highly respected, by Klima and Bellugi-Klima (1966). It was described in Chapter 2, pp. 15–16. You may recall that they had found that children develop negation in three stages:

1. Placing the negative word outside the main part of the sentence, e.g. *No want milk*.
2. Sentence-internal negation, but without '*do*-support' – that is, without putting in the word *do* to attach *not* (*-n't*) to; e.g. *I not want milk*.
3. Sentence-internal negation with *do*-support; e.g. *I do not want milk*.

Genie stayed in Stage 1 for almost three years, then moved to a mixture of Stage 2 and Stage 3 types – that is, alongside utterances like *I do not have red pail*, there would be ones like *Ellen not learn PE in school* and *Curtiss not sick*. Normal children stay in Stage 1 for a matter of weeks or sometimes months, but a delay of almost three years before moving on from that stage represents an extraordinary degree of retardation in this feature of the language. Nor did she ever master negation.

Her attempts to master questions were even less successful. As we saw in Chapter 2, one variety of English questions are called Wh questions, because they normally start with a 'Wh word' such as *who, what, when, where, why*. Curtiss comments that Genie's attempts to construct such questions led to the most ill-formed, least English-like structures that she produced. For example:

● Where is may I have a penny? (? = May I have a penny and where is it?)
● Where is tomorrow Mrs L? (? = Where will Mrs L be tomorrow?)
● I where is Graham cracker on top shelf? (? = I want a Graham cracker. Where are they? Are they on the top shelf?

Yet Genie appeared to understand questions, even if she couldn't construct them.

She lacked the ability to form the majority of the most central structures of English. She couldn't form relative clauses, like *The person who's coming tomorrow* . . ., or passive sentences like *The postman was bitten by the dog*; and, as we have just seen, she couldn't form questions or negative utterances efficiently. Furthermore, she didn't express differences of tense (present and past); didn't use modal auxiliaries (like *shall, will, can, would, could, should, must, may, might*); and, apart from *I, you* and *me*, didn't use pronouns – that is, didn't use *he, she, it, him, her, they, them, we, us*, etc.

Most children learn the main sentence structures of English in about two and a half years (between 18 months and 4 years). Four years after she began combining words, Genie's speech was still largely telegraphic. 'The great vocabulary explosion has simply not occurred,' commented Curtiss.

It's true that the teaching of Genie was interrupted when the research grants dried up, and some might want to argue that eventually, if that hadn't happened, she might have reached a stage where she was using language normally. There's a lot of evidence to suggest that that isn't true.

But Curtiss (1977: 204) has this to say:

> Genie's language is far from normal. More important, however, over and above the specific similarities and differences that exist between Genie's language and the language of normal children, we must keep in mind that Genie's speech is rule-governed behavior, and that from a finite set of arbitrary linguistic elements she can and does create novel utterances that theoretically know no upper bound. These are the aspects of human language that set it apart from all other animal communication systems. Therefore, abnormalities notwithstanding, in the most fundamental and critical respects, Genie has language.

Genie had provided answers to the questions about the critical period. Krashen's claim that the age at which language acquisition occurs doesn't matter, and his prediction that Genie would learn language normally, were shown to be wrong. And the weak version of Lenneberg's claim that there was a critical period that came to an end by the onset of puberty seemed to have been shown to be correct – or would have been if Genie had been a normal child.

On the other hand, Genie was not a normal child, and the physical, mental and emotional abuse that she suffered may have meant that she had brain damage. She was given many tests to see if that was true, but none of them seemed conclusive.

What can we say, then, in answer to the question as to whether Genie acquired language, and acquired it normally? The passage from Curtiss quoted above shows that she thinks Genie had acquired language, but hadn't acquired it fully. It seems to me that we can barely allow Genie into the category of those who have acquired language, and certainly we can't allow her into the category of those who have acquired it naturally and fully. Linguists are likely to divide on whether Curtiss's argument is persuasive. So we'd have to say she's an unclear case.

There is a manifest contrast, however, between (a) the children who are deaf signers and those who are speaking children of profoundly deaf parents, on the one hand, and (b) Genie on the other hand; for whereas the former both fall fairly clearly within the boundaries of those who acquire a language normally, the latter does not.

Notes

1. That is, hearing children actually say 'you' when they mean themselves.
2. The names in this real-life case have been changed to preserve the privacy of the people involved.
3. This section draws heavily on the information provided by Curtiss (1988), Curtiss *et al.* (1974), Fromkin (1975), Fromkin *et al.* (1974) and Garmon, (1994).
4. See discussion of the critical period for language learning, a little later in the chapter.

12. Was Dr Dolittle[1] lying?

12.1 Natural animal communication

Animals don't normally communicate with us in English or any other human language, but they have communication systems of their own which are sometimes quite intricate, and which are naturally acquired. Mightn't they all be languages, even if they're not human ones? Is there any essential difference between our human communication systems and animal ones?

Bees are a useful example to take to examine this question, since they have a fairly complex system of communication. An Austrian named Karl von Frisch (1886–1982) became fascinated by the way bees seemed to be able to communicate messages to each other, and he observed them intently between 1945 and 1948. He was intrigued by the fact that when one bee found some food, the message seemed to be passed very effectively to the other bees from the same hive, which were then able to go straight to the food source.

To make his observations easier, he made some special hives with glass fronts on them, so that he could see inside. Each hive contained only one honeycomb. He noticed that when bees returned from a food source, they would do 'dances' on the vertical surface of the honeycomb.

There were two types of dances. In the first one, the bees followed a leader around in a circle, so von Frisch called that one a 'circling' dance. In the second dance, each bee would run in a straight line, wagging its abdomen rapidly from side to side, then make a turn. Von Frisch called this one a 'wagging dance'.

The bees became more and more excited as they danced; then at some point they would go off in search of the food. Not unreasonably, von Frisch concluded that the dances represented a signalling system. After a lot more observation, he worked out that there were several signalling systems going on.

1. *The smell of the food.* Some of the nectar or pollen would stick to the feet of the bee that first found the food, and the smell of it would tell the other bees what kind of food it was.

2. *The vigour of the dance.* The more vigorous the dance was, the more extensive the supply of food was. As the supply diminished, the dance would slow down. The bees would then send out working parties that were just the right size for dealing with the supply available.

3. *Type of dance.* Von Frisch stained one group of bees blue and trained them to feed only a few metres from the hive. He stained another group red and trained them to feed about 300 m away. When they returned to the hive, all the blue bees did circling dances, and all the red bees did wagging dances. That must have been a very satisfying result for von Frisch, because it meant he had virtually cracked the code: the type of dance had something to do with the distance from the hive of the feeding-place.

   He then began to move the food source that was nearer to the hive a little further away each day, and also began to move the one that was 300 m away a little closer in each day. At a distance between 50 and 100 m from the hive, the blue bees switched from a circling dance to a wagging dance, and the red bees made the opposite switch. There was obviously a critical distance that differentiated the two dances. Apparently, different groups of bees (especially ones in different districts) have different 'critical distances', as though there are different 'dialects'.

4. *Frequency of turns in the dance.* The frequency of turns in the wagging dance gives more accurate information about the distance of the food source than the type of dance does. Von Frisch found that when the food was about 100 m away from the hive, the bee made about ten short turns in 15 seconds, whereas when the food was 3000 m away, it made only three long turns in 15 seconds. So the more turns there were, the closer the food was.

5. *Orientation in the dance.* The bees seemed to have a good idea not only of the distance, but also of the direction of the food. Bees navigate by the sun, and they can do this even if the sky is completely overcast. If a bee is caught and put in a box for a few minutes, it will fly straight to the hive when it's released; but if it's kept in the box for an hour, it will have difficulty finding its way, because it continues to fly at the same angle to the sun's direction as when it was caught. But in that time the earth's position has changed in relation to the sun.

As already mentioned, the honeycomb on which the bees dance in the hive is vertical. When the sun, as seen from the hive, appears to be just above the feeding place, as shown in Figure 12.1(a), the straight part of the dance is vertical, with the head up: ↑ . On the other hand, when the feeding place is in just the opposite direction from the sun, as shown in Figure 12.1(b), the straight part of the dance is vertical with the head down: ↓ . Finally, when the food is not on the line between the hive and the position of the sun at all (as shown in Figure 12.1(c)), the bee indicates the horizontal angle between the sun and the food by dancing at the same angle on the honeycomb:↘ .

Figure 12.1 Communication among bees: the orientation of the dance under different conditions (see text)

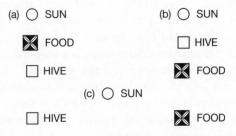

Now, that is a remarkable communication system that the bees use. Can we call it a language? We could call it that, as long as we made clear whether we were using 'language' in the same sense as when we talk about human 'language'. But the bees' communication system has important differences from any human language, and it might be less confusing if we chose another name for it. We might think of it as one example of animal communication, but reserve the name 'language' for the human verbal communication system. But let's leave that question open for a bit longer.

Here's why: human languages are capable of generating an infinite number of sentences (see Chapter 3), whereas animal communication is not capable of doing that in the same sense. It's true that bees can theoretically generate an infinite number of messages, but they're all of the same structure: 'There is food of type W in amount X at distance Y from here in direction Z.' So the system is infinite only in the sense that there are an infinite number of points along a continuum. This is similar

203

to the fact that there are an infinite number of points on a pitch range that the human voice can hit when it screams. But that's a fairly trivial infinitude compared with that of human language, which can generate an infinite variety of structures.

Many other animals apart from bees have interesting communication systems, but bees will serve to make the point.

12.2 Can animals be taught a human language?

A surprisingly large number of dog-owners seem to believe that their dog(s) can understand, albeit not actually use, human language. It's worth examining what such a claim means. It frequently means that when the owner picks up the lead and says 'Will we go for a walk?', the dog gets excited and shows all the signs of being anxious to go. But if the owner said, 'Will we stay at home today and not go for a walk?', using an intonation pattern like the usual one, it's likely that the dog would still react the same way. So perhaps it's only the single word *walk* that (s)he reacts to. Or perhaps it's not even that. Perhaps it's the intonation pattern in the voice, or the time of day, or the sight of the master/mistress picking up the lead, or all of these.

But true believers will say at this point that it's not as simple as that: their dog responds appropriately to many utterances. Like *Sit* and *Stay* and *Come* and *dinner*, etc. Well, how many utterances does (s)he respond appropriately to? Six? Twelve? Some dozens? I'm willing to believe any of these answers, but if the owner says hundreds, I'll be more dubious.

I want to suggest that there's a difference between being able to respond to some dozens of utterances 'appropriately' and being able to analyse those utterances linguistically and extract an accurate meaning. A dog can't do the latter. Even your dog. Furthermore, as Bertrand Russell (1948: 74) wrote, 'A dog cannot relate his autobiography; however eloquently he may bark, he cannot tell you that his parents were honest though poor. A man [i.e. a human being] can do this.'

However, many scientists have dreamt of being able to teach animals to talk, and there have been many attempts. Let's remember, first of all, that parrots and other talking birds don't use language; they just imitate. The scientists referred to above wanted to teach animals to do more than that.

12.2.1 SOME EARLY EXPERIMENTS WITH CHIMPANZEES

The favourite targets of such teaching have been chimpanzees, because of their intelligence and their similarity to human beings. They're usually females, because male chimpanzees are more aggressive and more difficult to handle. The experiments in which they figure have often been carried out by academic couples. In some cases this is because the chimpanzee has had to become part of the household.

Back in the 1930s one such academic couple, Winthrop and Luella Kellogg, raised a female chimp called Gua alongside their infant son Donald. At the age of 16 months, Gua could respond appropriately to about 100 words, which was more than Donald could at that age. Very worried parents, I imagine. Gua, of course, never did try to speak any of these words.

In the 1940s another American academic couple, Keith and Cathy Hayes, tried to raise a female chimp called Vicki in their home. She also learned to respond to a large number of words and with great difficulty could mouth the words 'mama', 'papa' and 'cup'. I've seen this process, which was captured on film, on a television programme, and I can swear that it would take loving 'foster parents' to recognize the words for what they were supposed to be.

Now we come forward to the 1960s, when a third academic couple, Alan and Beatrice Gardner, had a female chimp called Washoe. (Washoe is the name of a county in Nevada.) They made the realistic assumption that it was unlikely that chimpanzees could be taught to talk, since they don't have a suitable vocal tract; they therefore tried to teach Washoe to communicate via American Sign Language. As we've seen, signs in ASL are directly related to meanings and don't work through English or any other spoken language.

In 1969, when she was 4 years old, Washoe could use some 85 signs appropriately, allegedly often initiated 'conversations' and could produce sequences up to five signs long. The sequences, however, were not necessarily sentences, though they sometimes expressed something that could be regarded as a sentence. They could occur in virtually any order, and it wasn't obvious that there was any change in meaning to match a change of order. This, of course, is rather different from the way in which a human language like English or ASL works.

12.2.2 THE PREMACKS AND SARAH

Washoe was to be far outstripped in performance by a 'genius' chimp called Sarah, owned by yet another academic couple, Ann and David Premack. Like the Gardners, the Premacks accepted that chimpanzees couldn't be taught to talk, but instead of using ASL signs as 'words', they used coloured plastic shapes (see Premack and Premack, 1972; Premack, 1977).

Sarah built up a large vocabulary of 'words', and learned to 'read' them and 'write' with them. The Premacks claimed that she used them with 75–80 per cent accuracy.

They describe in detail how a trainer taught her the word 'give'. The first step was to place a piece of banana in front of her where she could reach it. She took it and ate it, and the process was carried out repeatedly. After this became routine, a pink plastic square, which was to be the 'word' for *banana*, was placed near Sarah, and the piece of banana was put in a place where she couldn't get it. She had to learn to put the plastic square (which had metal on the back of it) on to a magnetic board at the side of her cage. No doubt this was achieved more or less by trial and error at first, but after a number of repetitions it became routine.

None of the plastic shapes was iconic – that is, none of them betrayed their meaning either by their shape or their colour: a banana isn't pink, and it isn't square.

When this procedure had become routine with the banana, the trainer taught her a similar routine with apples. The plastic symbol for 'apple' was a blue triangle.

Then a symbol representing the verb 'give' was introduced. Now, in order to get a piece of apple, Sarah had to place the two plastic shapes representing 'give apple' on the magnetic board at the side of the cage. If she put 'apple give' she was not rewarded. Then she was taught a plastic shape to represent her name, 'Sarah', and she had to put the three 'words' *give banana/apple Sarah* before she would be rewarded with the food. Finally, she was taught a plastic shape for her trainer's name, Mary, and she then had to use four plastic shapes to get what she wanted: *Mary give apple/banana Sarah*. At each step, after a number of trials she achieved what was wanted, with a high rate of success.

They taught her other verbs which contrasted with *give*: *wash, cut, insert*, etc. When Sarah signalled 'wash apple', the apple was taken to a bowl of water and washed. In this way, say the Premacks, Sarah learned what action went with what verb.

At this point, we should pause and ask whether we can accept that the plastic shapes are 'words', or that the sequences of them are 'sentences'. Clearly there are enormous differences between what Sarah was doing and what little children do when they learn words. At the time of the *Scientific American* article (Premack and Premack, 1972), the Premacks' approach was as follows:

> Why try to teach human language to an ape? In our own case the motive was to better define the fundamental nature of language. It is often said that language is unique to the human species. Yet it is now well known that many other animals have elaborate communication systems of their own. It seems clear that language is a general system of which human language is a particular, albeit remarkably refined, form. Indeed, it is possible that certain features of human language that are considered to be uniquely human belong to the more general system, and that these features can be distinguished from those that are unique to the human information-processing regime. If, for example, an ape can be taught the rudiments of human language, it should clarify the dividing line between the general system and the human one. (p. 92)

With this ambition in mind, the Premacks pressed on into what they thought were more and more human-like properties of language. They presented three objects, two of which were alike (e.g. two cups and a spoon.) Sarah had to place a particular plastic shape between the two that were alike, and so the meaning of that shape was said to be 'same'. She also had to place another shape between those that were not alike, and this shape was said to have the meaning 'different'.

Next, a 'question mark' (a plastic shape which looked nothing like the usual question mark) was placed between two objects. The question which had been implicit in the previous tests was thus made explicit, according to the Premacks. They said the meaning of this 'interrogative' element was, for example, 'What is the relation between cup A and cup B?' Sarah was given the plastic shapes that meant 'same' and 'different', and had to make a choice. Even more interestingly, Sarah was able to carry out this procedure with numerous objects which had not been used in her training, which suggests she had a generalized conception of what the interrogative shape meant.

A further step into complexity was taken when shapes were introduced to represent the meanings 'name of' and 'not name of'. Sarah was required to place 'name of' or 'not name of' between a plastic shape and a real object (for example, the plastic shape for 'apple' and a real apple,

207

or a plastic shape for 'apple' and a real banana). Sarah learnt to do this with a high degree of accuracy.

It would certainly seem that Sarah was achieving much more than the earlier chimps, Gua, Vicki and Washoe. The Premacks claim that this was 'teaching language with language'. But we must again stop and ask ourselves whether that was really what was happening. After all, no language, in the human sense, was involved. Should we conclude, nevertheless, that Sarah was learning to handle a form of language that could be compared with human language? We'll reserve judgement on this for a bit longer.

And now, the *pièce de résistance*. The Premacks wanted to see if Sarah could handle what is known in linguistics as constituent structure (see Chapter 6) – that is, they wanted to see if she could analyse a 'sentence' into the parts that make up its structure. They taught her to carry out the following instructions (as represented by strings of plastic shapes):

'Sarah insert apple pail'
'Sarah insert banana pail'
'Sarah insert apple dish'
'Sarah insert banana dish'

So far, there was no great advance on what she had already done many times, and she performed successfully. The next step was similar, except that two instructions were given in the same sequence:

'Sarah insert apple pail Sarah insert banana dish'

Again, she was successful in carrying out the instructions. But now came the big step. Note first how we as human beings can delete repetitions in sentences. So instead of saying 'Put the apple in the pail; put the banana in the dish', we can say 'Put the apple in the pail (and) the banana in the dish'. She was confronted with a string of plastic shapes:

'Sarah insert apple pail banana dish'

In order to 'read' this instruction correctly, Sarah would have to know that 'pail' goes with 'apple' and not with 'banana'. In other words, she would have to recognize that the constituent structure was as in (a) and not as in (b) (which would not be structurally well formed);

208

(a)   Sarah insert apple pail || banana dish
(b)   Sarah insert apple || pail banana dish

After suitable training, she managed to do it.

These experiments carried out by the Premacks were certainly remark-able. Nevertheless, there are important differences between what Sarah did and what human beings can do – a fact which the Premacks admit.

The most obvious difference is that plastic shapes aren't words,[2] though they share with phonological words the property of being arbitrarily related to their meanings. (There isn't any reason why the English word 'apple' should mean *apple*, nor any reason why a blue plastic triangle should mean *apple*.) There is excellent evidence that representations of phonological words are stored in the brain, along with their meanings, but no evidence that representations of plastic shapes are, in the case of the chimpanzees who participated in the Premacks' experiments.

Roger Brown (1973) comments, in relation to Sarah's handling of the sequence *Sarah insert banana pail apple dish*:

> it is important to remember that not English words but tokens were used. There is something mesmerizing for the native speaker about the sight of the words which makes it easy to attribute all the linguistic knowledge we bring to such strings to the performance with tokens. (p. 45)

Brown also comments on the very structured nature of the training Sarah received:

> In general Sarah's paradigms seem to function as a set of independent carefully programmed language games. She has almost never (Premack tells me there have been a couple of exceptions) had sessions in which she received several sorts of sentences and never apparently sessions in which any one of all the kinds of sentences she presumably understands might be presented. (p. 48)

He says it reminds him of a two-week course in Japanese that he took once, in which 'a very ingenious teacher programmed her lessons in an almost Skinnerian way'.

Phonological words play a role in the language faculty of the brain, but there is no evidence that plastic shapes do, as David Premack admits. They don't have grammatical functions like 'subject' and 'object', and for that reason alone cannot be used in human-like language operations. (See Chapter 6.)

In fact, David Premack seemed to learn a lot from Sarah's teaching. In the early 1970s, when the *Scientific American* article appeared, he seemed still half in love with behaviourism (see Chapter 3), and very hopeful of success in showing that what Sarah could do and what human beings could do were the same in kind, albeit different in degree. But by 1980 he was convinced that what Sarah was doing was not human-like, and that the plastic 'words' were different in kind from human words. What's more, he was convinced that behaviourism couldn't explain the nature of human language. See Premack (1980).

12.2.3 Duane Rumbaugh and Lana

There have been many other studies with apes to see if they can learn a human-like language. Duane Rumbaugh, working at the Yerkes Regional Primate Center in Georgia, trained a chimp named Lana to communicate by tapping the keyboard of a computer, using symbols rather than alphabetic letters. She also learnt hundreds of symbols.

After more than thirty years of such experiments, most linguists were convinced that apes cannot even go close to learning a language with the full complexity of human languages. And no other type of animal could, either. There is good reason to believe that the difference between animal communication systems and human language may be not just a matter of degree, but one of kind. It might be sensible, then, to preserve the word 'language' for human language.

In popular television programmes there are often attempts to convey the idea that dolphins, whales, apes, spiders and many other species use language. Until recently, all the best evidence seemed to say that they don't, although they have complex communication systems of their own. It seemed possible, therefore, to place these sorts of 'language-learning' feats of animals outside the bounds of language acquisition.

12.2.4 Savage-Rumbaugh and Kanzi

But new questions have been raised in the past few years with some investigations of the talents of bonobos. Bonobos are a species of ape that were ignored for a long time because it was thought they were virtually the same as chimpanzees, to whom they are closely related, and whom they strongly resemble, except that the bonobos are smaller, and somewhat different behaviourally. Savage-Rumbaugh and Lewin (1994) and Savage-Rumbaugh *et al.* (1998) describe a bonobo named Kanzi who can respond to a large number of sentences of English. He's able to respond appropriately to questions by typing the answers on a computer keyboard which contains colourful abstract symbols called lexigrams. He could do this without receiving any explicit training – just by listening while the trainers tried (not very successfully) to train his foster-mother.

Although Kanzi sends messages by typing lexigrams on his computer keyboard, he can often receive them just by listening to the English words spoken by his human companions.

Adjacent to the primate laboratory are 50 acres (20 ha) of forest, which are available for use. Savage-Rumbaugh says that apes in their wild state spend much of the day travelling around the forest looking for food, and for this reason she tried to build Kanzi's vocabulary around these activities. Trails were made, and food was placed in coolers at certain stations in the forest, and renewed each day. The same kind of food was always in the same place, and each stopping-place had a name and a lexigram symbol to represent it. Each day the human carers moved around the forest with Kanzi, 'just as if we were a small group of bonobos searching for food in the wild' (Savage-Rumbaugh *et al.*, 1998: 30).

Kanzi would often travel on the shoulders of one of the humans in the group, and would gesture and move the person's head forcefully with his hands if he wanted her to change direction. If this didn't get the desired result, he would lean his body in the direction he wanted to go, which made it difficult for the person to go any other way.

He was able to use the lexigrams to announce where he wanted to go, and then guide the humans there. It was quite clear, then, that he had mental representations that allowed him to plan the future. He was also able to take them to a particular station even if the humans had merely referred to it in speech. He could take short cuts through the forest (leaving the trails) that they couldn't have done. It's clear that Kanzi is a very interesting animal. And his sister, Panbanisha, is able to perform in similar ways.

Savage-Rumbaugh *et al.* (1998: 207) summarize the things that they can and cannot do, and it makes an interesting list. Below I give a slightly shortened description of the main items. They are based on the kinds of interactions with Kanzi which are described on pp. 65–73 of *Apes, Language and the Human Mind*.

In the first place, Kanzi and Panbanisha can differentiate English phonemes and they understand that sequences of them constitute words.

Second, they recognize the words when they are spoken rapidly in sentences, even where the correct interpretation depends on knowledge of previous utterances.

Third, they have learnt the written symbols that are associated with many of the spoken words, and can use them for purposes of communication, even though they can't speak.

Fourth, they comprehend certain syntactic aspects of utterances: for instance, that the pronoun *it* can refer to a previous sentence, and that word order can be used to signal different relationships, so that Kanzi biting Sue is not the same as Sue biting Kanzi. They understand pronouns of possession such as *mine* and *yours*; expressions of time, such as *now* and *later*; words that express states, such as *hot* and *cold*; that one clause within a sentence can modify another part of the same sentence (e.g. *Get the ball that is outdoors, not the one that is here.*).

Savage-Rumbaugh *et al.* are just as specific in spelling out certain things that the two bonobos cannot do. In the first place, they cannot speak the words, though they have tried to. Second, they cannot match the extremely rapid language-learning performance of normal human children. Third, they have not gone as far as normal human beings. Fourth, they have less short-term memory capacity than normal human children, so that it's more difficult for them to imitate sequences of utterances or actions with only minimal exposure.

On p. 206 Savage-Rumbaugh *et al.* say, 'Given the overwhelming weight of the evidence, the conclusion that apes have a capacity for language can no longer be evaded.' But on p. 181 an even stronger claim is made: 'The linguistic competencies displayed by Kanzi and Panbanisha potentially undermine the assumptions that undergird much of modern linguistics, psychology and philosophy.'

The linguistic skills of Kanzi and Panbanisha all emerged prior to 3 years of age. Other bonobos who were exposed to human speech after that age did not acquire the ability to comprehend it. Kanzi and Panbanisha organized their perceptions of speech in a different manner from their siblings, who did not interact with people before the critical age. Savage-Rumbaugh *et al.* comment (p. 213), 'What these facts reveal, in a rather unequivocal manner, is that language is not innate in any meaningful sense of the word "innate".'

The stakes are high in this argument, then, and the claims made in this book and earlier works by Savage-Rumbaugh and her colleagues have caused strong reactions. Pinker (1994a) dismissed the reported linguistic achievements of Kanzi as being only marginally better than the achievements of ordinary chimpanzees, though that was before the two most recent books, Savage-Rumbaugh and Lewin (1994) and Savage-Rumbaugh *et al.* (1998). Other dismissive criticisms (of earlier work) were made by Wallman (1992).

For a review which has appeared since the publication of Savage-Rumbaugh *et al.* (1998), see Smith (1999). Smith admits that Kanzi can communicate with human beings, at least partly through the medium of English. However, he says, 'The extent to which this communication exploits the kind of grammar standardly attributed to humans is less clear, and the authors seem surprisingly, and explicitly, reluctant to find out (p. 9).'

It would have been easy to test Kanzi's abilities, since he does have 'a large vocabulary, a considerable intelligence, and a willingness to interact with humans' (*ibid.*). Such evidence as there is is mainly anecdotal, and the interpretations given could be challenged.

On one occasion Kanzi was told to 'put some water on the carrot'. His response to this was to throw the carrot outside – and this was counted as a correct response because 'it was raining very heavily at that moment, and tossing the carrot our into the rain was certainly a satisfactory means of getting it wet'. In the light of such judgements, Smith seems justified in lamenting that 'the criteria for a "correct response" are not spelt out' (*ibid.*).

In any case, a generous judgement of Kanzi's reported performance would put him on a par with the average 2-year-old. There is not even any evidence, Smith says, that Kanzi's language system 'obeys the principles of UG [Universal Grammar] (such as structure dependence) characteristic of all stages of language acquisition in children' (*ibid*).

Most people who are adherents of generative linguistics will probably find this a strong argument – even a conclusive one, perhaps. However, it's a strongly theory-dependent argument. By that, I mean that it's only as strong as generative linguistics is, and there are different views on that.

There are repeated complaints by Savage-Rumbaugh *et al.* (1998) that critics of the claims made for Kanzi demand standards of proof that would not normally be demanded for other experimental work. In chapter 4, which is said to be mainly by Savage-Rumbaugh, the following statement appears (p. 181):

> Rarely in science has the presentation of data been subject to so much dispute or discrediting ... Those scientists who are not yet ready to entertain the possibility that a group of animals may be proficient in the capacities of language and reasoned thought have made the data itself the focus of concern.

Stuart Shanker, who is said to be the main author of Chapter 2 of Savage-Rumbaugh *et al.* (1998), has this to say (p. 78):

> No matter how much evidence Savage-Rumbaugh might amass, the skeptic will always respond that Kanzi is not *really* 'encoding' and 'decoding' propositions; he just acts as if he is. An animal, the skeptic assures us, may possibly be conditioned or taught to use sounds to obtain certain ends, but by no means can it acquire *language*; the ability to use sentences to communicate thoughts. And it would appear that nothing that Savage-Rumbaugh has done – or *can* do – could refute this argument. The assertion ... is a consequence of a characteristically modern picture of language as our uniquely human birthright.

It's important to note that Savage-Rumbaugh *et al.* (1998) are not claiming that Kanzi and his sister have language to the full extent that humans have it, or anything like it. The central question, according to Shanker (p. 94ff.) is whether there is a 'bifurcation' of the animal kingdom which puts humans in a qualitatively different category from all the other animals, or whether there is a 'continuum', so that even if animals cannot match human performance in language (a fact that is agreed on all sides), what they can do is of the same kind, only more limited.

It's an argument that has been going on for decades, and looks like going on for more decades yet. In his excellent chapter, Shanker does persuade me that part of the reason for the strong resistance to Savage-Rumbaugh's claims is the existence of strongly entrenched ideas, such as the idea that human beings are unique in being the only species to have language. On the other hand, it doesn't persuade me that that's the only reason for the resistance, as I think the authors of this book would like me to believe. After all, when a book claims to overturn the basis of modern linguistics, psychology and philosophy, scholars have the right – even the duty – to look very sceptically at it.

Meanwhile, interesting experiments are going forward. For example, a team at the Mount Sinai School of Medicine's Department of Otolaryngology, led by Dr Patrick Gannon, have plans to monitor activity in the language regions of the brain of a bonobo such as Kanzi, using magnetic resonance imaging (MRI) and positron emission tomography (PET) (see Chapter 10). In particular, they want to see what happens while the bonobo is engaged in tasks involving communication (Gannon *et al.*, 1998).

The main focus of interest is the planum temporale (PT), an area which in the human brain is involved in communications. It is widely regarded as a key component of Wernicke's area of the brain. The part of the chimpanzee's brain that is involved in communications (gestures, grunts and hoots) is structurally the same.

Other researchers say that even if these experiments show that the system of communication in apes is more complex than previously thought, it still won't amount to language, in the human sense. This work should add an extra dimension to the debate.

Another interesting line of research is the use of the 'preferential looking procedure', which will be described in Chapter 13 as a means of testing what was going on in the brains of human babies. King (1996), in a review of his book, discusses the suggestion of Marc D. Hauser that this procedure is 'an elegant entry into the mind of the nonlinguistic organism'. As we shall see in Chapter 13, the 'preferential looking procedure' tests how long babies look at certain objects or events. They tend to look longer at 'impossible' events (such as a ball passing through a solid table) than at 'possible' events. Hauser proposes ways in which the preferential looking test can be applied to primates in order to learn more about their cognition. He and his colleagues have already carried out such tests, in fact, with macaques.

I intend to watch this debate with interest over the next few years. All the linguistic and philosophical beliefs I've held for a good many years make me want to reject Savage-Rumbaugh's claims, and yet Shanker, in particular, has convinced me that the whole question deserves to stay open for a bit longer. I find this fence quite comfortable.

Notes

1. Dr Dolittle was the main character in a series of books for children written by Hugh Lofting, the first of which appeared in 1920. The doctor's most important characteristic was that he claimed to be able to 'talk to the animals', and understand them, too.
2. For an interesting discussion of the issues, see Premack (1990).

13. 'Bootstrapping' – A

13.1 Introduction

In recent years important discoveries have been made about the abilities of very small infants (Mehler and Dupoux, 1990, 1994). So far the research has revealed that children 'know' a lot more, at a much younger age, than anyone previously imagined. Much of the research has concerned infants only a few months old, or a few weeks, or even a few days.

Various studies have dealt with what infants 'know' about language, the physical world, mathematics, psychology and notation. How can this be? How can researchers get inside the minds of babies to find out what they know about these matters? Some very clever techniques have been developed which indicate what *seems* to be going on.

The first involves the use of the sucking reflex as an indicator of what the baby's attending to. The baby is made to suck on an artificial nipple attached to a machine which measures the strength of the sucking.[1] What it measures is non-alimentary sucking; the nipple doesn't deliver milk or any other substance.

When a new object is shown to the baby, it sucks more vigorously, apparently from interest. But as it continues to look at the object, interest gradually becomes less, and the sucking becomes less vigorous. Then a different object is presented. If the baby sucks more vigorously again, we can conclude that it perceives the new object as different from the previous one. The 'objects' can be toys, designs on screens, or anything that the baby can see. And a similar technique can be used with sounds and with tactile stimuli.

In the case of visual designs, the experimenter can vary the size, shape, colour, etc. to test the baby's reactions as indicated by the sucking reflex. If a blue circle is shown to the baby until it becomes habituated to it and its sucking becomes less vigorous, and then a red

216

circle replaces the blue one, the baby can have one of two reactions. If it goes on sucking at the same rate, we can conclude that it doesn't perceive any difference, and that perhaps it therefore can't yet distinguish red from blue. On the other hand, if its sucking suddenly becomes more vigorous, we can conclude that it has perceived the difference and is interested in the change of colour.

The second technique for exploring what the baby is conscious of is to measure the duration for which the baby looks at a stimulus. If the same stimulus is shown repeatedly, the baby's looking time will become shorter and shorter as it becomes habituated to the object, but if a new stimulus replaces the old one, the baby's looking time may become longer, indicating that it perceives a difference and is showing renewed interest. If the attention span doesn't change, then presumably the baby perceives no difference. The observers who are recording the looking time must not know which particular display is being presented on any trial, so that the measurement will be as objective as possible.

There's a third technique for exploring what the baby's conscious of, which doesn't involve habituation and dishabituation. It's called the 'preferential looking' method. This label could easily be misconstrued. It doesn't mean 'a method that looks preferential', but 'a method that assesses which of two images or objects the baby prefers looking at'. Two different displays are shown to the baby simultaneously, and observers record the time during which the eyes are focused on each one. Thus an assessment is made of which one the baby prefers to look at.

These techniques have been applied to a number of different issues.

13.2 Knowledge of the physical world

I'll take an example of what infants know about the physical world, just to give you the flavour. Elizabeth Spelke, who is a pioneer in this field, comments (1985: 325), 'Human adults perceive the boundaries and the complete shapes of objects with an ease that is remarkable, for those boundaries are not reflected, in any simple way, in the pattern of light at the eye.'

What if one object is partly hidden by another one that is in front of it? Adults seem to be able to tell, without difficulty, that there are two objects and not just one combined one, and to perceive where the boundaries of each object lie. What about small infants? In order to find out what infant perceptions were like, Spelke carried out a number of

217

experiments with 4-month-old babies, involving the preferential look-ing method I've already described.

Figure 13.1 Infant perception test: schematic depictions of (a) the habituation display, and (b) the test displays of a partly occluded object
After P.J. Kellman and E. S. Spelke, Perception of partially occluded objects in infancy. *Cognitive Psychology*, 15 (1983). By kind permission of the publisher and authors. Copyright © 1983, Academic Press.

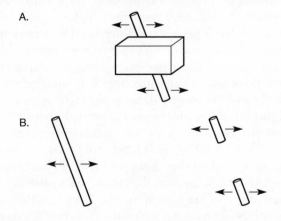

One, detailed by Kellman and Spelke (1983) and Spelke (1985),[2] involved a block-like object and a rod which moved to and fro behind the block (see Figure 13.1a). As the figure shows, the top and the bottom of the rod were visible, but the middle part was not. A number of trials were carried out, which lasted as long as the baby kept looking at the display. If the baby looked away for 2 seconds, that trial was ended.

For the first few trials, the babies tended to keep looking for 10 to 30 seconds, and then their looking times became shorter. They had 'habituated' to the display. When their looking time had diminished to half of what it had previously been, the block was removed and the babies were shown two different displays, which alternated. The two displays are shown in Figure 13.1B.

If the infant had seen the rod in Figure 13.1A as a single object, partly hidden by the block, then the habituation that had occurred with respect to this display should carry across to the complete rod on the left-hand side of Figure 13.1B, and consequently the infant should find the discontinuous rods on the right-hand side of Figure 13.1B more interesting to look at. On the other hand, if the infant had seen the display in Figure 13.1A as involving two separate short rods, one above and one below the block, the habituation that occurred should carry across to the display with the gap, and so the infant should prefer looking at the complete rod.

Adults see the rod as one connected object behind the block, since the two pieces move in unison and match up in colour and shape. The infants looked longer at the rod with the gap, which provided evidence that they also saw the rod as a connected whole behind the block.

That is only one of a number of experiments of this general kind. It is a clever experiment; it and others like it have certainly increased our knowledge of how infants perceive objects.

In the mid-1980s a number of experiments by Renée Baillargeon and colleagues (Baillargeon, 1986; Baillargeon *et al.*, 1985, 1990) showed that infants as young as 5 months understand that objects continue to exist when they're hidden from sight (say by another object). This is contrary to the claim by Piaget (1937, 1954) that, although the infant can grasp objects at between 3 and 6 months of age, it is not until the age of 9 or 10 months that (s)he does an active search for objects that have disappeared, and not until then that the infant has the concept of objects being permanent.

In one experiment reported by Baillargeon *et al.* (1985), infants aged 5 months were shown a screen that 'moved back and forth through a 180-degree arc, in the manner of a drawbridge'. However, most drawbridges that I have seen depicted can't move through 180 degrees, but only through about 90, so it might be better to forget about the drawbridge. Let's just restrict ourselves to saying it's a screen which, from a base position on the ground, can move through an arc of 180 degrees as if it were on a hinge. The infants were habituated to this sight, and then a box was placed in a central position behind the screen, at first visible but becoming hidden as the screen was raised to hide it. Next the babies were shown two events, one of which was possible and the other impossible.

In the 'possible' event, the screen was raised until it hid the box, and then it stopped. In the 'impossible' one, the screen continued moving until it went through the space occupied by the box.

The infants looked longer at the impossible event than at the possible one, showing that there was something surprising about it which

219

occupied their attention longer. From these results, the authors drew two main conclusions: (a) that the infants understood that the box continued to exist after it was hidden by the screen, and (b) that they expected the screen to stop when it reached the occluded box, and when it didn't do so they reacted as if they were surprised or puzzled.

This experiment refutes Piaget's claim about the chronology of object permanence.

13.3 Discrimination of language sounds

Let's begin by asking how good babies are at discriminating sounds, up to the age of 6 months.

They can tell the difference between a voiced sound like /g/ and the equivalent 'voiceless' one, in this case /k/; between two sounds that differ only in their place of articulation (e.g. /b/ and /g/); and between two sounds that differ only in their manner of articulation, such as /d/ and /n/ (Jusczyk, 1997: 69).

How do we know? The same techniques of measuring attention that were described earlier can be used for these tests, too. Jusczyk and Thompson (1978) describe some experiments in which the aim was to see whether 2-month-old infants could detect the difference between two contrasting stop consonants in sequences of two syllables.

First of all, the investigators wanted to see whether it made any difference to the perception of the infants whether the two sounds were contrasted in initial position or in medial position (in the middle of the sequence). So, for a time the infants were exposed to the stimulus [Bada], and the sucking rate was measured. When the sucking rate had decreased by 25 per cent or more (indicating that the baby had become habituated to that sequence), the stimulus changed to [Gada], and new measurements were made of the sucking rate. The increase in the sucking rate after the change showed that the baby had noticed the change and was attending more eagerly to the new stimulus.

Although experiments have focused more on consonants than on vowels, there is also evidence that infants can discriminate between various kinds of vowels.

A few years ago, in a television programme called *Language and the Brain*, Patricia Kuhl, of the University of Washington, presented a more visual technique of demonstrating children's ability to discriminate sounds than the ones I've discussed above. An infant who was

15 months old listened to an adult voice say the vowel [i] repeatedly: [i] – [i] – [i] . . . At a certain point, the vowel changed to [a] and the child looked to one side, just a fraction of a second before a bright, active, interesting toy lit up on that side. The fact that the child looked in that direction *before* the toy lit up and became active meant that she must have known what was going to happen. And the only clue to that was the fact that the vowel changed from [i] to [a]. She'd obviously been through this routine before, but that wouldn't help her to know the exact instant when the toy would go into action. That had to be because she recognized the change of vowel; so obviously she could discriminate between the two vowels. Another very clever device to show what was going on in a baby's mind.

But the demonstration didn't end there. In the next run-through, different voices were used saying the first vowel (this time [a]): a man's voice, a woman's voice and a child's voice. The voice just before the change of vowel was a man's, but the voice that came in on the change of vowel to [i] was a child's. It made no difference. The infant again turned her head in the direction of the toy just before the toy became active.

Now, as Patricia Kuhl pointed out, this is truly remarkable. The physical sounds of the three different voices were quite different from each other, yet the baby was able to filter out these differences and concentrate on the change of vowel quality. In other words, the baby generalized the sound [a] to embrace three different productions of it by three different voices. Nevertheless, there's also evidence that infants are sensitive to differences between speakers.

13.4 From speech sound to syntax

A particularly interesting question that's been explored in very recent times is: how do children get from the stage where they can only make sounds to the stage where they can use utterances with grammatical structure? Though it might seem a simple question, it is, of course, a tantalizingly difficult one. If we could find an answer to it, we would have solved one of the greatest scientific problems in existence. That's why a great number of very good researchers have spent a lot of time on this problem.

One of the main thrusts of research has been to explore whether the prosody of speech gives any clues as to where phrase boundaries occur in

221

utterances. (Prosody refers to the rhythm of speech, which involves such things as stress and vowel length. Stress, in turn, may involve pitch changes (intonation), loudness, and so on.)

The idea is that babies may pick up the prosodic patterns in the speech around them and extract clues from them which would help them to sort out the phrasing of an utterance and ultimately lead them to an appreciation of grammatical structure.

Mehler *et al*. (1988) report on an experiment in which 4-day-old French infants and 2-month-old American infants were able to distinguish between utterances in their native languages and ones in another language. This seems an astonishing claim, but is well supported by the experiment.

The paper begins by pointing out that a crucial task for the infant is to distinguish speech from a host of other noises that occur in the environment: noises from animals, machines, trucks, bells, etc. Then there is the additional task of dealing with the variation that occurs in speech in rate of utterance, voice quality, accent, and so on. And they must do all this so as never to treat two utterances from different languages as if they belonged to the same language. As the authors say (p. 144), 'If utterances from several different languages are classified as belonging to the same language, then inappropriate generalizations may be drawn about the regularities that hold within the native language.'

They wanted to use the same voice throughout the experiment, so they used a bilingual who sounded like a native speaker in the two languages that were to be used (in the judgement of native speakers of both). She was fluent in both French and Russian, so the experimenters recorded samples of her speech in those two languages and presented them to 4-day-old French infants. There were 40 such children, all from monolingual families. The investigators had to test 64 babies in order to obtain 40 subjects. Four babies were excluded for crying, sixteen for failing to suck for three consecutive samples, and four for failing to habituate within 30 trials. (It seems young to be a failure in life . . .)

The bilingual speaker recorded samples of her speech in the two languages, in which she gave an account of part of her life. The same events were covered in each language. She didn't know what the speech samples were to be used for. Fifteen different samples were chosen for each language, which lasted varying times from 13 to 22 seconds. An artificial nipple was used to record the sucking responses of the infants.

There isn't sufficient space here to describe in detail the eight experiments that were carried out. The main result was that the French children were able to tell French from Russian even though they were only 4 days old, and responded differently to the two languages. When two unfamiliar languages were used, the children weren't able to discriminate one from the other.

How do the children manage to discriminate between a familiar and an unfamiliar language? The authors discuss whether prosodic factors might be the key. However, they say, 'We are *not* presently in a position to say that infants rely solely, or even principally, on prosodic information to distinguish intact native language utterances from foreign ones. Nevertheless, this is an interesting line of investigation.'

There are many other papers which attempt to justify the 'prosodic bootstrapping hypothesis'. Hirsch-Pasek *et al.* (1987) studied 7- to 10-month-old infants to see how sensitive they were to acoustic properties which correlated with clause units.

Pauses were inserted at clause boundaries in sample recorded utterances, taken from speech directed by a mother to her 19-month-old daughter (motherese). Then, by way of contrast, pauses were also inserted in matching sample utterances, only this time not at clause boundaries, but at points internal to the clauses. The infants attended longer to the utterances in which the pauses were at clause boundaries. The authors conclude that 'The prelinguistic infant apparently possesses the means to detect important units such as clauses, within which grammatical rules apply' (p. 269).

For an excellent collection of papers discussing the 'prosodic bootstrapping hypothesis', see Morgan and Demuth (1996). If you then have an appetite for more, there are a lot of useful references given in that book. One of the best chapters in the volume is by Fernald and McRoberts (1996). Near the beginning, the authors say (p. 365):

> The appeal of the prosodic bootstrapping hypothesis is easy to understand. If the boundaries between syntactic constituents in speech were indeed reliably marked by constellations of prosodic features such as pauses, pitch contours and vowel lengthening, this acoustic punctuation could potentially be useful to the child beginning to learn language.

But although the hypothesis has been very popular with researchers, the data to support it are not very compelling, and rest 'on a selective use of indirect evidence' (p. 365).

223

Fernald and McRoberts challenge the frequently made claim that in adult-directed speech, boundaries of clauses and phrases are regularly shown by pauses, changes of pitch and lengthening of speech segments. They examine the evidence carefully, and decide that, as far as pauses are concerned, the studies commonly quoted 'do not provide convincing evidence for the potential value of pauses as cues to syntax for the infant' (p. 370). They argue further that it isn't clear how adults would use the elongation of speech segments as cues 'without first working out various other aspects of the sentence, and it is certainly not obvious that infants should be able to do so' (p. 372).

The chapter continues in this way, analysing and dismissing the arguments for all the alleged markers of syntactic structure. Then Fernald and McRoberts say:

> Thus we have not learned much new about the prosodic fine structure of ID [infant-directed] utterances that is relevant to the discovery of syntax. . . . And the central argument of Newport et al. (1977) is as relevant today as it was then: whatever their pragmatic merits, the modifications in maternal speech do not provide easy access to phrase structure trees.
>
> This is not to say that prosody is unimportant in revealing language structure – only that its potential role has been oversimplified in the prosodic bootstrapping debate as we see it. (p. 384)

In Chapter 7 we discussed the idea of a discovery procedure, and saw that it was not possible to arrive at one. In many ways, the prosodic bootstrapping hypothesis has involved yet another attempt to provide a discovery procedure. So far it hasn't succeeded, though maybe it will one day. It's rather more sophisticated than the simple example of a failed discovery procedure we examined in Chapter 7, and its proponents accept that there are some innate properties. As we will see, though, in Chapter 15, allegations of innateness are not beyond challenge, either.

You're this far into the book and you still don't know how children construct their first utterances. Furthermore, there will still be a certain amount of mystery about it when you've finished reading the book, since no one knows the full answer. But don't go away: there are a lot of interesting things to learn yet about how children acquire language.

13.5 Acquisition of vocabulary

Let's move away from the phonetic end of the spectrum and look at the other end, where children are learning some words. Suppose that children begin by learning what individual words mean. Notice that they do have to do this: the words can't be innate, or all languages would have the same vocabulary. But that doesn't mean that the concepts with which the words are associated couldn't be innate, or partly innate.

The most likely thing is that children leap to an understanding of the early words by hearing them in a situation where it's obvious what the meaning is. I have in mind the sort of situation where the child's mother holds out a ball while saying the word 'ball'. It may take a while, but after a time the child gets the idea.

You probably already know the story of Helen Keller. When she was 19 months old, she caught scarlet fever, which left her blind and deaf. When she was 7, her parents employed a tutor for her, named Anne Sullivan. Sullivan turned out to be a brilliant teacher of her unusual pupil. First she taught Helen the manual alphabet, in which each letter has a code, and which is signed on to the back of the hand. One day she took Helen to a water-pump and let the water fall on the child's hand, while signing each letter of 'water' on to the back of her hand. Helen, who was very intelligent, suddenly had a great revelation. First she recognized that her tutor was spelling out the name of what was flowing on to her hand, and then it came to her: 'Everything must have a name.' She is said to have run around touching things and asking Anne Sullivan what the name of each thing was. She subsequently learnt to speak and to understand what people were saying by putting her fingers against their lips while they were talking. In adult life she lectured and wrote very successful books. In one of them she recalled the day she had that revelation.

What I want to suggest is that every child must have a revelation of a similar kind, but since most of them can see and hear normally, they have it a lot earlier, and with less difficulty.

Some modern experiments, such as the one described by Baldwin (1993), have established that infants of only 16 to 19 months learn to match spoken labels to objects. (In some cases infants a good deal younger than 16 months can do it.) That isn't as straightforward as it might sound.

Suppose the child hears a new label and understands that there's something in the surrounding context to which it's being applied. How

225

does (s)he know *which object* it's being applied to? Perhaps the child's mother might touch the object she's naming; but that won't help much if the child's looking at something else at that moment. In fact, it might lead her/him to make a wrong identification of the word with what (s)he's gazing at. Of course, wrong mappings of this kind could seriously impede learning, and produce confusion.

As Baldwin suggests, however, this can be overcome to some extent if the mother notices what the child is looking at, and then names the object that is in focus.

Baldwin found that, even at 16 to 19 months, children were able to be active in looking for cues as to which object was meant. She found that if there was a discrepancy between what the child was looking at and what was named, the child was more likely to look at the experimenter to see the direction of her gaze than if there was no discrepancy. Other non-verbal clues help the child, too; for example, the mother might point to the object she means, or hold it out for the child's inspection, or the context might be such that there is really only one object that could be meant. Baldwin (1993: 146) comments:

> The findings provided clear support for an early appreciation of the linguistic significance of the speaker's nonverbal cues. Infants did not tend to make mapping errors when they were introduced to novel labels under discrepant labeling conditions. Rather, they tended to select the visible toy when it was the correct referent ... but not when it was an incorrect referent.

So let's suppose that by such experiences, the child gradually develops the beginnings of a vocabulary, and gets to know the meanings of a number of words. It's still a long way from there to talking in sentences, and the crucial question is 'How does the child now make progress towards that goal?' We'll take that question up in the next chapter.

Notes

1. More precisely, it measures the amplitude of the sucking.
2. For further examples of Spelke's work, see Spelke (1988, 1990, 1995).

14. 'Bootstrapping' – B

14.1 Semantic and syntactic bootstrapping

Grimshaw (1981: 174) made a very interesting suggestion about how children make progress in learning vocabulary. She pointed out that there's good evidence that, quite early in their linguistic development, children understand notions like 'object' (thing) and 'action', and that the child might make use of these in arriving at syntactic (grammatical) categories. She assumed, as most other linguists do, that much of what goes on in the child's mind is unconscious.

Grimshaw's suggestion was that if a word is the name of an object, the child might (unconsciously) assign it to a category which a linguist would describe as 'noun'. If a word describes an action, it would be assigned to a different category, which linguists call 'verb'.

As we have seen in Chapter 6, not all nouns refer to objects (e.g. 'love'), and not all verbs refer to actions (e.g. 'own'). Furthermore, 'action' is a noun, not a verb, as we might expect if all words that refer to actions are verbs. Nevertheless, the majority of nouns that a young child would meet are probably objects, according to Grimshaw. In any case, if a noun or verb crops up which doesn't conform to the child's notions, then it will just have to be ignored.

The views expressed by Grimshaw were picked up by Pinker (1982) and extended. Like Grimshaw, he supposes that the child provisionally assumes 'that words for perceptible concrete objects are nouns, words for actions are verbs, and words correlated with the specificity of objects in discourse are determiners' (p. 678). He further assumes that the child first of all hears nouns and verbs in isolation from each other, when they are accompanied by the objects and actions to which they refer, and that subsequently the learner 'hears determiners plus nouns in situations where the specificity of the noun was already known. Then the categorisation of each word could be deduced' (p. 678).

Thus the child learns the categories from what (s)he has already learnt about the meanings of words. But beyond that, the child can now work out the order of the categories in a sentence – can work out that a sentence like *cats drink milk* has the order NOUN–VERB–NOUN.

There is more to it than that, since sentences not only contain a certain word order, but also require the grouping of words into phrases. Pinker's explanation of how the child acquires a knowledge of the phrase structure of sentences involves an appeal to certain innate knowledge about it. He believes the child has a pathway into the grammatical structure of sentences via the knowledge that (s)he has already acquired of word meanings. This process has come to be known as 'semantic bootstrapping'.

Once the child has come to understand something of the positions of word classes in sentences, then (s)he can incorporate new words into, say, the class 'noun' – words like *dream* and *measles* that would not have met the simple definition of 'physical object' that (s)he started with. That definition, then, is used only as a starter, and is later expanded. Likewise, verbs can be expanded from the simple concept of action words, to embrace states (such as *own*, *have*) as well.

In support of the simple differentiation of nouns and verbs as representing 'physical objects' and 'physical actions' at first, Pinker cites the interesting work reported by Feldman *et al.* (1978). Deaf children who are isolated from other users of sign language invent some signs of their own: pointing signs are used to represent objects, while iconic signs are used to represent actions. An iconic sign is one that suggests its meaning by mime: for instance, as we saw in Chapter 11, crying might be represented by fingers being drawn from the eyes down along the cheeks. The fact that deaf children also make a basic distinction between physical objects and actions suggests that this is a readily available distinction which may be innate.

Lila Gleitman (1990) has claimed that as well as using word semantics to acquire syntax (semantic bootstrapping), children use verb syntax to learn verb semantics, a process which she calls syntactic bootstrapping. (See also Landau and Gleitman, 1985.) Note that Gleitman doesn't try to refute Pinker's claim that word semantics is used by children to bootstrap themselves to a knowledge of syntax; rather, she claims that syntactic bootstrapping and semantic bootstrapping both occur.

228

Gleitman sets forth some interesting arguments for her views, but Pinker (1994b) doesn't accept them and gives detailed counter-arguments. It's a debate that will no doubt continue, and it isn't easy to predict the final outcome. We won't examine Gleitman's arguments or Pinker's responses here; those who would like to know more about them should study them first-hand by reading Gleitman (1990) and Pinker (1994b).

14.2 'Constraints' on word learning

There used to be an anecdote current among linguists, about a linguist who was trying to record and analyse the language of a tribe somewhere in Africa. By gesturing, he somehow managed to convey to a member of the tribe that he wanted him to say what certain objects were called, in his language. The linguist pointed to a tree, in order to elicit the word for that. 'Ugu-ugu' the man said, and the linguist recorded it in his notebook. Next, he pointed to a rock. 'Ugu-ugu', the informant said. The linguist wrote that in his notebook, too, but remarked in his notes that this word had at least two meanings. Then he pointed to the river. 'Ugu-ugu', he was told. He wrote that down, too, but began to be suspicious about the apparent paucity of words in this language. By the time he had asked about a dozen objects and had always received the reply 'ugu-ugu', he was *highly* suspicious. He eventually found out that 'ugu-ugu' was the word for a finger, so that whatever he pointed to, the informant thought he was asking what the word for *finger* was. I can't guarantee that this story is true, though it may be and I'd really like it to be.

Some years ago the American philosopher Willard Quine (1964) made a highly relevant point about such elicitation techniques. He asked the reader to imagine a situation in which a linguist is trying to elicit the native word for 'rabbit' by pointing to a rabbit. The informant says 'gavagai', and Quine asks how the linguist is to know whether 'gavagai' means the whole rabbit or just a part of it, like a leg, or the mouth, or the tail. For that matter, it could mean just a fleeting glimpse of a rabbit. And although Quine doesn't say so, 'gavagai' might even mean 'sick' or 'pregnant'.

A similar point is relevant if a mother points to a tree and says to her child 'tree', or 'That's a tree.' How does the child know that the word 'tree' doesn't refer to a branch, or a leaf, or a twig, or the trunk? Or, for that matter, to the mother's finger? And if a bird happens to emerge from the foliage just at that moment, it could perhaps refer to the bird. You can see the difficulty. It's a difficulty that's caused an enormous amount of discussion in recent years, in writings about the way children acquire words and come to an understanding of their meanings.

As Waxman (1994: 230) put it:

> How do infants so rapidly learn that a given word (e.g., flamingo) may apply to a particular whole object and may be extended to other members of that object category (e.g., other flamingoes), but not to salient properties of the object (e.g., its long neck or unusual colour), to salient actions in which it is engaged (e.g., feeding its young) or to salient thematic relations (e.g., a flamingo and sand)? If children had to rule out these and countless other logically possible candidate meanings, word learning would be a formidable task indeed.

Notice that the last sentence implies that word learning is not a formidable task, and, in the sense that virtually every child achieves it, it apparently isn't. But consider what children have to do in order to learn a word. They must notice that there's a certain sequence of sounds which is used repeatedly, and must notice that it seems to be a word. Also, they must recognize that it's the same word each time they hear it (though that's risky, since some different words sound the same – like *flour* and *flower*). They must also have the concept to which the word refers. Of course, they're likely to have many other concepts, too, so they have to be able to figure out which one belongs to this word. But, as Waxman says, the task of selecting which possible meaning goes with which sound sequence would be impossibly hard if there were no clues.

Many linguists and psychologists believe that that help comes from inborn 'biases' or 'constraints' in the brain, which make the child prefer certain kinds of answers to others. The general idea of constraints was put forward over thirty years ago by Noam Chomsky (see Chapter 6). The constraints he suggested then, however, were to do not with word learning but with syntax. Chomsky would almost certainly not agree with the particular proposals put forward by Waxman and others. In fact, he's much more radical in his suggestions, as we shall see a little later.

Well, what are these 'biases' that are said to be built into children's minds?

230

14.2.1 THE WHOLE-OBJECT BIAS

It's been claimed that one of the 'biases' is that children expect that the first word they hear applied to a novel object will be the name for the whole object, and not for one of its parts (Markman, 1991). Thus in the case of the mother who pointed to a tree and said 'tree' or 'That's a tree', the child would expect 'tree' to refer to the whole object she was pointing to. If a bird flies out just at the instant when she points, then there is the possibility of a misunderstanding, but then that's always a possibility. This constraint is often known as the whole-object constraint (or bias).

14.2.2 THE TAXONOMIC BIAS

Another 'bias' or constraint is that the child will be predisposed to believe that that word will also apply to any other object of the same kind – that is, that the word *dog* can refer not only to a particular dog that someone may be pointing at, but also to any member of the whole class of similar individuals. This is sometimes known as the taxonomic constraint[1] (Markman, 1991).

14.2.3 THE MUTUAL EXCLUSIVITY BIAS

A third 'bias' that children are said to have is that any given object will have only one label or name. This is sometimes known as the mutual exclusivity constraint. Thus if a child is shown two objects and he/she knows the name for one of them, and if an unfamiliar word is used for one of them, the child will assume that the novel word refers to the object whose name is not known (Markman, 1991).

14.2.4 THE SHAPE BIAS

A fourth 'bias' was proposed by Landau *et al.* (1988) and dubbed the shape bias. Clark (1973) had also mentioned the same matter. Landau *et al.* were concerned with the question of how children judge two or more items to be the same, so that they will apply the same label to them. They did experiments (involving adult as well as child subjects)

231

which showed that shape was an important factor in judging class membership. The adults would not put items in the same lexical category as a standard one if they differed from it in shape, though if they differed from the standard one in either size or texture, they didn't reject them. Children showed a similar bias, though less marked. Landau *et al.* comment:

> Our data are thus consistent with previous findings of a shape emphasis in early word learning [Clark, 1973]. However, the results extend and clarify previous findings by suggesting that the bias is not equally strong in all cases. First, there was a developmental trend: the bias increased in strength and generality from 2 to 3 years of age and more markedly from early childhood to adulthood. (p. 316)

Soja *et al.* (1991) reported experiments designed to show that children who have not yet learnt any syntax already make a crucial distinction between individuated whole objects and non-solid substances, and that this distinction plays an important role in their learning of new words. They rejected the claim of Landau *et al.* (1988) that shape is crucial in projecting noun meanings. Their experiments show that 2-year-olds ignore shape when a newly heard noun refers to a non-solid substance. So do 5-year-olds and adults. In addition, young children use many abstract nouns, and the question of shape is irrelevant for them.

Playing devil's advocate, Soja *et al.* (1991) then suggest that Landau *et al.* (1988) might have meant that shape is relevant only when the referent is a solid object. But even this isn't so. They say:

> Data from [Keil, 1989] show that adults, and even early elementary-aged children, are robustly sensitive to how an animal came to get its shape in deciding what that animal is. For example, adults and 10-year-olds are certain that if an antelope were to get a long neck by plastic surgery, it would not become a giraffe, even if the surgeon made it physically indistinguishable from a giraffe. (p. 207)

14.2.5 THE GRAMMATICAL CATEGORY BIAS

A fifth 'bias' or assumption that's been attributed to children is that they can learn something about a word's meaning from the grammatical category to which it belongs. You might feel it's unlikely that children of about 2 would know anything about grammatical categories; and you would be right, in the sense that children don't consciously know anything about them.

But recall the experiment reported by Katz *et al.* (1974) and described in Chapter 6 of this book. They showed that girls of only 17 months of age acted as though they knew the difference between proper nouns and common nouns. You'll recall that one group of girls were told that a particular doll was 'Dax', and the other group was told that the doll was 'a dax'. You may also recall that later, each girl from the first group was told, 'Show Dax to Mummy', and they each picked up the doll that had been shown to them in the first place. The girls from the second group were told 'Show a dax to Mummy', and they chose either of the dolls, seemingly at random.

There were more details, as you can see in Chapter 6, but overall the experiment suggested that the girls could tell the difference between a common noun and a proper noun even if they hadn't heard that particular one before.

Having now recalled some evidence that little children do act as though they have some (unconscious) knowledge of grammar, let's return to the main direction we were taking, which was to describe some of the biases or constraints that seem to guide the children's approach to vocabulary acquisition.

Waxman (1994) claimed that children assume they can learn something about a word's meaning from the grammatical category to which it belongs. She was especially interested in the linkages between word-learning and the organization of concepts in the brain, and in this connection she picked up some ideas expounded by Rosch *et al.* (1976).

For any object, there is a whole hierarchy of labels that can be applied to it. For instance, suppose someone has a dog – a golden retriever called Pilot (because he is owned by a blind woman). The name 'Pilot' refers to an individual, but the term 'golden retriever' is the name of a class of similar individuals. The class name ignores the differences between Pilot and other golden retrievers, like Rover and Diesel. To this extent it's an abstract term.

But Pilot could also be referred to as a 'dog', and this term ignores more differences among the members of its class than 'golden retriever' does. As well as ignoring the differences between Pilot, Rover and Diesel, it ignores those between golden retrievers and alsatians and corgis. It is therefore a more abstract term than 'golden retriever'.

Figure 14.1 Basic level: the 'basic' level in this hierarchy is the middle one

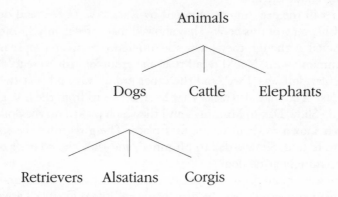

Above that, we can use the term 'animal' to refer to Pilot. 'Animal' is a still more abstract term than 'dog', because it ignores the differences between dogs and cattle and elephants. So there is a hierarchy of increasingly abstract labels that can apply to the same individual. Stuart Chase (1938, 1950) referred to this hierarchy as a 'ladder of abstraction'.

We can represent the hierarchy as shown in Figure 14.1. As you know, under 'retrievers' come individuals like Pilot, Rover and Diesel; but they have been left out of the diagram in Figure 14.1 because this is a hierarchy of *categories*, not individuals.

Eleanor Rosch *et al.* (1976) made a close study of such hierarchies, and called the middle level of the three the 'basic' level (in this case, dogs, cattle, elephants). Within the category 'dog', there are the subordinate categories retriever, alsatian, corgi, etc. On the other hand, 'dog' is itself a subcategory of the higher (superordinate) category 'animal', and so the hierarchy is a system of class inclusion. Rosch and her colleagues make much of the cognitive importance of the basic level.

The main point is that Rosch *et al.* (1976) claim that the basic level is the best one for toddlers to use in order to make the distinctions that are relevant to them. And Waxman (1994: 234) says, 'One of the most robust findings in the developmental literature is that preschool children succeed in classifying and labelling objects at the *basic* level long before they do so at other hierarchical levels.'

For many purposes the best term is one which allows us to identify the properties that would be shared by the members of that category; especially ones that would distinguish them from the members of other categories. It is claimed that *dog* is better for these purposes than *retriever*. It's true, I think, that many people would find it easier to say what the distinguishing characteristics of a dog are than to say what the distinguishing marks of a retriever (or, say, a chihuahua or a samoyed) are. On the other hand, Rosch and her colleagues claim, the term *animal* is too wide to allow us to identify the features closely enough. The basic-level terms, such as *dog*, then, seem to have particular value for thinking about real-world objects.

Nevertheless, researchers have also paid a lot of attention to the other, non-basic levels in hierarchies. The linkage between word learning and conceptual organization becomes particularly clear at these levels. We'll briefly look at the research reported by Waxman (1994). See also Waxman (1990) and Waxman and Gelman (1986).

Waxman's aim in her 1994 paper is to explore the relationship between the linguistic development that takes place during a child's vocabulary acquisition and the cognitive development. She refers to the innate biases that have been proposed, which we discussed above. The one she is particularly interested in is the bias towards being able to use the grammatical form of a new word (e.g. a count noun, a proper noun, or an adjective) to help work out its meaning.

She starts by assuming that young children are sensitive to precise relations between linguistic and conceptual development, and she goes on to give an account of experiments that demonstrate that there's a special link between count nouns, like block(s), dog(s), stick(s), etc., and the names of object categories. To put it simply, a child who hears a new count noun assumes it is the name of a category of objects.

Using a count noun seemed to assist the children to learn the name of an object; but the same was true of adjectives only at the young age level of 12 and 13 months. By $2\frac{1}{2}$ years of age, children treat nouns and adjectives differently, in the sense that they seem to assume that a count noun will be the name of a category of objects, but they don't make the same assumption about an adjective.

Waxman sums up the data to this point as follows (1994: 246):

Based on the data reviewed so far, I have suggested that the appreciation of a linkage between count nouns and object categories undergoes no devel- opmental change: it appears to emerge early, requiring little, if any, experience of the language. In contrast, an appreciation of specific linkage between other grammatical categories (e.g., adjectives, mass nouns, verbs) and meaning emerges later in development and may depend on language experience.

Finally, Waxman shows that the generalization about count nouns is consistent across languages, but that the other categories vary across languages, so that Spanish and English are quite different with regard to adjectives, for example. The principle about count nouns seems to be universal and therefore probably innate, and so does not depend on experience of language before it manifests itself, whereas the principles governing adjectives and other grammatical categories don't seem to be universal, but vary across languages; therefore they do depend on experience with language before manifesting themselves.

14.3 Criticisms of the 'bias' approach

Although the theory of 'constraints' or 'biases' has been very influential and has occupied centre stage during the past couple of decades, it has some trenchant critics. One of the most vigorous is Paul Bloom,[2] who, in Bloom (1993: 13), refers to the so-called whole-object and taxonomic constraints in the following terms:

> These constraints are posited to explain the acquisition of words that refer to kinds of whole objects (e.g. 'dog'), but the majority of lexical items acquired by children are not of this nature. Even 2-year-olds possess words that refer to specific individuals ('Fred'), substances ('water'), parts ('nose'), properties ('red'), actions ('give') and so on. This motivates further constraints that determine how words can relate to one another within the lexicon; these can lead children to override the whole object and taxonomic constraints.

One such constraint is the mutual exclusivity assumption, which says that each object can have only one label. Bloom points out that adults don't obey this constraint, since the fact that you sometimes call the dog Fido doesn't prevent you from also calling him a dog. It is possible, of course, that children obey this constraint until they reach a certain point of development, when they give it up.

Merriman and Tomasello (1995) point out that research on vocabulary acquisition has concentrated heavily on nouns, and has largely neglected verbs, adjectives and other word classes. In a powerful statement they draw attention to the fact that in recent years many scholars have discussed constraints on word learning as though they were 'given' – inborn in the child; consequently the child has the constraints from the very beginning. But a number of researchers reject that point of view and claim that the children learn general principles about words from the very act of dealing with new words. Such researchers prefer to refer to 'word learning principles' rather than 'constraints'. Merriman and Tomasello cite Merriman (1991) and Golinkoff *et al.* (1994) as examples. But he points out that such principles don't overcome the problem Quine posed with regard to word acquisition. (Remember 'rabbit' and *gavagai?*)

14.4 A more radical approach

All the approaches we've discussed so far have been concerned with the question of how the child establishes what the *reference* of a word is – that is, what it is in the world that the word refers to. But Noam Chomsky takes a much more radical approach. He has often taken positions which seem at first to be outrageously radical, but a few years later have come to be well accepted; so you shouldn't dismiss this one lightly. Chomsky (1996a: 22) claims:

> there need be no objects in the world that correspond to what we talk about, even in the simplest cases, nor does anyone believe that there are. About all we can say at a general level is that the words of our language provide complex perspectives that offer us highly special ways to think about things – to ask for them, tell people about them, etc. . . . *People* use words to refer to things in complex ways, reflecting interests and circumstances, but the *words* do not refer.

Of course, Chomsky gives examples of the facts that lead him to think this way. He points out that a house can be both concrete and abstract. If his house was demolished by a tornado, he could say that he rebuilt it somewhere else. Normally it would be said that *his house* and the pronoun *it* have the same reference – that is, refer to the same object. But the house that was destroyed is not the same house as was rebuilt, if we're talking about the concrete sense of *house*. Only in an abstract sense are both of them *his house*, and *it* refers only to the abstract sense. But that is puzzling, too, since you wouldn't want to say you built an abstract house.

London can also be both concrete and abstract. Chomsky goes on:

> it can be destroyed by a fire or an administrative decision. If London is reduced to dust, *it* – that is, London – can be *re*-built elsewhere and still be the *same* city, London, unlike my house, which won't be the same house if it is reduced to dust and *it* is *re*-built somewhere else.

We might add that this phenomenon occurs also with objects much smaller than London. Someone can say, 'The Theatre Royal burnt down, but they rebuilt it further down the road and renamed it the Lyrique.' Furthermore, as Chomsky also remarks, the motor of his car is different again. If it is reduced to dust, the same dust can't be used to rebuild that particular motor. If the dust is used for building a motor, it will be a different one.

We can easily think of other kinds of examples. Consider this fragment of conversation:

> 'Didn't your brother die?'
> 'I've never had a brother.'

It's clear that neither example of *brother* here refers to any object in the world. Nevertheless, in other circumstances there could be someone in the world who answered to the description 'your brother'. But notice that you couldn't teach a child the meaning of the word *brother* by pointing to such a person and saying, 'That's a brother. That's what a brother looks like.' And, of course, the so-called shape constraint would be utterly useless in helping the child recognize brothers in the future, so that (s)he would know whether to use the same word.

But Chomsky goes further than I have so far described, saying that what we know about even quite simple words, such as *house*, *London*, *it* and *same*, 'must be almost entirely unlearned' (1996a: 23). But if what we know is unlearnt, how could we have got to know it? Chomsky's answer is that this knowledge must be inborn; it must be part of what is 'wired into' our brains before birth.

Many readers will probably react by saying, 'But that's not credible'. Some of those readers will eventually come to find it credible, as many linguists and psychologists have done, and some never will (as some linguists and psychologists never have). But whether you believe it or not, it's a very important claim, one which has dominated much of the research over the past thirty or forty years. That isn't a reason why you should believe it, but it is a reason why you shouldn't reject it out of hand, without thinking about it further and reading more about it.

Neither Chomsky nor anyone else has ever filled in the details of the biological mechanisms by which inborn ideas are transmitted from generation to generation, or where they can come from. Chomsky doesn't pretend to know; he only claims that all the best evidence points in that direction.

Notes

1. *Taxonomic* is the adjective based on the noun *taxonomy*, which means 'classification'. So this constraint says that children are biased to expect that a new word will 'classify', or name a class of words.
2. See Bloom (1993) for an excellent collection of papers on language acquisition.

15. The best of both worlds?

15.1 Introduction

Chapter 4 described the work of Jean Piaget and his 'constructivist' account of cognitive development, including the development of language. We looked at some of the telling criticisms that had been made against constructivism, but mentioned that there were 'new Piagetians' who were developing Piaget's ideas in new directions. The most successful of these is Annette Karmiloff-Smith of University College London.

Karmiloff-Smith no longer subscribes fully to Piaget's views, and perhaps should no longer be called a Piagetian, since she has developed her own model. In it she joins some of Piaget's notions to some of those advanced by 'nativists'. A 'nativist' is someone who believes that certain language principles are innate. Chomsky is one such, as we have seen, and another is Jerry Fodor; he is an American psychologist and philosopher of psychology. Many people regard him as among the very best, if not the best, in both categories.

Fodor has always been a strong supporter of Chomsky and added his weight to the early struggle against behaviourism. He also took an extremely important role in the debate between Chomsky and Piaget (see Chapter 5). But Fodor is far from being *just* a supporter of Chomsky. His main concern has been to construct a model of how the mind works, and his efforts have been both impressive and highly influential.

In 1983 Fodor published *The Modularity of Mind*, a book which has been discussed a great deal ever since. It is this work which Karmiloff-Smith has picked up and married to Piaget's work – or, more accurately, she has married part of it to part of Piaget's work. Before we can appreciate her proposal, we need to consider what Fodor claims that is of interest to her.

15.2 Fodor: the modularity of mind

It's clear that the mind engages in a number of different kinds of activity. One kind deals with different inputs. What the eyes see, what the ears hear, what the nose smells, and so on all have to be registered in the brain and interpreted. Fodor (1983) argues that each of these inputs is processed by a different 'module' in the brain, and that all the modules work separately from each other. Another way of expressing this is to say that each module is 'domain specific'. The module that deals with the inputs from the eyes deals only with those; the module that handles inputs from the receptors that are sensitive to changes of temperature in the environment deals only with those; and so on. Importantly, Fodor claims that language belongs in the list of inputs, and therefore has its own module.

Modules have certain characteristics which define them, as well as that of being domain specific. One is that they are innate. Another characteristic is that their operation is mandatory – that is, they can't ignore the inputs, but have to process them. If your brain becomes aware of an utterance, it automatically processes it; likewise, if your eyes see something and input it to the brain, it will automatically be processed. Another characteristic is that although input processes are known to involve a number of levels, most of the levels are inaccessible to consciousness – in fact, only the final one is usually available.

Other properties of modules are that they work fast and automatically, and that each input system is associated with a fixed neural architecture – that is, it is 'hard-wired' in the brain. Yet another property is that modules have characteristic patterns of breakdown (pathological conditions). Also (and this is rather more speculative), input systems develop in a certain sequence and at a certain speed.

Finally – and very importantly – modules aren't subject to influence from other parts of the mind; nor can other parts of the mind gain access to their internal workings. In fact, other parts of the mind can only process a module's outputs. It's important to note that a module has to meet *all* the criteria for modularity, not just some of them. Why? Because Fodor defined them that way. He doesn't do it arbitrarily, of course, but argues for each one of them.

Let's consider the example which most concerns us here: language. The module that processes language is:

- domain specific – that is, it processes only language and not anything else (like, for example, vision);
- innate (at least according to Chomsky and Fodor);
- mandatory – that is, any language that is input *must* be processed; it can't be ignored. Certainly that is true of your own native language, but some limited processing may also occur if you hear a foreign language, though Fodor doesn't discuss this;
- composed of a number of different levels involved in processing language; but we are usually conscious only of the final one (if that);
- fast and automatic;
- associated with a fixed neural architecture (involving Broca's and Wernicke's areas of the brain, and others as well);
- subject to characteristic patterns of breakdown, e.g. aphasia;
- characterized by a certain developmental sequence and a certain developmental speed. (As already remarked, this is a little less certain than the other characteristics.)

In so far as these claims are correct, then, language meets all the criteria required for it to be processed by a module.

I've already mentioned that other parts of the mind don't have access to modules, and can only process their outputs. But what are these 'other parts of the mind'? Collectively, they are referred to by Fodor as 'central processing', and they include the system of already-held beliefs, as well as the 'encyclopedic knowledge' that we have all built up through experience, long-term memory, planning capacities, and so on. These can all have access to each other and influence each other. They are also slow and not mandatory (they don't *have* to react to inputs from any other parts of the mind). Central processing contrasts in these characteristics with the input modules.

It's important to realize that Fodor doesn't try to describe which physical parts of the brain contain the modules. That isn't possible in the present state of knowledge about the neural organization of the brain. Rather, he tries to sketch the kind of mental 'architecture' that seems to him to be required by the facts.

15.3 Karmiloff-Smith: *Beyond Modularity*

Annette Karmiloff-Smith (1992) accepts some of these suggestions of Fodor's about the 'architecture' of the mind, but she departs from him in two important particulars. Fodor holds that the modules are completely 'prespecified' in the newborn child – that is, all their details are innate. By contrast, Karmiloff-Smith claims that the set of characteristics of the modules reach their full specification only through development that occurs after birth, rather than being totally prespecified. There is a process of 'modularization' which occurs repeatedly as the child develops. Karmiloff-Smith also maintains that the distinction between modules and central processing isn't as strict as Fodor claims.

Karmiloff-Smith thinks that the infant's born with a certain number of innate predispositions to process certain kinds of inputs; in other words, the brain is 'tuned' to receive certain kinds of inputs and process them. Although these predispositions are domain specific (they respond to only one kind of input), they will later become available to domain-general processes – what Fodor calls central processing. But the predispositions are not strictly modular, in Fodor's sense. At birth the brain is somewhat 'plastic' – capable of being moulded in different ways. And any parts of it that are plastic cannot contain knowledge that is hardwired at birth.

Over time, certain brain circuits are selected to process particular kinds of inputs. As Karmiloff-Smith, (1992: 5) puts it, 'Nature specifies initial biases or predispositions that channel attention to relevant environmental inputs, which in turn affect subsequent brain development.' Thus her 'predispositions' differ from Fodor's 'modules' in not being fully specified at birth (or before). Rather, they develop.

Karmiloff-Smith admits that the claim that there's a process of modularization is pretty speculative, and she doesn't develop it any further in her book. She says the choice between her view and Fodor's can only be determined by 'future research using on-line brain-activation studies with neonates and young infants' (p. 5). If Fodor's right about the modules being fully specified at birth, she says, the experiments should show that from the very beginning (when the infant first responds to inputs), 'specific brain circuits are activated in response to domain-specific inputs'. On the other hand, if she's right and there's a gradual process of modularization, 'activation levels should initially be relatively distributed across the brain, and only with time ... would specific circuits always be activated in response to domain-specific inputs'.

Karmiloff-Smith stresses that it's important not to confuse modules and domains. A 'module' is an information-processing unit in the brain, but a 'domain' is the set of mental representations relevant to a particular area of knowledge (language, number, visual inputs, etc.). So to say that modules are domain specific means that they each process a different kind of information.

15.4 The input from Piaget's theory

It is of interest that Karmiloff-Smith was originally a Piagetian who worked in Piaget's department at the University of Geneva. She was there for thirteen years, but says she was regarded by the other Piagetians there as something of a rebel. That would perhaps help to explain why she has now rejected much of Piaget's model. But she extracted from the model the part that she felt was right, and still holds with it. That is the part she wants to wed to part of Fodor's theory. Let's now look at the details.

Piaget's model of children's development was 'domain general'. It's important to understand what that means. Remember, a domain consists of a set of mental representations to do with a particular area of knowledge – for example, language, number, physics, etc. If development is 'domain general', it means that it takes place simultaneously and uniformly in all the domains. Piaget consistently denied that any linguistic structures or principles were innate, and even denied any maturational constraints (which would have implied that the constraints were innate). Language didn't develop independently of other cognitive developments; it developed as a result of the operations of sensori-motor intelligence, which was responsible for all cognitive development. Karmiloff-Smith rejects these beliefs of Piaget's. She also rejects his belief that cognitive development proceeds in 'stages'.

But since I have said that she wants to marry some of Piaget's claims to some of Fodor's, the obvious question is, which of Piaget's views does she accept? First, the view that mental structures are actively constructed by the child, though she doesn't believe that it's done through 'sensori-motor intelligence'. Furthermore, although Chomsky has been quite scathing in rejecting constructivism, Karmiloff-Smith thinks that Chomsky's claim that there are innate linguistic principles is not incompatible with constructivism – given certain provisos. First, you have to add to constructivism the claim that there are innate predispositions to process certain kinds of sensory inputs. That means the predispositions are domain specific, of course – that is, each of the domains develops separately from the others, in its own way and at its own pace.

It follows that what is prespecified must be less detailed than nativists like Chomsky and Fodor would claim. Furthermore, there must be a progressive process of *modularization*, to build the modules, which are not prespecified.

We've already seen that Fodor claims that the modules that process inputs to the mind are 'domain specific'; however, we cannot say that he thinks that *development* is domain specific, because he believes that the modules are fully developed by birth (or before). By contrast, Karmiloff-Smith believes that cognitive development continues after birth, but takes from Fodor the idea that the modules that develop are domain specific.

That is the nature of the 'marriage' she proposes between a part of Piaget's theory and a part of Fodor's. We'll defer until a little later a consideration of whether it's a happy marriage, uniting the best of both worlds.

15.5 Evidence from children

Karmiloff-Smith concedes that there are certain facts that seem to support Fodor's notion that the principles that guide learning are innate and domain specific. For example, children who suffer from a condition called Williams' syndrome[1] are typically severely retarded with respect to numbers, spatial cognition and problem-solving but are relatively normal with respect to language, face recognition and 'theory of mind' (discussed below).

Autistic[2] children may have only one deficit, that of 'theory of mind', while the rest of the cognitive processes are relatively unimpaired. If the mind were domain general, we would expect that any deficits would show up right across the spectrum of mental processes.

However, Karmiloff-Smith (1994: 697) remarks, 'Whether autism and Williams' syndrome involve domain-specific representational deficits or computational deficits, or both, remains an open question.'

But what is this 'theory of mind' in children, that I've referred to above? The main point is that children develop the ability to form ideas about what other people are thinking and feeling, and what their intentions are. As readers will be aware, adults certainly have this ability, and it plays a very important role in the life of the mind, and hence of society.

Certain tests have been devised to assess whether children have an adequate theory of mind. One of these is a hidden object test, sometimes called the 'Sally-Anne' test. Two children are involved; let's call them Emma and Scott. While they're both in the room, the investigator hides a toy – say, by putting it in a drawer. One of the children (let's choose Emma) is sent out of the room, and while she's out, the investigator moves the toy from the drawer to another hiding-place – let's say under a cushion on the couch – making sure that Scott sees the change clearly. The investigator then asks Scott to predict where Emma will look for the toy when she comes back into the room. Children of about 3 or less will say 'under the cushion', because they don't seem to be able to distinguish what the other child knows from what they themselves know. But children of 4 or over will say 'in the drawer', because that's the knowledge they (correctly) attribute to the other child. A child who can pass this test has an adequate theory of mind. That is only one of a battery of tests that can be used for this purpose.[3]

Smith and Tsimpli (1995) give a fascinating account of a man named Christopher who was born in 1962, and who is a so-called 'savant'[4] – that is, a person who has one outstanding mental ability, though showing severely limited abilities in other areas of mental performance. He has been like this from early childhood. His outstanding ability is that of learning languages: he can read, write and communicate in fifteen or twenty of them. Yet his other cognitive abilities are very limited. There are also savants who show outstanding musical or mathematical ability, although they have disabilities in other cognitive domains. The existence of savants is further evidence that cognitive skills are domain specific.

Of course, that doesn't remove all the mysteries about savants and their abilities. One man, who was shown on television a few years ago, was able to say immediately (and correctly) on what day of the week a given date in the distant future or past would fall – even if it was some centuries away; yet he was unable to do simple arithmetic. There is still a great deal for scientists to learn about the operations of the mind, but they have started to make some progress.

246

Karmiloff-Smith also points out that brain damage in adults provides further evidence of domain specificity. Disorders of higher cognitive functions caused by brain damage typically affect only one domain – say, language, number or face-recognition – while the other domains remain relatively intact.

But Karmiloff-Smith (1992: 9), citing Chomsky (1988), comments that the more domain-specific properties there are in the infant mind, the less creative and flexible the later system will become. It therefore becomes important for us to explain the flexibility of subsequent cognitive development. She goes on: 'It is implausible that development will turn out to be entirely domain specific *or* domain general ... development clearly involves a more dynamic process of interaction between mind and environment than the strict nativist stance presupposes.' Don't miss the fact that Karmiloff-Smith has just made a very important declaration: she does not agree with 'the strict nativist stance'.

15.6 Representational Redescription

Karmiloff-Smith, like most other cognitive psychologists, believes that knowledge is given some sort of mental representation. In principle, it could be a language-like representation or a mental-image representation, or perhaps some other kind.

Fodor (1975) believes that there is a special 'language of the mind' or 'language of thought' which is used for representations. (Not everyone accepts that.) Such a language of the mind would not be the same as any actual spoken language like English; it would be a universal 'language' used in the minds of all human beings, whatever their native language. Fodor claims that the output of all modules is put into this language of thought before being passed to the central processing system – the part of the mind that deals with knowledge and beliefs.

Karmiloff-Smith challenges this claim. She says some knowledge is innate and some is acquired through interaction with the environment. In either case, a great deal of it (and at first all of it) is unconscious. This is what Karmiloff-Smith calls 'implicit' knowledge. It is, of course, represented in the mind, even though it is inaccessible to the mind's conscious processes. This level of representation is called the I-level (Implicit level). Karmiloff-Smith (1992: 20) says, 'At level I, representations are in the form of procedures for analysing and responding to stimuli in the external environment.'

Before knowledge can be thought about or manipulated, she says, it has to be re-represented in a new format which lends itself to those processes; or, to use her terminology, it has to be 'externalized'. She proposes that there are three levels of externalization, which she dubs E1, E2 and E3. At the E3 level, the knowledge is conscious and can be expressed in words, analysed, discussed, and so on. E1 and E2 are steps along the way to this, but we won't concern ourselves with them here. Progress towards explicit knowledge involves several re-representations, one for each level. Thus there are four levels of representation in all: Implicit (I), Explicit-1 (E1), Explicit-2 (E2) and Explicit-3 (E3). Karmiloff-Smith comments (1992: 20), 'These different forms of representation do not constitute age-related stages of developmental change. Rather, they are parts of a reiterative cycle that occurs again and again within different microdomains and throughout the developmental span.'

Earlier (p. 6) she explains what she means by 'microdomains':

> I shall retain the term 'domain' to cover language, physics, mathematics and so forth. I will also distinguish 'microdomains' such as gravity within the domain of physics and pronoun acquisition within the domain of language. These microdomains can be thought of as subsets within particular domains.

Making use of this sort of machinery, Karmiloff-Smith presents a model of children's cognitive development called Representational Redescription, or RR for short.

Earlier in the book (Chapter 5) I discussed the fact that a great deal of knowledge of language is unconscious, even in adults. Such knowledge never gets beyond the level of I-represention. Any knowledge that becomes conscious and can be put into words will have come to be represented at the E3 (external) level.

15.7 Is the marriage successful?

We must now consider whether the marriage of Piagetian and Fodorian theory really does give the best of both worlds, and whether it is a happy marriage. The answer is that it's too early to be completely sure. In the past, women's magazines tended to present the idea that all problems ended at the altar, and then the couple would live happily ever after. A more realistic view is that at the point of marriage it hasn't yet been determined whether they'll live happily ever after, and that marriage is only the beginning of a whole lot of challenges.

It's similar with the marriage that Karmiloff-Smith has arranged between parts of Fodor's theory and parts of Piaget's. It would be a mistake to think that this marriage means that there will be no more problems, as Karmiloff-Smith would be the first to admit. But many cognitive scientists regard it as an exciting event for the future promise that it holds, and have found *Beyond Modularity* the most stimulating book in their field for many years.

Not that everyone is convinced by it. The journal *Behavioral and Brain Sciences* has a special format for presenting research that is the focus of attention and debate. First the researcher presents a 'précis' of the work involved, then it's subjected to what is called an 'open peer commentary', in which a large number of recognized scholars belonging to the field in question write comments on the work that is in focus. Then the focused author replies to the points made. Karmiloff-Smith was featured in this way, the comments being about her book *Beyond Modularity* (Karmiloff-Smith, 1994). In 1997 *Behavioral and Brain Sciences* published a continuation of the 1994 commentary (Karmiloff-Smith, 1997), in which three more scholars discussed *Beyond Modularity* and were replied to by Karmiloff-Smith.

The comments in the 1994 publication were diverse. One scholar, David Estes (p. 715), predicts 'that this book will be recognised as a landmark, one that provides further evidence for the maturity of developmental psychology and its potential for illuminating not only the course of cognitive development but the nature of the human mind as well'. By contrast, Susan H. Foster-Cohen (p. 716) claims that 'Karmiloff-Smith's position that there is emergent modularity for language is untenable, both empirically and logically.' And there are all shades of opinion in between.

It isn't surprising that there is this difference of opinion. Those who are staunch defenders of either Piaget or Fodor are bound to disagree with the synthesis proposed by Karmiloff-Smith. On the other hand, her theory is so different from what immediately preceded it that it has excited a good many scholars by its stimulating ideas.

There is a very insightful review of Karmiloff- Smith (1992) by N. V. Smith (1993). He pays tribute to the elegance of Karmiloff-Smith's basic hypothesis, but suggests that her conclusions about modularity don't follow. He points out (p. 99) that 'virtually everything we know about our first language is not only inaccessible to conscious introspection by the child, but remains inaccessible to the adult; that is, most of our linguistic knowledge never progresses to the E2–3 level'. This means that the details of the language module have already been determined before Representational Redescription begins to occur. Consequently, Representational Redescription can't play a significant role in developing those details.

In particular, children who are still at the Implicit level (I) have mastered the major part of the syntax of their language. In fact, Karmiloff-Smith admits that language cannot depend on Representational Redescription but that 'if you have Representational Redescription, you can go beyond language learning, to become a mini-linguist'.

She gives the following example of a child acting like a mini-linguist (Karmiloff-Smith, 1992: 31):

'What's that?'
(Mother: 'A typewriter.')
'No, you're the typewriter, that's a
    typewrite.'

(Yara, 4 years)

She comments that the child who does this 'is not just learning a lexicon, but analysing features of that lexicon as a linguist'.[5]

Citing this, Smith (1993: 100) comments that,

This makes the domain of syntax, and some other parts of the language faculty, relatively unpersuasive as evidence for going beyond modularity. Indeed, it is revealing that in her chapter on 'The child as a linguist' K-S discusses syntax only in the context of her (extremely cogent) critique of Piaget. . . . None of the areas of language that K-S looks at in any detail falls within either the syntactic or the phonological core.

At the time of the writing of this chapter, Karmiloff-Smith had not published a reply to these criticisms. But that, of course, doesn't mean she has been convinced by them or defeated by them. Smith is arguing from a strict nativist point of view, and the basic assumptions of Karmiloff-Smith and strict nativists are so different (as she shows in her answers to other nativists (Karmiloff-Smith, 1994, 1997) that it's difficult for either side to convince the other or to score decisive victories. The debate is likely to go on for a long time yet.

15.8 Connectionism

Klahr (1992) discusses approaches to the study of cognitive development and makes a distinction between 'soft-core' and 'hard-core'
approaches. The hard-core approaches are ones that use computers to
simulate the way in which children accomplish certain tasks; soft-core
approaches are ones that do not. Researchers at both ends of the
spectrum may accept the same theoretical assumptions and methodological practices, but they will interpret them differently. At the
soft-core end of the spectrum, there is likely to be less precision.

Karmiloff-Smith (1992: 175) points out that in *Beyond Modularity*
she has described the Representational Redescription model in verbal
terms, and that this way of doing things puts it at the soft-core end of
Klahr's spectrum.

Well, what's wrong with describing her model in words? The trouble
is that words, although extremely powerful tools for communicating,
can also be vague and ambiguous. They don't have the kind of
exactitude that, say, mathematics has – necessarily so, because if they
did have, they wouldn't be as flexible as they are in communication.
Words are adequate for expressing general principles, Karmiloff-Smith
claims, but when an attempt is made to specify precise mechanisms, a
computer simulation of what happens in the child's brain is more
precise and better.

For this reason, towards the end of *Beyond Modularity*, Karmiloff-
Smith ties her model in with connectionism. Connectionism is a model
of representation used in a number of sciences, including developmental
psychology. In the latter, it models children's development (and many
other phenomena) by means of networks. The networks are meant to
bear some resemblance to the brain, though it's true that the resemblance isn't very close. The brain contains a complicated network of cells
called neurons, which are chained together by elongated pieces of
nerve cell called axons and dendrites. Similarly, a network of the kind
studied by connectionists consists of 'cells', represented by dots, and
connections between them, represented by lines with arrow-heads on
them.

I won't pursue connectionist theory here, since it would take us
beyond the purpose of this book. If you would like to learn more, you
can do so by reading an introductory work such as Bechtel and
Abrahamsen (1991); then, if your appetite's still strong, try Rumelhart
et al. (1986) and McClelland *et al.* (1986).

It should be noted, though, that the use of connectionist simulations for language has as many opponents as it has supporters.

15.9 'Rethinking innateness'

In 1996 six authors, including Annette Karmiloff-Smith, published a book called *Rethinking Innateness: A Connectionist Perspective on Development* (Elman *et al.*, 1996). We won't be dealing with the work as a whole, because it goes beyond the scope of this introductory book, but there are some very interesting things in Chapter 1 (called 'New perspectives on development') which are relevant to what Karmiloff- Smith is trying to do. We don't know how much input she had into that chapter, because all six authors accept responsibility for all the chapters, but it isn't difficult to believe that she was heavily involved. At any rate, it's consonant with what she has written in *Beyond Modularity*, but goes further.

The crucially interesting question that's raised in this chapter is: 'What do we mean when we say that something is innate?' The authors argue, persuasively in my opinion, that there are numerous things we might mean.

They cite two research findings that have led to the belief in recent decades that much of human development is based on innate principles. One such finding is that newborn infants have surprising abilities which were previously unsuspected (cf. Chapter 13 of the present book). The second finding is that many things that adults do can't be learnt – hence the knowledge on which they depend must be inborn, and simply triggered by experience. (Cf. descriptions in Chapter 13.)

As an alternative explanation, they argue that development takes place 'through the *interaction* of maturational factors, under genetic control, and the environment' (p. 1). You'll recognize that Piaget also advocated this position.

The 'genetic control' is, by definition, provided by the genes. But the real questions, say the authors, are how the genes provide this control, and what they do. There follow descriptions of how genes and cells work.

One of the most important parts of the chapter, from our point of view, is the section headed 'What does it mean to be innate?' (p. 20). They cite an immediate problem about answering this question:

First, calling a behavior innate does very little to explain the mechanisms by which that behavior becomes inevitable. So there is little explanatory power to the term. If all that is meant by saying a behavior is innate is that it is (under normal circumstances) inevitable, then we have gained little. (p. 21)

In the next section, called 'Ways to be innate: a framework', the authors try to be more specific about the ways innateness is manifested. Those who would like to pursue this rather technical issue can do so by reading *Rethinking Innateness*. The main point I wish to make here is that some new and important thinking is going on about the notion of innateness.

One piece of their discussion can be described fairly simply. If mental representations are innate, it means they involve constraints on knowledge and behaviour which are 'hard-wired' into the brain. For example, Chomsky and other generative linguists have argued that basic principles of grammar are 'hard-wired'. But Elman *et al.* argue that such an arrangement is comparatively rare in higher organisms, which are more notable for the plasticity of their brains – that is, the ability of their brains to adapt to different needs.

Elman *et al.* claim that there has been a growing amount of evidence against innate representations. They cite a number of recent studies of vertebrate animals in which inputs to specific areas of the cortex have been changed (pp. 372–7).

For example, in ferrets, visual inputs to the retina have been redirected to the part of the cortex that deals with auditory inputs, which thus becomes responsive to visual stimuli. As the authors comment, although this suggests that 'the auditory cortex can see', we have no way of telling what the experience is like from the animal's point of view.

They go on (pp. 26–7), 'This suggests that cortex has far more representational plasticity than previously believed. Indeed, recent studies have shown that cortex retains representational plasticity into adulthood.'

There are other experiments in which pieces of cortex have been transplanted from one region to the other at an early stage of development. Such transplants have been done, for instance, with newborn rodents. In one series of experiments, neurons from the visual cortex were moved to the sensori-motor region and vice versa. The interesting question is whether the transplanted pieces take on the character of their original location, or that of their new location. The answer in this case was that the transplants developed in accordance with their new location. Again, the brain seems to be a lot more plastic than was once thought.

This, of course, is of considerable interest to Karmiloff-Smith, since it lends itself to her argument that specific modules develop after birth – which they can only do if the brain is to some extent plastic.

The first chapter of *Rethinking Innateness*, then, conveys the message that it isn't sufficient to say that certain principles are innate and leave it at that, since there are numerous ways in which the innateness could be built into the brain. But we must also pay attention to an important remark:

> We emphasize from the outset that the approach we take is not anti-nativist – far from it. Where we differ from some is that we view the major goal of evolution as ensuring adaptive *outcomes* rather than ensuring prior knowledge. ... We are prepared to call many universally-recurring patterns of behavior – in languages, for example – innate, even though we find them nowhere specified directly in the genome.[6] In this sense, our definition of innateness is undoubtedly broader than the traditional view. We also believe that it is richer and more likely to lead to a clearer understanding of how nature shapes its species. (p. 46)

Notes

1. Named after J. C. P. Williams, who made a study of four patients with a narrowing of the aorta. They were mentally retarded and were described as having an 'elfin-like' facial appearance, with upturned nose, an open mouth and thicker-than-usual lips. Unlike autistic children, such children are usually outgoing and friendly.
2. Autistic children show extreme withdrawal and lack strong, or any, emotional responses to those who deal with them. They may be mute or unable to use language satisfactorily for communication. They often have superior rote memory.
3. For further discussion, see Perner *et al.* (1987), Wellman (1990) and Carruthers and Smith (1996).
4. As Smith and Tsimpli point out, the pejorative term 'idiot-savant' was used in earlier times, but it now seems better to avoid the connotations of such a term.
5. Language that is used to analyse other language is sometimes called 'metalanguage'. That is what Karmiloff-Smith is describing here.
6. The genes in the set of chromosomes of an individual.

254

16. Conclusion

16.1 Conflicting basic assumptions

It's interesting to compare the basic assumptions underlying different approaches to the study of language acquisition.

The behaviourist approach of Skinner seeks to explain the phenomenon entirely in terms of inputs to the child from the outside world. All the others we've studied accept that the mind or brain plays an important role, and that it interacts in various ways with the outside world.

Chomsky, who has the strongest belief in innate principles of language, probably makes the least provision for interaction with the outside world. He's quite firm about interaction being necessary, but a minimal amount, he believes, is sufficient to awaken the innate principles that are already in the brain.

The others all allow the necessity for a greater degree of interaction between the brain/mind and the outside world. Where they differ is in the kind of interaction that they think is necessary. Piaget believes that sensori-motor activity (that is, activity involving the senses and the muscles) is the pathway by which knowledge enters the brain from the outside world, by leading the child to build mental structures (i.e. structures of knowledge).

The others would probably admit that sensori-motor activity provides one path to some knowledge, but not all knowledge, and above all, not knowledge about language. The interaction with the outside world is more varied and complex than that.

For Halliday and the proponents of motherese, interaction with other people, including most importantly the mother (or other care-giver), is an essential part of the process of acquiring (or learning) language. Yet there's a difference between Halliday and the motherese supporters. The latter put more emphasis on the syntactic and phonetic nature of the language that passes between adult and child; Halliday puts emphasis on the interpersonal relationship between the two. Not that either would deny that both things have validity.

There is a stronger difference, though. A number of the followers of motherese are quite happy with the idea of there being at least some innate component to the language acquisition process, whereas Halliday firmly excludes the idea of there being any specifically linguistic innate knowledge.

There is really a continuum of scholars from the pure 'motherese' followers at one end to the more tightly theoretical 'bootstrapping' proponents at the other end. And among the bootstrappers there are some who are quite strongly generative (Chomskyan).

Different again is Karmiloff-Smith, who, as we've seen, insists that modular knowledge isn't innate in the purest sense, but is acquired through exposure to the world and interaction with people.

So we have numerous variations on the internal and the external factors, and interactions between them. The internal factors are, it would seem, more mysterious than the external ones, though the problem with the external factors is that there are so many of them that it's difficult to know for certain which are the relevant ones.

16.2. Affinities

So what comes out of the different kinds of research that have been described? We've seen that many scholars have tried to solve the huge problem of how children come to acquire language. None of them has given the ultimate answer, though a number have provided strong illuminations of various kinds.

Is there any chance that someone will bring together the best illuminations from the different paradigms? I don't really believe so. Mostly, members of the different schools of thought have neither the time nor the inclination to read each other's work, or to debate with each other, and if they did, they wouldn't be persuaded. In order to make progress within their own model, they have to plough deeply in the one direction. This is understandable, but it means that different schools tend to be insulated from each other. That phenomenon isn't confined to the disciplines of linguistics and psychology, of course.

Leaving that aside, though, how much is there in common among any of the schools? I believe there are certain affinities. Annette

Karmiloff-Smith has tried to blend some of Piaget's and Fodor's (and Chomsky's) ideas, and then take the resultant mixture into the connectionist paradigm. In doing so, she has also drawn on a good deal of the fairly recent research on infant cognition. That's an ongoing project, and an interesting one.

I believe there are also affinities between some of the ideas advanced by Halliday and some of those advanced by writers on motherese. I'm thinking, for example, of the careful tracing of the relationship between mother (or other) and child.

Skinner's account of language acquisition seems to be pretty dead today, but apparently not everyone agrees. A correspondent to the Piaget e-mail list on 4 March 1997 claimed that 'collaboration and integration across schools has been going on between Piagetians and Skinnerians', and he named some of the people involved.[1] It just goes to show that there are counter-revolutionaries out there, awaiting their chance.

The same correspondent, on 28 February 1997, said that the problem with Chomsky and Fodor was that they thought that behaviourists believed that there was a mechanical association between a stimulus and a response. He then went on to suggest that the way in which neural networks provide a loose connection between behaviour and events is very close to the loose connection that Skinner proposed. Some of the people who are critical of neural (connectionist) networks would also say this, but would mean the words to have negative connotations (unjustly, I think).

16.3 Mind and brain

There's been dramatic progress in recent years with regard to methods of exploring the functioning of the brain. I'm thinking especially of imaging techniques (see Chapter 10). It's to be expected that as we develop more and more technical methods for finding out what's going on in the brain, and what the real functions are of its various parts, some of the matters that seem mysterious about the brain at present will become less so.

Not everyone is so concerned about the physical location of language. Lecours and Joanette (1985: 327) report Jacques Mehler as remarking, in private correspondence, that 'it has of late become fashionable among experimental psychologists to state that "it does not matter much whether one's language is biologically represented in one's brain or in either of one's little fingers" '. Lecours and Joanette then announce that their chapter will pertain 'to certain aspects of the cerebral rather than the digital representation of language'.

They're right, of course. Most of the work that linguists do wouldn't be changed one iota if we found that language was represented in one of the little fingers, though our conception of the internal architecture of little fingers would change, no doubt.

16.4 What I've left undone

I haven't dealt with all shades of thought in this book; there are too many, and I've had to limit the extent of my coverage. I'm aware that Vygotsky and Bruner may be considered significant omissions, at least by some.

I'm aware, on the other hand, that there will be some who'll want to ask why I included this or that school, but I'm prepared to defend my choices. I'm comforted by the fact that different people will be upset about the inclusion or exclusion of different schools.

I'm aware, too, that I've limited my attention mainly to one language, English; yet I believe that cross-language studies are very important for research in child language, as they are for linguistics generally. But no book can cover everything, and I've had to make my choices.

There are new directions of research which I haven't followed in this book, usually because they're too difficult for an introductory text. Into this category come Chomsky's minimalist theory (Chomsky, 1995b) and connectionist ideas on language (see references given in Chapter 15).

16.5 For the future: bet the farm on these

And now, my tips for directions to look for interesting future activity:

1. As always, don't take your eyes off Chomsky. Ever.
2. There's likely to be more and more work examining language in the light of evolution. Philip Lieberman has been producing books in this field for some years, including, most recently, Lieberman (1998).

Deacon (1997) argues that the brain and language evolved together, and that 'languages are far more like living organisms than like mathematical proofs'. He says we ought to study them in the same way we study the structure of organisms: in evolutionary terms.

A number of other writers have also been concerned recently to look at language in evolutionary terms. Anne Fernald showed her interest in it in work that's described in Chapter 7. Chapter 2 of Bickerton (1995) is devoted to language and evolution, and there are, of course, other works in this vein.

3. In the next few years, there are likely to be further exciting technical discoveries which will give scientists more access to the brain, and some of these will give new opportunities for exploring the relation between language and the brain.

4. The questions about different notions of innateness will be sharpened and pursued further. This is one of the questions about language that in principle should be able to be solved one day. If so, it will mark the end of arguments for and against innateness. I don't think there'll be a simple yes/no answer; the questions will change.

5. The question of plasticity will continue to be explored.

6. Questions of bootstrapping and the relationship between mother and child will continue to be explored profitably.

That won't be all, of course. Probably, unimaginable paths will open up, so I'm not going to try to imagine them.

16.6 Last words

So here we are, nearly at the end. When you came into this book, you may have thought that you'd now learn not only the truth, but the whole truth, about how children acquire/learn language. Perhaps you're disappointed to find that I can't give you that; I can only tell you what various scholars have said about the problem. But if this were a physics book or a biology book, you wouldn't expect that anyone could tell you the ultimate truth about any phenomenon – that there would be a final answer at the end of the book. So why should we expect the sciences of linguistics and psychology to be any different?

Notes

1. I refrain from identifying either the correspondent or the people he refers to, because the publication status of letters to e-mail lists has never been fully resolved. Correspondents often write in haste, and might not want to be quoted elsewhere. On the other hand, they might be disappointed that they are not identified. If so, my apologies.

References

Baillargeon, Renée (1986) Representing the existence and the location of hidden objects: object permanence in 6- and 8-month-old infants. *Cognition*, 23, 21–41.

Baillargeon, Renée, Marcia Graber, Julia Davos and James Black (1990) Why do young infants fail to search for hidden objects? *Cognition*, 36, 255–84.

Baillargeon, Renée, Elizabeth S. Spelke and Stanley Wasserman (1985) Object permanence in five-month-old infants. *Cognition*, 20, 191–208.

Baldwin, D.A. (1993) Infant contributions to the achievement of joint reference. In Paul Bloom (ed.), *Language Acquisition: Core Readings* (pp. 129–53). New York: Harvester Wheatsheaf.

Bechtel, William and Adele Abrahamsen (1991) *Connectionism and the Mind: An Introduction to Parallel Processing in Networks.* Oxford: Blackwell.

Beeman, Mark and Christine Chiarello (1997) *Right Hemisphere Language Comprehension: Perspectives From Cognitive Neuroscience.* Hillsdale: Erlbaum.

Beilin, Harry (1975) *Studies in the Cognitive Basis of Language Development.* New York: Academic Press.

Bellugi, Ursula (1967) The acquisition of negation. Unpublished PhD dissertation, Harvard University.

Bellugi, U., K. van Hoek, D. Lillo-Martin and L. O'Grady (1993) The acquisition of syntax and space in young deaf signers. In Dorothy Bishop and Kay Mogford (eds), *Language Development in Exceptional Circumstances* (pp. 132–49). Hove, UK: Erlbaum.

Bever, Thomas G., Jerry A. Fodor and William Weksel (1965) Theoretical notes on the acquisition of syntax: a critique of 'contextual generalization'. *Psychological Review*, 72, 467–82.

Bickerton, Derek (1995) *Language and Human Behavior.* Seattle: University of Washington Press.

Bisiach, E., E. Capitani, C. Luzzatti and D. Perani (1981) Brain and conscious representation of reality. *Neuropsychologia*, 19, 543–52.

Bisiach, E. and C. Luzzatti (1978) Unilateral neglect of representational space. *Cortex*, 14, 129–33.

Bloom, Lois (1970) *Language Development: Form and Function in Emerging Grammars.* Cambridge, MA: MIT Press.

Bloom, Lois (1973) *One Word at a Time.* The Hague: Mouton.

Bloom, Lois (1991) *Language Development from Two to Three.* Cambridge: Cambridge University Press.

Bloom, Paul (ed.) (1993) *Language Acquisition: Core Readings.* New York: Harvester Wheatsheaf.

Bloomfield, Leonard (1933) *Language.* New York: Holt, Rinehart & Winston.

Boden, M. (1979) *Piaget.* London: Fontana.

Bohm, David (1983) *Wholeness and the Implicate Order.* London: Ark Paperbacks.

Bowerman, Melissa (1973) *Early Syntactic Development: A Cross-linguistic Study with Special Reference to Finnish.* London: Cambridge University Press.

Braine, M.D.S. (1963a) On learning the grammatical order of words. *Psychological Review*, **70**, 323–48.

Braine, M.D.S. (1963b) The ontogeny of English phrase structure: the first phase. *Language*, **39**, 1–13.

Brown, Roger (1970) *Psycholinguistics.* New York: Free Press.

Brown, Roger (1973) *A First Language: The Early Stages.* London: Allen & Unwin.

Brown, Roger (1977) Introduction. In Catherine Snow and Charles Ferguson (eds), *Talking to Children: Language Input and Acquisition* (pp. 1–27). Cambridge: Cambridge University Press.

Campbell, Robert L. and Mark H. Bickhard (1987) A deconstruction of Fodor's anticonstructivism. *Human Development*, 30, 48–59.

Caplan, David (1987) *Neurolinguistics and Linguistic Aphasiology.* Cambridge: Cambridge University Press.

Carey, Susan (1978) The child as word learner. In Morris Halle, Joan Bresnan and George A. Miller (eds), *Linguistic Theory and Psychological Reality* (pp. 264–93). Cambridge, MA: MIT Press.

Carruthers, Peter and Peter K. Smith (1996) *Theories of Theories of Mind.* Cambridge: Cambridge University Press.

Carson, Benjamin S., Sam P. Javedan *et al.* (1996) Hemispherectomy: a hemidecortication approach and review of 52 cases. *Journal of Neurosurgery*, June, 1–14.

Carter, Rita (1998) *Mapping the Mind.* London: Weidenfeld & Nicolson.

Chase, S. (1938, 1950) *The Tyranny of Words.* London: Methuen.

Chiarello, C., C. Burgess, L. Richards and A. Pollock (1990) Semantic and associative priming in the cerebral hemispheres: some words do, some words don't ... sometimes, some places. *Brain and Language*, 38, 75–104.

Chomsky, Carol (1969) *The Acquisition of Syntax in Children from 5 to 10.* Cambridge, MA: MIT Press.

Chomsky, Noam (1959) A review of *Verbal Behavior*, by B. F. Skinner. *Language*, 35, 26–58.

Chomsky, Noam (1964a) Formal discussion of 'The Development of Grammar in Child Language'. In Ursula Bellugi and Roger Brown (eds), *The Acquisition of Language* (pp. 35–9). Chicago: University of Chicago Press.

Chomsky, Noam (1964b) A review of B.F. Skinner's *Verbal Behavior*. In Jerry A. Fodor and Jerrold J. Katz (eds), *The Structure of Language: Readings in the Philosophy of Language*. Englewood Cliffs: Prentice-Hall.

Chomsky, Noam (1965) *Aspects of the Theory of Syntax*. Cambridge, MA: MIT Press.

Chomsky, Noam (1967) Untitled prefatory note to reprint of his review of Skinner's *Verbal Behavior*. In Leon A. Jakobovits and Murray S. Miron (eds), *Readings in the Psychology of Language*. Englewood Cliffs: Prentice-Hall.

Chomsky, Noam (1968) *Language and Mind*. New York: Harcourt, Brace & World.

Chomsky, Noam (1972) *Language and Mind* (enlarged edition). New York: Harcourt, Brace, Jovanovich.

Chomsky, Noam (1976) *Reflections on Language*. London: Temple Smith.

Chomsky, Noam (1979) *Language and Responsibility*. Lewes: Harvester Press.

Chomsky, Noam (1988) *Language and Problems of Knowledge*. Cambridge, MA: MIT Press.

Chomsky, Noam (1995a) Language and nature. *Mind*, 104(413), 1–61.

Chomsky, Noam (1995b) *The Minimalist Program*. Cambridge, MA: MIT Press.

Chomsky, Noam (1996a) *Power and Prospects: Reflections on Human Nature and the Social Order*. St Leonards (Sydney, Australia): Allen & Unwin.

Chomsky, Noam (1996b) Language and thought: some reflections on venerable themes. In his *Power and Prospects* (pp. 1–30). St Leonards (Sydney, Australia): Allen & Unwin.

Chomsky, Noam (1997) *Perspectives on Power*. Montreal: Black Rose Books.

Christie, Frances (1985) *Language Education*. Geelong: Deakin University Press.

Clark, Eve V. (1973) What's in a word? On the child's acquisition of semantics in his first language. In T.E. Moore (ed.), *Cognitive Development and the Acquisition of Language* (pp. 65–110). New York: Academic Press.

Collins, Harry and Trevor Pinch (1993) *The Golem: What Everyone Should Know about Science*. Cambridge: Cambridge University Press.

Curtiss, Susan (1977) *Genie: A Psycholinguistic Study of a Modern Day 'Wild Child'*. New York: Academic Press.

Curtiss, Susan R. (1988) Abnormal language acquisition and grammar: evidence for the modularity of language. In L. M. Hyman and C. N. Li (eds), *Language, Speech and Mind: Studies in Honor of Victoria A. Fromkin*. New York: Routledge & Kegan Paul.

Curtiss, Susan R., Victoria A. Fromkin *et al.* (1974) The linguistic development of Genie. *Language,* 50, 528–54.

Damasio, Antonio R. (1994) *Descartes' Error: Emotion, Reason, and the Human
Brain.* New York: Avon Books.

Dax, Marc (1865) Lésions de la moitié gauche de l'encéphale coincidait avec
l'oubli des signes de la pensée (lu au Congrès méridional tenu à Montpellier
en 1836). *Gazette Hebdomadaire de Médecine et de Chirurgie,* 2(2nd series),
259–62.

Deacon, Terence W. (1997) *The Symbolic Species: The Co-evolution of Language
and the Brain.* New York: Norton.

De Joia, Alex and Adrian Stenton (1980) *Terms in Systemic Linguistics: A Guide
to Halliday.* London: Batsford.

Dennis, M. and H. Whitaker (1976) Language acquisition following hemidecortication: linguistic superiority of the left over the right hemisphere.
Brain and Language, 3, 404–33.

de Villiers, P. and J. de Villiers (1979) Form and function in the development
of sentence negation. In *Papers and Reports on Child Language Development*
(no. 17, August, 57–66), Department of Linguistics, Stanford University.

Elman, Jeffrey L., Elizabeth A. Bates *et al.* (1996) *Rethinking Innateness: A
Connectionist Perspective on Development.* Cambridge, MA: MIT Press.

Feldman, Heidi M., Susan Goldin-Meadow and L. Gleitman (1978) Beyond
Herodotus: the creation of language by linguistically deprived deaf children. In A. Lock (ed.), *Action, Gesture and Symbol: The Emergence of Language*
(pp. 253–74). New York: Academic Press.

Ferguson, Charles A. (1977) Baby talk as a simplified register. In Catherine
Snow and Charles A. Ferguson (eds), *Talking to Children: Language Input and
Acquisition.* Cambridge: Cambridge University Press.

Fernald, Anne (1989) Intonation and communicative intent: is the melody the
message? *Child Development,* 60, 1497–510.

Fernald, Anne (1992) Meaningful melodies in mothers' speech to infants. In
H. Papousek, U. Jurgens *et al.* (eds), *Nonverbal Vocal Communication: Compar-
ative and Developmental Approaches* (pp. 262–82). Cambridge: Cambridge
University Press.

Fernald, Anne (1993) Human maternal vocalizations to infants as biologically
relevant signals: an evolutionary perspective. In Paul Bloom (ed.), *Language
Acquisition: Core Readings* (pp. 51–94). New York: Harvester Wheatsheaf.
This paper was originally published in Barkow *et al.* (eds) (1992), *The
Adapted Mind: Evolutionary Psychology and the Generation of Culture.* Oxford:
Oxford University Press.

Fernald, Anne and Gerald McRoberts (1996) Prosodic bootstrapping: a critical
analysis of the argument and the evidence. In James L. Morgan and
Katherine Demuth (eds), *Signal to Syntax: Bootstrapping from Speech to
Grammar in Early Acquisition* (pp. 365–88). Mahwah, NJ: Erlbaum.

Ferreiro, E. (1971) *Les relations temporelles dans le langage de l'enfant*. Geneva: Librairie Droz.

Ferreiro, E. and H. Sinclair (1971) Temporal relations in language. *International Journal of Psychology*, 6, 39–47.

Fodor, Jerry A. (1975) *The Language of Thought*. New York: Crowell.

Fodor, Jerry A. (1983) *The Modularity of Mind*. Cambridge, MA: MIT Press.

Forman, George E. (1982) A search for the origins of equivalence concepts through a microanalysis of block play. In George E. Forman (ed.), *Action and Thought* (pp. 97–136). New York: Academic Press.

Fromkin, Victoria A. (1975) An update on the linguistic development of Genie. In D. P. Dato (ed.), *Georgetown University Round Table on Language and Linguistics 1975: Developmental Psycholinguistics, Theory and Applications*. Washington, DC: Georgetown University Press.

Fromkin, Victoria A., Stephen D. Krashen *et al.* (1974) The development of language in Genie: a case of language acquisition beyond the 'critical period'. *Brain and Language,* 1, 81–107.

Gallaway, Clare and Bencie Woll (1994) Interaction and childhood deafness. In Clare Gallaway and Brian J. Richards (eds), *Input and Interaction in Language Acquisition* (pp. 197–218). Cambridge: Cambridge University Press.

Gannon, Patrick J., Ralph L. Holloway *et al.* (1998) Asymmetry of chimpanzee planum temporale: humanlike pattern of Wernicke's brain language area homolog. *Science*, 279 (9 January), 220–2.

Garmon, Linda (1994) *Secret of the Wild Child*. Boston: WGBH.

Gazzaniga, Michael S. (1988) *Mind Matters: How Mind and Brain Interact to Create our Conscious Lives*. Boston: Houghton Mifflin.

Geschwind, Norman (1969) The work and influence of Wernicke. In R.S. Cohen and M. W. Wartofsky (eds), *Boston Studies in the Philosophy of Science*, vol. 4 (pp. 1–33). Boston: Reidel.

Gleitman, Lila R. (1990) The structural sources of verb meanings. *Language Acquisition*, 1, 3–55.

Gleitman, Lila R., Elissa L. Newport and H. Gleitman (1984) The current status of the motherese hypothesis. *Journal of Child Language*, 11, 43–79.

Golinkoff, R. C. Mervis *et al.* (1994) Early object labels: the case for a developmental lexical principles framework. *Journal of Child Language*, 21, 125–55.

Greenfield, Patricia M. and Joshua H. Smith (1976) *The Structure of Communication in Early Language Development*. New York: Academic Press.

Greenfield, Susan (1997) *The Human Brain: A Guided Tour*. London: Weidenfeld & Nicolson.

Gregory, Richard L. (1987) *The Oxford Companion to the Mind*. New York: Oxford University Press.

Grimshaw, Jane (1981) Form, function, and the language acquisition device. In C.L. Baker and J.J. McCarthy (eds), *The Logical Problem of Language Acquisition* (pp. 165–82). Cambridge, MA: MIT Press.

Gruber, Howard E. and J. Jacques Voneche (1977) *The Essential Piaget*. Northvale, NJ: Aranson.

Gruber, Jeffrey S. (1976) *Lexical Structures in Syntax and Semantics*. Amsterdam: North-Holland.

Haldane, Elizabeth and G. R. T. Ross (1931) *The Philosophical Works of Descartes*, vol. 1. New York: Dover.

Halliday, M.A.K. (1961) Categories of the theory of grammar. *Word*, 17, 241–92.

Halliday, M.A.K. (1967–68) Notes on transitivity and theme in English: parts 1 and 2. *Journal of Linguistics*, 3.1.37–81; 3.2.199–244; 4.2.179–215.

Halliday, M.A.K. (1973) *Explorations in the Functions of Language*. London: Edward Arnold.

Halliday, M.A.K. (1974) Answers in interview. In Herman Parret (ed.), *Discussing Language* (pp. 81–120). The Hague: Mouton.

Halliday, M.A.K. (1975) *Learning How to Mean: Explorations in the Development of Language*. London: Edward Arnold.

Halliday, M.A.K. (1978) Meaning and the construction of reality in early childhood. In Herbert L. Pick and Elliot Saltzman (eds), *Modes of Perceiving and Processing of Information* (pp. 67–96). Hillsdale: Erlbaum.

Halliday, M.A.K. (1979) One child's protolanguage. In Margaret Bullowa (ed.), *Before Speech: The Beginnings of Interpersonal Communication* (pp. 171–90). London: Cambridge University Press.

Halliday, M.A.K. (1984) Language as code and language as behaviour: a systemic-functional interpretation of the nature and ontogenesis of dialogue. In Robin P. Fawcett, M.A.K. Halliday, S.M. Lamb and A. Makkai (eds), *The Semiotics of Culture and Language*, vol. 1., *Language as Social Semiotic* (pp. 3–35). London: Pinter.

Halliday, M.A.K. (1991) The place of dialogue in children's construction of meaning. In Sorin Stati, Edda Weigand and F. Hundsnurscher (eds), *Dialoganalyse III: Referate der 3 Arbeitstagung, Bologna 1990*, vol. 1 (pp. 417–30). Tübingen: Niemeyer.

Halliday, M.A.K. (1994) *An Introduction to Functional Grammar* (2nd edn). London: Edward Arnold.

Halliday, M.A.K. and Ruqaiya Hasan (1976) *Cohesion in English*. London: Longman.

Hellige, Joseph B. (1993) *Hemispheric Asymmetry: What's Right and What's Left*. Cambridge, MA: Harvard University Press.

Hirsch-Pasek, Kathy and Rebecca Treiman (1982) Doggerel: motherese in a new context. *Journal of Child Language*, 9, 229–37.

Hirsch-Pasek, Kathy, Deborah G. Kemler-Nelson *et al.* (1987) Clauses are perceptual units for young infants. *Cognition*, 26, 269–86.

Holder, M. K. (1997) Expert answer to an on-line question in the *Scientific American* page on the World Wide Web. *Scientific American*.

Horning, J.J. (1969) A study of grammatical inference. Unpublished doctoral dissertation, Stanford AI Project.

Hyams, Nina (1986) *Language Acquisition and the Theory of Parameters.* Dordrecht: Reidel.

Hyams, Nina (1992) A reanalysis of null subjects in child language. In Jürgen Weissenborn, Helen Goodluck and T. Roeper (eds), *Theoretical Issues in Language Acquisition: Continuity and Change in Development* (pp. 249–67). Hillsdale: Erlbaum.

Joanette, Yves, Pierre Goulet and Didier Hannequin (1990) *Right Hemisphere and Verbal Communication.* New York: Springer-Verlag.

Joynt, R.J. (1964) Paul Pierre Broca: his contribution to the knowledge of aphasia. *Cortex*, 1, 206–13.

Jusczyk, Peter W. (1997) *The Discovery of Spoken Language.* Cambridge, MA: MIT Press.

Jusczyk, Peter W. and Elizabeth Thompson (1978) Perception of a phonetic contrast in multisyllabic utterances by 2-month-old infants. *Perception and Psychophysics*, 23(2), 105–9.

Karmiloff-Smith, Annette (1992) *Beyond Modularity: A Developmental Perspective on Cognitive Science.* Cambridge, MA: MIT Press.

Karmiloff-Smith, Annette (1994) Précis of *Beyond Modularity: A Developmental Perspective on Cognitive Science. Behavioral and Brain Sciences*, 17, 693–745.

Karmiloff-Smith, Annette (1997) Commentary on Annette Karmiloff-Smith (1994). *Behavioral and Brain Sciences*, 20(2), 359–77.

Katz, Nancy, Elizabeth Baker and John MacNamara (1974) What's in a name: a study of how children learn common and proper names. *Child Development*, 45, 469–73.

Keil, F.C. (1989) *Concepts, Kinds and Cognitive Development.* Cambridge, MA: MIT Press.

Kellman, P.J. and Elizabeth Spelke (1983) Perception of partly occluded objects in infancy. *Cognitive Psychology*, 15, 483–524.

Kimura, D. (1961) Cerebral dominance and the perception of verbal stimuli. *Canadian Journal of Psychology*, 15, 166–71.

Kimura, D. (1964) Left–right differences in the perception of melodies. *Quarterly Journal of Experimental Psychology*, 16, 355–8.

Kimura, D. (1988) Review of *What the Hands Reveal about the Brain*, by Howard Poizner, Edward S. Klima and Ursula Bellugi. *Language and Speech*, 31(4), 375–8.

Kimura, D. (1993) Sex differences in the brain. *Mind and Brain: Readings from Scientific American* (pp. 79–89). New York: Freeman.

King, Barbara J. (1996) The communication continuum: review of *The Evolution of Communication*, by Marc D. Hauser. *Semiotic Review of Books*, 7(3), 2–3.

Klahr, David (1992) Information-processing approaches to cognitive development. In Marc H. Bornstein and Michael E. Lamb (eds), *Developmental Psychology: An Advanced Textbook* (pp. 273–335). Hillsdale: Erlbaum.

Klima, Edward S. and Ursula Bellugi-Klima (1966) Syntactic regularities in the speech of children. In J. Lyons and R.J. Wales (eds), *Psycholinguistics Papers: The Proceedings of the 1966 Edinburgh Conference* (pp. 183–219). Edinburgh: Edinburgh University Press.

Klima, Edward S. and Ursula Bellugi (1979) *The Signs of Language*. Cambridge, MA: Harvard University Press.

Krashen, Stephen (1973) Lateralization, language learning and the critical period: some new evidence. *Language Learning*, 23, 63–74.

Kress, Gunther (1976) *Halliday: System and Function in Language*. London: Oxford University Press.

Landau, Barbara S. and Lila R. Gleitman (1985) *Language and Experience: Evidence from the Blind Child*. Cambridge, MA: Harvard University Press.

Landau, Barbara, Linda B. Smith and S.S. Jones (1988) The importance of shape in early lexical learning. *Cognitive Development*, 3, 299–321.

Lecours, André Roch and Yves Joanette (1985) Keeping your brain in mind. In Jacques Mehler and Robin Fox (eds), *Neonate Cognition: Beyond the Blooming Buzzing Confusion*. Hillsdale: Erlbaum.

Lenneberg, Eric H. (1967) *Biological Foundations of Language*. New York: Wiley.

Levelt, W.J.M. (1975) What became of LAD? In W. Abraham (ed.), *Ut Videam: Contributions to an Understanding of Linguistics, for Pieter Verburg on the Occasion of his 70th Birthday*. Lisse: Peter de Ridder Press.

Lieberman, Philip (1998) *Eve Spoke*. New York: Norton.

Loreno, Orlando, and Armando Machado (1996) In defense of Piaget's theory: a reply to 10 common criticisms. *Psychological Review*, 103, 1, 143–64.

MacNamara, John (1972) Cognitive basis of language learning in infants. *Psychological Review*, 79, 1–13.

Markman, Ellen M. (1991) The whole object, taxonomic, and mutual exclusivity assumptions as initial constraints on word meanings. In S. A. Gelman and J. Byrnes (eds), *Perspectives on Language and Thought* (pp. 72–106). New York: Cambridge University Press.

Martin, J, R. (1992) *English Text: System and Structure*. Philadelphia: Benjamins.

McClelland, James L., David E. Rumelhart and the PDP Research Grouup (1986) *Parallel Distributed Processing: Explorations in the Microstructure of Cognition*, vol. 2: *Psychological and Biological Models*. Cambridge, MA: MIT Press.

McGlone, J. (1978) Sex differences in functional brain asymmetry. *Cortex*, 14, 122–8.

McGlone, J. (1980) Sex differences in human brain asymmetry: a critical survey. *Behavioral and Brain Sciences*, 3, 215–63.

McNeill, David (1970) *The Acquisition of Language: The Study of Developmental Psycholinguistics*. New York: Harper & Row.

Medawar, Peter (1961) *The Strange Case of the Spotted Mice: And Other Classic Essays on Science*. Oxford: Oxford University Press.

Mehler, Jacques and Emmanuel Dupoux (1990) *Naître humain*. Paris: Editions Odile Jacob.

Mehler, Jacques and Emmanuel Dupoux (1994) *What Infants Know: The New Cognitive Science of Early Development* (Patsy Southgate, trans.). Cambridge, MA: Blackwell.

Mehler, Jacques, Peter Jusczyk *et al.* (1988) A precursor of language acquisition in young infants. *Cognition*, 29, 143–78.

Menn, Lise and Carol Stoel-Gammon (1995) Phonological development. In Paul Fletcher and Brian MacWhinney (eds), *The Handbook of Child Language* (pp. 335–59). Oxford: Blackwell.

Merriman, William E. (1991) The mutual exclusivity bias in children's word learning: a reply to Woodward and Markman. *Developmental Review*, 11, 164–91.

Merriman, William E. and Michael Tomasello (1995) Introduction: verbs are words too. In Michael Tomasello and William E. Merriman (eds), *Beyond Names for Things: Young Children's Acquisition of Verbs* (pp. 1–18). Hillsdale: Erlbaum.

Miller, George A. (1970) *The Psychology of Communication*. Harmondsworth: Pelican.

Mogford, K. (1993) Oral language acquisition in the prelinguistically deaf. In Dorothy Bishop and Kay Mogford (eds), *Language Development in Exceptional Circumstances* (pp. 110–31). Hove, UK: Erlbaum.

Morgan, James L. and Katherine Demuth (eds) (1996) *Signal to Syntax: Bootstrapping from Speech to Grammar in Early Acquisition*. Mahwah, NJ: Erlbaum.

Newport, Elissa L., Henry Gleitman and L.R. Gleitman (1977) Mother, I'd rather do it myself: some effects and non-effects of maternal speech style. In Catherine Snow and Charles A. Ferguson (eds), *Talking to Children: Language Input and Acquisition* (pp. 109–49). Cambridge: Cambridge University Press.

Ornstein, Robert (1997) *The Right Mind: Making Sense of the Hemispheres*. New York: Harcourt Brace.

Otero, C.P. (1988) *Noam Chomsky: Language and Politics*. Montreal: Black Rose Books.

Painter, Clare (1984) *Into the Mother Tongue: A Case Study in Early Language Development*. London: Pinter.

Perner, J., S.R. Leekam and H. Wimmer (1987) Three-year-olds' difficulty with false belief: the case for a conceptual deficit. *British Journal of Developmental Psychology*, 5, 125–37.

Piaget, Jean (1937) *La construction du réel chez l'enfant*. (Publishing details not available).

Piaget, Jean (1953) *The Origin of Intelligence in the Child* (Margaret Cook, trans.). London: Routledge & Kegan Paul.

Piaget, Jean (1954) *The Construction of Reality in the Child* (Margaret Cook, trans.). New York: Basic Books.

Piattelli-Palmarini, Massimo (1979) *Théories du langage, théories de l'apprentissage: le débat entre Jean Piaget et Noam Chomsky*. Paris: Seuil.

Piattelli-Palmarini, Massimo (1980) *Language and Learning: The Debate Between Jean Piaget and Noam Chomsky*. Cambridge, MA: Harvard University Press.

Piaget, Jean (1954) *The Contruction of Reality in the Child* (Margaret Cook, trans.). New York: Basic Books.

Piattelli-Palmarini, Massimo (1995) Ever since *Language and Learning*: afterthoughts on the Piaget–Chomsky debate. In Jacques Mehler and Susana Franck (eds), *Cognition on Cognition* (pp. 361–92). Cambridge, MA: MIT Press.

Pinker, Steven (1979) Formal models of language learning. *Cognition*, 7(3), 217–83.

Pinker, Steven (1982) A theory of the acquisition of lexical interpretive grammars. In Joan Bresnan (ed.), *The Mental Representation of Grammatical Relations* (pp. 655–726). Cambridge, MA: MIT Press.

Pinker, Steven (1994a) *The Language Instinct: How the Mind Creates Language*. New York: Morrow.

Pinker, Steven (1994b) How could a child use verb syntax to learn verb semantics? *Lingua*, 92, 377–410.

Poizner, Howard, Edward S. Klima and Ursula Bellugi (1987) *What the Hands Reveal about the Brain*. Cambridge, MA: MIT Press.

Posner, M.J. and M.E. Raichle (1994) *Images of Mind*. New York: Freeman.

Premack, Ann J. and David Premack (1972) Teaching language to an ape. *Scientific American*, 227, 92–9.

Premack, David (1977) *Intelligence in Ape and Man*. New York: Halsted.

Premack, David (1980) Representational capacity and accessibillity of knowledge: the case of chimpanzees. In Massimo Piattelli-Palmarini (ed.), *Language and Learning: The Debate between Jean Piaget and Noam Chomsky* (pp. 205–30). Cambridge, MA: Harvard University Press.

Premack, David (1990) Words: what are they and do animals have them? *Cognition*, 37, 197–212.

Quine, Willard V.O. (1964) Meaning and translation. In Jerry A. Fodor and Jerrold J. Katz (eds), *The Structure of Language: Readings in the Philosophy of Language* (pp. 460–78). Englewood Cliffs: Prentice-Hall.

Raichle, Marcus E. (1994) Visualizing the mind. *Scientific American*, April, 36–42.

Richards, Brian J. and Clare Gallaway (1994) Conclusions and directions. In Clare Gallaway and Brian J. Richards (eds), *Input and Interaction in Language Acquisition* (pp. 253–69). Cambridge: Cambridge University Press.

Rosch, Eleanor, C.B.Mervis *et al.* (1976) Basic objects in natural categories. *Cognitive Psychology*, 8, 382–439.

Rumelhart, David E., James L. McClelland and the PDP Research Group (1986) *Parallel Distributed Processing: Explorations in the Microstructure of Cognition, vol. 1: Foundations.* Cambridge, MA: MIT Press.

Russell, Bertrand (1948) *Human Knowledge: Its Scope and Limits.* London: Allen & Unwin.

Savage-Rumbaugh, Sue and Roger Lewin (1994) *Kanzi: The Ape at the Brink of the Human Mind.* New York: Wiley.

Savage-Rumbaugh, Sue, Stuart G. Shanker and T.J. Taylor (1998) *Apes, Language and the Human Mind.* New York: Oxford University Press.

Schiff-Myers, N. (1987) Hearing children of deaf parents. In Dorothy Bishop and Kay Mogford (eds), *Language Development in Exceptional Circumstances* (pp. 47–61). Hove, UK: Erlbaum.

Schlesinger, Izchak M. (1971) The production of utterances and language acquisition. In D. I. Slobin (ed.), *The Ontogenesis of Grammar.* New York: Academic Press.

Skinner, B.F. (1957) *Verbal Behavior.* Englewood Cliffs: Prentice-Hall.

Slobin, Dan I. (ed.) (1971) *The Ontogenesis of Grammar.* New York: Academic Press.

Smith, N.V. (1994) Review paper, *Beyond Modularity: A Developmental Perspective on Cognitive Science* by A. Karmiloff-Smith. *European Journal of Disorders of Communication*, 28, 95–105.

Smith, N.V. (1999) Bonobos. *Glot International*, 4(3), 9.

Smith, Neil and Deirdre Wilson (1979) *Modern Linguistics: The Results of Chomsky's Revolution.* Brighton: Harvester Press.

Smith, Neil and Ianthi-Maria Tsimpli (1995) *The Mind of a Savant: Language Learning and Modularity.* Oxford: Blackwell.

Snow, Catherine (1972) Mothers' speech to children learning language. *Child Development*, 43, 549–65.

Snow, Catherine E. (1986) Conversations with children. In P. Fletcher and M. Garman (eds), *Language Acquisition* (pp. 69–89). Cambridge: Cambridge University Press.

Soja, Nancy N., Susan Carey and Elizabeth S. Spelke (1991) Ontological categories guide young children's inductions of word meaning: object terms and substance terms. *Cognition*, 38, 179–211.

Spelke, E.S. (1985) Preferential-looking methods as tools for the study of cognition in infancy. In G. Gottlieb and N.A. Krasnegor (eds), *Measurement of Audition and Vision in the First Year of Postnatal Life: A Methodological Overview* (pp. 323–63). Norwood, NJ: Ablex.

Spelke, E.S. (1988) Where perceiving ends and thinking begins. In Albert Yonas (ed.), *Perceptual Development in Infancy*, vol. 20 (pp. 197–234). Hillsdale: Erlbaum.

Spelke, E.S. (1990) Principles of object perception. *Cognitive Science*, 14, 29–56.

Spelke, E.S. (1995) Initial knowledge: six suggestions. In Jacques Mehler and S. Franck (eds), *Cognition on Cognition* (pp. 433–47). Cambridge, MA: MIT Press.

Sperry, R.W. (1974) Lateral specialization in the surgically separated hemispheres. In F.O. Schmitt and F.G. Warden (eds), *The Neurosciences: Third Study Program* (pp. 5–13). Cambridge, MA: MIT Press.

Springer, Sally P. and Georg Deutsch (1989) *Left Brain, Right Brain* (3rd edn). New York: Freeman.

Tarrter, Vivien C. (1998) *Language Processing in Atypical Populations*. Thousand Oaks, CA: Sage.

Templin, Mildred C. (1957) *Certain Language Skills in Children: Their Development and Interrelationships*. Minneapolis: University of Minnesota Press.

Toth, Nicholas (1987) The first technology. *Scientific American*, 256(4), 104–13.

Wallman, J. (1992) *Aping Language*. Cambridge: Cambridge University Press.

Waxman, Sandra R. (1990) Linguistic biases and the establishment of conceptual hierarchies: evidence from preschool children. *Cognitive Development*, 5, 123–50.

Waxman, Sandra R. (1994) The development of an appreciation of specific linkages between linguistic and conceptual organisation. *Lingua*, 92, 229–57.

Waxman, S.R. and R. Gelman (1986) Preschoolers' use of superordinate relations in classification and language. *Cognitive Development*, 1, 139–56.

Weissenborn, Jürgen (1992) Null subjects in early grammars: implications for parameter-setting theories. In Jürgen Weissenborn, Helen Goodluck and Thomas Roper (eds), *Theoretical Issues in Language Acquisition: Continuity and Change in Development* (pp. 269–99). Hillsdale: Erlbaum.

Wellman, H.M. (1990) *The Child's Theory of Mind*. Cambridge, MA: MIT Press.

Wernicke, Karl (1874) The aphasic symptom complex: a psychological study on an anatomical basis. In R.S. Cohen and M.W. Wartofsky (eds), *Boston Studies in the Philosophy of Science*, vol. 4 (pp. 34–97). Boston: Reidel.

Wexler, Kenneth and Peter W. Culicover (1980) *Formal Principles of Language Acquisition*. Cambridge, MA: MIT Press.

Index

accommodation (Piagetian) 45–6
adjective 95
adult language 62, 144–7
  adult-to-adult 105–7, 113
  adult-to-child 111
    see also baby-talk (BT); 'motherese'
  adult-to-dog 123–4
age and language development 12–17, 195,
  199, 212
ambiguity 91
American Sign Language (ASL) 185–9, 205–6
animal communication 66, 201–15
aphasia 156, 157–63, 190
apraxia 191
article *see* determiner
articulation and speech apparatus 28
ASL *see* American Sign Language (ASL)
assimilation (Piagetian) 45, 46
attention factors 107, 217
autism 245

babies and speech
  early speech 1–10, 12, 101–2
  and mother 30–2, 39, 125
  see also infants; preferential looking procedure
baby-talk (BT) 104, 105, 106
Baillargeon, Renée 219
Baldwin, D.A. 225–6
bees and communication 201–4
behaviourism 31, 32–6, 62, 64
  in language acquisition 36–9, 210, 257
behaviourist linguists of 68
Beilin, Harry, tests 52–7
Bellugi, Ursula 15–16, 185, 186, 188, 190,
  191, 197
Bever, Thomas G. 118–19, 120
biases 231–7
bilingualism 102
biological clock, human 77

Bloomfield, Leonard 35–6
Bohr, Niels 52
bonobos, experiments with 210–15
'bootstrapping' 19, 26, 256
  infant knowledge 216–20
  speech sound 220–1
  syntax 221–4
  vocabulary 225–6, 227–8
brackets, bracketing 91–4
brain
  functions of 243–4, 245, 255–6
  and language 214–15, 241–2, 257–8
  lateralization 173, 195–6
  neurological studies of 169–81
  plasticity of 253–4
  and signing 190–1
  and speech 151, 155–7, 169
brain damage 246–7
brain hemispheres 151–67 .
  hemispherectomies 171–4
  'split-brain' surgery 169–71
  tests 178–81
brain scans 175–8, 215
Braine, Martin 9–10, 117, 118
Broadbent, Donald 178
Broca, Paul 155, 157, 159–61, 176
Brown, Roger 108, 116, 209

caregiver register 104
caretaker speech 104
child-directed speech (CDS) 104, 121
children
  deaf 183, 184–91, 228
  with deaf parents 183, 184, 192–3
  deprived 183, 193–9
  and grammar 121
  and mother's speech 109–12, 112–15
  and participation 132–3
  preschool 12–13, 17, 234
  utterances 12–17, 117, 224

INDEX

chimpanzees, experiments with 205–10
Chomsky, Noam 8, 42, 83–103, 120,
    230, 255
    competence and performance 70–2
    ideal speaker-listener 69–71
    and innateness 75–84, 95, 108, 115, 238–40
    mentalism of 67–77
    and minimalism 258
    and Piaget 78–81
    scientific method 67–9
    and Skinner 62–6
    theories of 64, 85–6, 99, 108, 111, 113
    unconscious knowledge 72–5
    word use 237–8
Chomskyan revolution 67, 69
clarifying process 105, 106, 107
clause 93, 94, 109, 113
clause boundaries 223–4
closed class 9, 10
cognitive growth and development
    and language 44, 256–7
    sensori-motor 45–7, 79, 244
    stages 47–58
    tests 52–7
cognitive growth theory 44–60, 240
cognitive revolution 67
competence 70–1
complex sentences 94, 107
complexity, measurement of 109–10, 111
computers and language 65
conceptual development 234–5
conditioning 63
conjunction 95
connectionism 251–2, 257, 258
consonants 20–3, 27, 220
constituent structure 90–6, 208
constraints 97
    see also biases, innate principles
constructivism 240, 244–5
conversational participation 108, 134
count nouns 235–6
cross-language studies 258
cues, verbal and non-verbal 226
Culicover, Peter W. 116–17, 121
Curtiss, Susan 193, 195, 197, 199

Dax, Marc 157, 158–9, 176
deaf persons 66, 183–93, 228
deictic terms 115, 124, 189
deixis 189
Dennis, M. 172–4
deprived children 183, 193–9
derivational length 113
Descartes, René 65–6
determiner 90, 91, 92, 95

dialect 24, 84–5
dialogue 143–4
dichotic listening tests 178–9
dictionary 88
    see also lexicon
diphthongs   23
discovery procedure 117–20, 121–2, 224
doggerel (adult-to-dog speech) 123–4
domain specificity 244–7

elicitation techniques 229
emotion, communication of 125, 126
environmentalist approach 130
evolution 126–7
expansions 115
experimentation, ethics of 110
expressive processes 105, 106, 107
external influences 84

facial expression 125, 126
feedback 107, 121
Ferguson, Charles 105, 106, 107
Fernald, Anne 124–7, 224
Fodor, Jerry 80, 81, 240–2, 243
foreign language 222
formal system, formalism 129
Frisch, Karl von 201–2

gender and skills 165–7
generative linguistics 28, 80–1, 119, 213
gesture, use of 7, 137
Gleitman, Henry 121, 123, 228, 229
Gleitman, Lila 107, 113–16, 121, 228–29
grammar 6, 84–6, 96–7, 188–9
    basic essentials 86–96
grammatical category bias 232–6
grammatical structure 143–4

Halliday, M.A.K. 129–47, 255, 256
handedness 163–5
hierarchy words, basic level 233–5
Hirsch-Pasek, K. 123–4, 223
holophrastic sentences 6, 7

iconic sign 228
ideal speaker-listener 69–71
imperatives 113, 114
infant-directed (ID) speech 104, 126
infants
    knowledge 216–20
    speech and language 220–8
    see also babies; 'bootstrapping'
innate language capacities 75–7, 78–80, 95,
    224, 238–9

innate language component 116–17, 120
innate principles 75, 81–4, 96–100, 240, 245, 252–4
inputs 62, 241, 243, 245
intensifier 95
International Phonetic Alphabet 20
interrogatives 17, 107, 113, 124, 198
intonation 3, 7, 106, 124–5, 126
introspection in language study 67, 68
intuitions about language 68, 69, 92

Kanzi 210–15
Karmiloff-Smith, A. 131, 240, 240–54, 256
Katz, N. 95, 233
Keller, Helen 225
Kimura, Doreen 179, 190–1
Klima, E.S. 15, 197
Krashen, Stephen 195–6, 199
Kuhl, Patricia 220–1

language 85, 195–6, 214
language acquisition 183, 195, 199, 255–6
language capacity 75–7
language-specific features 114
Lenneberg, Erich 195, 199
lexicon 86, 121
lexigrams 211
linguistic research, future 258–9
linguistic rules, structure dependent 69, 80, 99–100, 213
lip-reading 184–5

materialist/mechanistic theory 35–6
meaning see semantics
mental development and language 83–4
mental faculties 31
mentalism 62–6, 67–77
methodology 251
microdomains 248
Miller, George 39, 41
mistakes 42, 72, 99, 121
model utterance 39
modelling 107
modification 111
modifiers 106, 118
modularity of mind 241–2, 243–4, 245, 249–50
morphemes 114, 188
mother tongue see native language
'motherese' 104–5, 108, 116–17, 123–7, 255–6
study of 108–15, 118, 120–7
multiple-word utterances 12–17, 117
mutual exclusivity bias 231, 236

native language 26–7, 40, 62, 102, 105, 222

nativists 240
negative utterances 15–16, 114, 197–8
Newport, Elissa 112–15
nonsense word 117–18
noun 87–90, 95, 96, 227–8
noun phrase 92–5, 118, 189
nursery talk/ language 104

object (grammatical) 113, 189, 209
objectivity 69
open class 9–10
order of events 59–60
order of mention 59–60, 189, 228

parameters 100–2
parentese 104, 108
passive 56, 60
Pavlov, Ivan 32, 36
performance 70, 71
phonemes 26, 27, 28
phones 26, 27, 28
phonetics 20, 106, 186
see also sounds of the language
phonological words 209
physical world, perception of 217–20
phrase structure 90–6
Piaget, Jean 131, 219, 220, 255
and Chomsky 78–81
cognitive growth theory 44–60, 240
domain general development 244–5
and language development 58–60
Piagetian school 44, 58–60, 81–2, 240, 244
Piattelli-Palmarini, Massimo 80–1
Pinker, Steven 227–9
pitch 3, 9, 106, 124–5
pivot grammars 9, 10, 117, 118
planum temporale (PT) 215
Poizner, Howard 188, 189, 190, 191
predicate 92, 93
preferential looking procedure 215, 217
preposition 95
prespeech 133
principles see innate principles
'pro-drop' languages 101
pronoun 101, 106, 110, 189
'prosodic bootstrapping hypothesis' 223, 224
prosody of speech 221–2, 223
protolanguage 133–41
puberty 195, 199

Quine, Willard 229

reductionists 167
redundant speech 111

INDEX

reflex (Piagetian) 45
reinforcement 63
repetition 5, 106, 110, 111, 115
Representational Redescription (RR) 247–8, 250, 251
response 62, 63
Rosch, Eleanor 234–5
routines, teaching of 108
Royaumont debate 78–81
rules, child's formulation of 121
Russell, Bertrand 204

'Sally Anne' test 246
samples of speech ('corpus') 68
Sarah 206–210
'satellites' see modifiers
Savage-Rumbaugh, Sue 210–215
savants 246
scientific method 32–4, 67–9
'semantic bootstrapping' 228
semantics 131–2, 137–41, 142, 144, 145
sensori-motor intelligence 45–7, 79, 244
sentence 85–6, 90–6, 99, 101, 198
sentence-nodes 113
Shankar, Stuart 214, 215
sign language 66, 183–5, 189–91, 193, 228
  ASL 185–9, 205–6
simplified register 105
simplifying processes 105–6, 107
Skinner, B.F. 36–9, 62, 67, 84, 130, 255, 257
  and Chomsky 62–6
slang, teenage 10
Smith, N. 213
Snow, Catherine 108–12, 115, 116, 120–3
social aspects and influences 129–31
social semiotic 134–5
sociolinguistics 129, 130
sound signals 99
sounds of the language 20–8, 220–1
  see also phonetics
speech rate 106
Spelke, Elizabeth 217–219
Sperry, Roger 170
stimuli, response to 62, 63
stress 23–5, 126

structural unit boundaries 111
structure dependence see linguistic rules
subject (grammatical) 92, 93, 113, 189, 209
Sullivan, Anne 225
symbolic communication 135, 136
'syntactic bootstrapping' 228
syntactic level 186
syntactical constructions 6, 12–13, 221–4
systemic-functional grammar 147–8

teaching language 110, 113–15, 116, 120, 125
theory of mind 245–6
third-person concept 110
time, concept of 59–60
topic areas 106
Toth, Nicholas 163–4
Treiman, Rebecca 123–4
two-word utterances 6, 8–10, 12, 117

unconscious knowledge 72–5, 99
Universal Grammar (UG) 213

variables see parameters
verb 87–90, 95, 106, 109, 114, 228–9
verb phrase 93, 95
verb system 13–15
verbal operant 63
vocabulary 5, 17–19, 197, 225–8, 229–30
  biases 231–7
vocabulary explosion 6, 12, 141, 198
vowels 22, 23, 220–1

Wada, Juhn 180
Watson, J.B. 32
Waxman, S.R. 230, 233, 234, 235–6
Wernicke, Karl 155, 157, 161–3, 176, 215
Wexler, K. 116–17, 121
'Wh' questions 17, 139, 141, 198
Whitaker, H. 172–4
Williams' syndrome 245
word classes 86–7, 95, 227–8
  position of 117–19, 121, 228
word learning 237
word use (reference) 237–8